Cleveland Amory ▷ ▷ ▷

Marilyn
Greenwald

Cleveland Amory

MEDIA CURMUDGEON & ANIMAL RIGHTS CRUSADER

▷ UNIVERSITY PRESS

OF NEW ENGLAND

HANOVER &

LONDON ◁

UNIVERSITY PRESS OF NEW ENGLAND
One Court Street, Lebanon, NH 03766
www.upne.com
© 2009 by University Press of New England
Printed in the United States of America
5 4 3 2 1

Library of Congress Cataloging-in-Publication Data
Greenwald, Marilyn S.
Cleveland Amory : media curmudgeon and animal rights
crusader / Marilyn Greenwald.
     p.   cm.
Includes bibliographical references and index.
ISBN 978–1–58465–681–4 (cloth: alk. paper)
1. Amory, Cleveland. 2. Social historians—United States—
Biography. 3. Animal rights activists—United States—
Biography. 4. Critics—United States—Biography. 5. Television
criticism—United States. 6. Journalists—United States—
Biography. 7. Boston (Mass.)—Biography. I. Title.
CT275.A6856G74   2009
974.4'61092—dc22
[B]   2009000996

University Press of New England is a member of the
Green Press Initiative. The paper used in this book meets
their minimum requirement for recycled paper.

▷ *For Tim*

▷ CONTENTS

Illustrations follow page 72.

Cleveland Amory ◁ ◁ ◁

▷ ▷ ▷ Introduction

I used to write about Mrs. Astor and her horse.
Now I just write about the horse.
► CLEVELAND AMORY

*C*leveland Amory was the type of man who inspired in reporters odd recollections and vivid turns of phrase. Near the end of Amory's sixty-year career as a writer, editor, and activist, one magazine reporter noted that it seemed as though his entire life had been "recorded in print or on video-tape, either by himself or by someone else." As another reporter noted on the occasion of his death, in her last recollection of him he was "beaming like a new father at a smelly, grouchy goat," one of thousands whose rescue from Navy sharpshooters he had just arranged through a complex and innovative roundup involving air guns and netting. Still another writer related the tale of the oblivious Manhattan carriage driver who had the misfortune to angrily kick his horse as Amory sat in a nearby car. Amory jumped out of the car and grabbed the man by the neck. "You miserable idiot!" Amory yelled. "If you ever kick that horse again, I personally am going to beat you to a pulp." This when Amory was in his sixties.

When recounting the lengths Amory would go to in order to save animals (i.e., airlifting wild burros out of the Grand Canyon, "painting" baby seals in Canada with organic red dye to render their skins useless to furriers), one writer described him as a man "you wouldn't want to be in charge of making a Sophie's choice between you and your pet burro."

Writers could afford to be eloquent when discussing Amory because the man himself gave them a lot of raw material. At six feet three and, for much of his life, past 250 pounds, Amory, with his baritone voice and big blue eyes, was larger than life, physically and metaphorically. He was also quick with a cutting response and completely fearless. And like most genuinely fearless people, he did not even realize he was fearless. He took on the hunting and fur lobbies long before it was fashionable, and, with his humor and persistence, made it fashionable, literally, for many to do the same. "You'd kill your own mother if she had four legs," he would tell hunters; or, to a group that was brutally slaughtering pigeons for sport, "You'd kill your own mother if she had wings." Once, when explaining in an interview that most states' wildlife departments were controlled by hunters and trappers, he dryly referred to the Michigan Department of Natural Resources as the "Department of Nuts with Rifles." This kind of attitude earned him a lot of enemies — many of whom were armed. He took great pride in their vast numbers.

When one of his longtime friends and colleagues, Lewis Regenstein, was asked if he ever feared for Amory's life in the twenty-five years they worked together, his response was quick: "All the time." Did Amory fear for his own life? "Never," Regenstein said.

Amory was a man who was self-aware. Some writers, like William Zinsser, who knew Amory when both were still in school, mused about why a former editor of the *Harvard Crimson* would give up a promising writing career (he had written two best-selling books about New England society before he was forty, and his first, *The Proper Bostonians*, created a sensation) to focus on animals. In fact Amory never gave up writing — but he himself acknowledged that the craft he studied and practiced much of his life ultimately became secondary to him, trumped by his efforts to protect animals. "I used to write about Mrs. Astor and her horse," he would joke. "Now I just write about the horse."

When he was in middle age, Amory, inadvertently perhaps, reinvented himself when he became the regular television critic for *TV Guide*. The small ink-drawn sketch that accompanied his column became a staple to the millions of readers of the magazine. Almost overnight and for more than a decade, Amory became *the* expert about the fast-growing medium of television in the 1960s and 1970s. And, as could be expected, he pulled no punches when offering his opinions of new shows, although each year he ran a column of readers' reactions to his assessments. These were his favorite columns. Amory was at his caustic best when replying to criticism of *his* criticism.

And a half dozen years after he left *TV Guide*, when he was in his sixties and at the age when most people would retire, he reinvented himself again — this time as the writer of in-depth celebrity profiles for the Sunday newspaper supplement *Parade*. Because of Amory's longtime friendship with many of the celebrities, these profiles were sometimes unusually revealing. Again, he was read regularly by millions.

Amory's single-minded dedication to his cause, like that of many serious activists, was not triggered by one or two events but was instead developed and cultivated by certain people, events, and circumstances in his life. He said throughout his life that his concern for animals was spawned by a beloved and compassionate aunt who used to take in stray and abused animals and give them a home, even though neighbors ridiculed her for her efforts. When he was a boy, the same aunt introduced him to the animal lover's bible, *Black Beauty*. As a young man, he also said, he was shocked into participating in animal-protection activities after witnessing a bullfight in Mexico, which struck him, despite the pageantry, as little more than raw brutality.

But Amory's upbringing as a blue-blooded Yankee also shaped his views. Although his family started out with money and had social status, he and his siblings were raised with a certain sense of social responsibility that instilled in them a duty to help those less fortunate than they, or to contribute to society in general. Amory as a young man made a lot of money chronicling the activities and mind-set of well-heeled New Englanders, but in the process he came to realize that some of those he wrote about wasted their lives summering, wintering, and in general frittering away their time with a superficial existence that benefited few if anyone. This idea was driven home to him after he spent a few months in France with the Duke and Duchess of Windsor; the pampered couple seemed to have little to do with their time and, to his way of thinking, led shallow and empty lives.

Amory got to a point where he simply stopped writing full-time about America's blue bloods, although it had been a lucrative vocation for him. But it did change his way of thinking about the role of each person in society, and it made him contemplate the social responsibility of human beings. Amory's animal-protection activities gradually consumed all his time in one way or another, and it was into those efforts that he channeled his brilliance, his energy, and his aptitude for persuasion and public relations. Those activities gave him a reason for being, and a reason to get out of bed every morning.

Even on the surface, Amory's life did, indeed, provide lots of raw material for writers. His list of famous "contacts" — which he began to develop as a student at Harvard, where some of his classmates would become leaders in government, literature, and national affairs — expanded more when he wrote a best-selling book about blue-blood society. This suddenly cemented the young man's status as an authority on the subject and led to a glamorous way of life that consisted of cocktail parties, guest appearances on talk shows, and lucrative speaking engagements. This was a man who attended baseball games with Cary Grant and sailed on the Onassis yacht. His list of famous friends and acquaintances grew even more in his second reincarnation as a television critic for the nation's biggest magazine; Amory, it seemed, knew everyone who was anyone.

It is this "perfect storm," perhaps, this convergence of creativity, intelligence, drive, and famous friends that allowed him to become a pioneer in the animal-rights movement, and that led to his garnering great publicity for a movement that, before he came to it, was directed by genteel leaders who did not quite know how to guide it out of the shadows. Amory's method of operation when trying to persuade others of his point of view was to "use" his famous friends — who considered his a worthy cause — as well as his penchant for humor mixed with a little scandal to create a slightly outrageous claim that would be sure to get publicity. And, because he came to the movement in late middle age, he knew instinctively that he must groom others to carry on after he was gone — that was one of his pivotal missions.

All this made Amory much loved and much despised. Some of those who disagreed with him claimed that Amory was an egotist whose goal was, ultimately, publicity for himself. While he did indeed often seek the limelight, he did it for the cause. And he and the cause were one and the same. When he first became interested in animal protection as a young man, Amory might have been considered a radical; he was angry at some existing humane groups because he felt they did very little to change laws that could further animal rights, and that they spent too much time and energy feathering their own personal nests. As time went on, though, Amory's tactics were seen as much more moderate. He did not believe, for instance, in unlawfully freeing animals from captivity or invading the personal space of those with whom he disagreed. If he saw a woman on the streets of a big city wearing animal fur, Amory was not one to deface the fur or verbally abuse the woman. Instead, he found a better way to persuade her to abandon the fur: he simply remarked very loudly to his companion, "Just what I told you — it makes her look so fat!"

Many of Cleveland Amory's friends believe that while he certainly loved and understood animals, he was able to help them because he loved and understood people more. And that may well have been the case, although the cruelty he had seen and heard about in his life would have left many people jaded. But cynicism was not productive, and his energy was better spent elsewhere — often to inject humor into otherwise decidedly unfunny events.

Take, for example, the animal trainer who had abused elephants. After Amory accused him of the mistreatment, the trainer tried to appease Amory by telling him he would give his best elephant to the Fund for Animals' animal sanctuary, Black Beauty Ranch, so the fund could use it as a stud. The trainer did not know that the purpose of the ranch was to save injured animals and not breed them. "Mister, at the Fund for Animals, we don't believe in breeding animals," Amory told him. "And after meeting you, we don't believe in breeding humans, either."

Chapter 1 ▷ ▷ ▷ The Ultimate Outsider

> Cleveland was the embodiment of the saying that
> one person can make a difference.
>
> ▶ LEWIS REGENSTEIN at the memorial service
> for Cleveland Amory

*W*hen Cleveland Amory began his usual five-minute commentary on NBC's *Today* show one morning in the early fall of 1963, it was business as usual for NBC executives — or so they thought. The tall, auburn-haired Amory was, at age forty-six, a best-selling author who had established himself as a social critic, journalist, and man-about-town in Manhattan. His charm, wit, and access to the rich and famous made him popular on the lecture and talk-show circuits nationwide, and his articles were regular fixtures in national magazines like the *Saturday Review, Harper's*, the *Saturday Evening Post*, and others. His wry observations about life in general, his puns, and his dry humor had made him a favorite with viewers of the morning news show and with readers.

Little did NBC president Julian Goodman know that his morning would end with a switchboard lit up by hundreds of irate callers. And many more unhappy viewers sent letters as the week progressed. Little did Amory know that the day would end with his unceremonious firing by NBC. No two-week notice for Amory; he was asked to vacate the premises immediately. His eleven-year stint at *Today* was over.

▷ ▷ ▷ Amory's experience with the *Today* show is emblematic of his career: his writing and social criticism made him a household name during the 1960s and 1970s, and he certainly had a more promising writing and broadcasting career ahead of him at this time. But a more pressing interest would gradually take up more and more of his time.

Born in 1917 in the summer resort of Nahant, Massachusetts, to a distinguished blue-blooded family of Boston merchants, he had, through his breeding, an easy entry into upper-class Boston society. By 1947, the thirty-year-old Amory had published a best seller, *The Proper Bostonians*, which chronicled the activities and mind-set of that society with, to put it mildly, unusual candor. The iconoclastic and irreverent Amory — the perfect "insider-outsider" — was not one to toe the party line when it came to most things, including Boston society. His book was one of the first major works to portray the first families of Boston as the pathologically insular and comically quirky group that they were, but Amory was not petty or mean by nature, and ultimately his book had staying power and was read and enjoyed even by some its subjects. By 1963, it was in its eighteenth printing.

Amory's firing by *Today* came as a shock to him, even though he had been warned a few months earlier by *Today* show personnel that they did not like the direction his supposedly lighthearted commentary had occasionally taken. It came as a shock to him even though he had not received prior script approval that day, after *Today* personnel had earlier insisted that he get it. It came as a shock to him even though the usually intuitive Amory must have realized that even some people sympathetic to what had become his calling in life — animal rights — did not want to hear about abused animals as they ate their morning cereal.

By the time Amory left *Today*, he had written three best-selling books about society, was a regular columnist for the *Saturday Review*, had authored a book of fiction, and had written many articles in some of the most prestigious magazines in the country. By 1963, he was fortunate enough — and talented enough — to mesh his jobs and obsession with animal rights, and he had some degree of peace in his life. Eventually, his activities for animal rights and his interest in the cause began to overshadow his writing and broadcasting career, and, some believe, hurt him professionally. But his is a story that poses questions about celebrities' responsibility to the public, and it illustrates a clash between one person's moral convictions and his job. Was it permissible for Amory to use his platform as a social and arts critic to air his views about animal rights, or did step over the line? Did he, as a true believer, hurt his own career?

"He knew everyone. People always returned his calls," Amory's longtime friend and attorney Edward Walsh said about Amory's access to well-known people all over the country. But Walsh said Amory had an ability to connect with people that was virtually uncanny. "Cleveland had this incredible, wonderful sense of how to move people," Walsh said. "He loved animals, almost unconditionally. But he loved people more." Walsh, like many others, became a friend of Amory's almost by accident; the two men met briefly in the mid-1970s when Walsh conducted some routine legal work for the animal-rights group that Amory founded, and the next thing he knew he was in the activist's inner circle. Amory began inviting him to ball games and social events and began calling him on the phone to chat.

According to Marian Probst, who was Amory's assistant and close friend for more than thirty years, he was hard to resist: "You'd meet him and next thing you know, you were working for him," she said only half jokingly, because that's what happened to her. Those in his inner circle — including his stepdaughter, Gaea — were used to Amory's regular and chronic phone calls, usually during sporting events or films. He loved keeping his friends on the phone and "watching" these events with them, offering running commentary. For someone whose name was a fixture in newspaper columns around the country, Amory was remarkably easygoing and down-to-earth. A tireless speaker who traveled around the country talking about society, American culture, television, animals, and just about anything that crossed his mind, Amory by the early 1960s also was king of all media, appearing on television talk shows and offering commentary regularly on radio. His talks were filled with anecdotes about his brushes with the famous, tales of the quirks of America's painfully polite blue bloods, and good-natured complaints about modern life.

Several factors contributed to Amory's achievements and celebrity: he had a quick mind, tremendous verbal agility, boundless energy, and a guileless nature that kept even his criticism from sounding bitter or mean. An imposing six feet three inches tall with a substantial frame, he had thick, curly, reddish-brown hair and large blue eyes. Often a bit disheveled later in his life, he was described by reporters over the years as "handsome" and, as he aged, "like an unmade bed." Once, he was compared (favorably) to a Newfoundland hound. As he grew older, Amory was not one to pay much attention to fashion, as a *Boston Globe* reporter implied in a 1989 article: "A hefty man, " he wrote, "in black jersey and jacket so rumpled he might have been on his way to the Yale game — not to watch, but to play."

But Amory's most pronounced trait — one that informed his activities and his thoughts — was a deep self-confidence and an unwillingness to back down when he was convinced he was right, which was much of the time. It was a trait that, by the time he died in 1998, contributed to his overall happiness and fulfillment. But it was also one that earned him many enemies, including legions of hunters, wildlife officials, researchers, and some doctors. But, as he would routinely say, he was not intimidated and often flattered because one is judged "by the quality of one's enemies."

Amory had been hired in 1952 by *Today* for $300 a show to offer periodic commentary about the American scene. He usually appeared every three weeks or so, and he had joined the pioneering morning talk/news show the year it debuted. *Today* officials had a policy to read in advance the content of such commentary, but they looked the other way when it came to Amory, who had been free to speak without such prior script approval because of the light nature of his remarks. That is, until 1963, when his commentary would periodically take a turn for the serious. And when he was serious, Amory inevitably talked about a subject that was growing nearer and dearer to his heart: animal rights. He offered his first commentary about the subject in the spring of 1963 after it came to his attention that the American Legion in Harmony, North Carolina, was sponsoring its annual "bunny bop." Participants would chase rabbits, catch them, and then beat them to death with sticks and stones.

Amory's long-held interest in animal rights stemmed, he said, from two events in his life: first, his childhood visits with a beloved aunt who cared for and loved many stray dogs and cats and who instilled in him the idea that animals have soul and intellect, and who introduced him to his favorite book, *Black Beauty*; and, second, from his days as a young newspaper reporter in Arizona in the 1940s when he covered a bullfight on the Mexican border. The barbarism of the event was deeply ingrained in the young man's mind, and it triggered in him a compulsion to stop cruelty to animals whenever he could. He began joining every humane society and animal-rights group he could find, only to believe that those groups had very little clout in actually reducing or publicizing widespread animal cruelty. As he traveled across the country in the 1950s and 1960s, he became increasingly aware that cities and civic groups often killed animals in the name of sport or fund-raising, yet few people knew that. By the early 1960s, Amory was growing more and more horrified — and obsessed — by what he heard and saw.

After learning about the "bunny bop" in North Carolina, Amory and Probst traveled to Harmony and engaged in a debate with its planners. There were many comical aspects to their trip there, and *Today* officials clearly expected to hear Amory's usual lighthearted commentary when he returned. What *Today* audiences heard was somewhat humorous, but mostly it was sarcastic and pointed. Instead of gentle commentary, Amory ridiculed the participants and noted sarcastically that it should be the participants and not the rabbits who should be hunted and killed. So many hunters existed that it would be humane to "thin their ranks," he said. Immediately following his commentary, many *Today* viewers let the management of the show know that they were not amused by Amory's flip comments. The switchboard lit up, and Amory was immediately reprimanded by a top network official who warned him never to offer such commentary again.

By this time in his life, Cleveland Amory had become a true believer of sorts. He was convinced that animal abusers — and his definition of the term included hunters, some scientists, and many self-described "naturalists" — were able to get away with their actions because the public was not fully aware of them. With his platform and access to the media, he apparently believed he could help change that. Within a few months of his hunt-the-hunters commentary, he once again took up the cause of animal rights without prior script approval, this time in a more serious way. He spoke at length on *Today* about the evils of vivisection — the abuse of animals in laboratory experiments. The issue had come up because Congress was considering several bills at the time that offered some protections for animals. While he did not necessarily oppose the use of animals in laboratory experiments, he believed that many were needlessly abused and treated inhumanely. Amory repeated some of the arguments he made in *Saturday Evening Post* and *Saturday Review* articles, describing to the *Today* audience how countless dogs, cats, and other domestic pets were routinely starved, burned, frozen, and otherwise tortured in some of the country's laboratories. Although many Americans may have been shocked and dismayed at the revelation, it was not necessarily what they wanted to hear while eating their cereal that morning. Outspoken scientists joined hunters in voicing their opposition to what they heard on the *Today* show and, once again, the NBC switchboard lit up. Only this time, Amory was given no warning or reprimand. He was out.

In 1988, Amory, then seventy-one, summarized his views about popularity in a response to a letter from a twenty-two-year-old man who sought his advice on how to succeed in life. The man wrote Amory that he was compiling comments about the subject from famous people in hopes of including them in a book. Amory's written response was divided into three related sections. First, he wrote, "Don't be afraid to be yourself." Second, "Don't be afraid to disagree, or, if necessary, to be a minority of one." And third, "Don't be dismayed, in a good cause, at the prospect of having enemies."

Still, Amory's path was not always a clear one for him, and it occasionally hurt him personally that not everyone shared his zeal for animal rights. In 1966, he even took on former first lady Jacqueline Kennedy, although he respected her and knew her socially, and had certainly been a fan of her husband. He made it known throughout his life that he greatly admired President Kennedy, a 1940 Harvard graduate, calling him, among other things, "the most disciplined mind that ever has occupied the White House since Thomas Jefferson." Amory even attended President Kennedy's famous birthday party celebration at Madison Square Garden in May 1962. Amory occasionally saw Jacqueline Kennedy at social events, and corresponded occasionally with Rose Kennedy. (He had sent her a copy of his book *Who Killed Society?* in 1960, and she responded with a cordial note written from the family's Palm Beach estate.)

Mrs. Kennedy had been in the middle of a much-publicized trip to Seville, Spain, where a popular sport was bullfighting on horseback. Mrs. Kennedy, an equestrian, had attended a bullfight and called it "exciting and beautiful," so the royals in Seville invited her to ride one of the horses used in bullfighting. Amory, who at the time was serving as president of the Humane Society of the United States, quickly issued a statement that was quoted in the *New York Times's* account of the event. Mrs. Kennedy ought to know better, he said: "This is a sad and singularly ironic footnote to our modern age of violence that Mrs. Jacqueline Kennedy, of all people, who has seen the barbarism of the present era at such tragic first hand, should now see fit to condone and even compliment the bullfight, which is one of the last relics of the barbarism of a past era."

Several months later, when Amory saw the former first lady at the opera, he tried to catch her eye from afar with a greeting. She saw him — and looked right through him with no acknowledgment. Amory, his friend and assistant Probst recalled, was crushed by the personal snub.

When it came to criticism of those he felt were abusers of animals, he was without fear or favor.

chapter 2 ▷▷▷ The First Resorts

> A good family is one that used to be better.
>
> ▶ CLEVELAND AMORY, *The Proper Bostonians*

$\mathcal{A}$s he grew up near Boston with his older brother and younger sister, Cleveland Amory, like others with his privileged social status, led a type of schizophrenic existence. His family had the money and taste to send their children to the best schools, live in the best houses, and wear the finest clothes. Yet the Amory children also were born into a no-frills life that stressed commitment and hard work: activities without purpose were frowned on. As an adult, Cleveland liked to tell the story about how, when the family spent summers in the resort town of Nahant, they swam at a point called Forty Steps. Supposedly for recreation, the children routinely descended the forty "seaweedy, slimy, stony, miserable steps." But after making that trek, they came not to soft, warm sand but to freezing-cold water. Cleveland once told his father that he did not find the whole adventure much fun. "It's not supposed to be fun," Robert Amory replied. "It feels so good when you get out." To Cleveland, the response was typical upper-class Bostonian: "That's what Bostonians like to do," he said. "Wear the hair shirt."

Cleveland Amory's upbringing at 956 Brush Hill Road in Milton, Massachusetts, about ten miles southwest of Boston, was typical for one of his social stature. In biographical material put out later in his life by one of his publishers, Harper & Brothers, he said that the population of the street "had always figured prominently in the activities of First Families [of Boston]." His father, Robert, had been a vice president of Spring Mills textiles, and his mother, Leonore Cobb Amory, came from a prominent family in Chicago. Although Amory's childhood was typical of that of an upper-crust Bostonian family, he spent much of his adult life and career satirizing aspects of the WASPY Boston upbringing, or at least pointing out its absurdities, gleaned from eighteen years as an insider. Whether others in his social class agreed with him was one thing. But they would have to admit that his observations were at least legitimate — his background gave him a unique and personal entrée into the intimate lifestyle of Boston's aristocracy.

In biographical material put out by his publishers, Amory always listed three of his favorite sayings. Two dealt with animals: "Man has an infinite capacity to rationalize his own cruelty" was one; "the mark of a civilized person is how he treats what's underneath him" was another. But a third dealt with the New England society about which he enjoyed writing early in his career: "A good family is one that used to be better." A true Boston Brahmin, Amory wrote, had a "merchant prince" — a patriarch who by the 1860s had earned the family fortune, usually making money in industry, and launched them into society. Often that wealth was achieved in textiles or seafaring.

Amory gleefully tells us in the book flap of *The Proper Bostonians* about the provincialism of Boston society and the emphasis on proper breeding. "This is the Boston where visitors from a strange, barbaric province called Iowa once were advised that 'here we pronounce it Ohio.'" The first anecdote in the book, in paragraph one on page one, describes a letter-of-recommendation request in the 1920s made by a Chicago banking house to a Boston investment firm about a young Bostonian the bank was considering hiring. The investment firm executives went on at length about the young man's pedigree; his mother was a Lowell, his father a Cabot, they assured the bank management, and his familial background beyond that was impeccable. In Chicago, though, that evidently carried little weight: "We were not contemplating using [him] for breeding purposes," the bank responded.

▷ ▷ ▷ Robert and Leonore Amory and their three children, Robert Jr., Cleveland, and Leonore, led a typical Bostonian existence — privileged yet austere. Born in 1888, Robert Amory came from a long line of Boston merchants and was a 1906 graduate of Harvard who also studied engineering at the Massachusetts Institute of Technology. (The Amory family initially settled in Charleston, South Carolina, in the seventeenth century.) At one time the president of the Nashua (New Hampshire) Manufacturing Co., a textile factory, Robert also was a former president of the National Association of Cotton Manufacturers. In 1910, Robert Amory married Leonore Cobb of Chicago, the daughter of Henry Ives Cobb, a prominent architect there. Leonore was the only daughter in a family of seven boys and was a University of Chicago graduate at a time when few women attended college. Despite her intellectual and social pedigree, it was difficult for Leonore to break into

Robert's world when she moved east to Amory's home at 323 Beacon Street in Boston's Back Bay. She was not a native Bostonian, although her family had a country home in Brewster, New York, and spent considerable time in New York. While Leonore had trouble adapting to the society into which she married, she was no shrinking violet. She was bright and outspoken, qualities that she may have passed down to her younger son, Cleveland, who was named after one of Leonore's brothers.

According to Robert and Leonore's grandson, the Amorys were Bostonians through and through. "They weren't Cabots or Lowells, but they were at the top of the social strata, imbedded with all of its narrowness and the other things," Rob Amory said. When Robert Amory's textile mill began faltering financially, it was purchased by business leader Royal Little's Textron and closed. Robert and Leonore, their children grown, were forced to became "ex-patriots" and move to New York, where Robert Amory became executive vice president of Spring Mills Inc., another textile manufacturer. Ultimately, the Amorys' stash of money dwindled, but their bloodline was permanent and their social status in Boston ingrained in the city's history. As Cleveland Amory would write as an adult, it was unimportant that the once-wealthy Amorys had lost much of their wealth (and indeed, he said, had to take in boarders to make ends meet); what was important was that it had been "good, sound nineteenth-century money — none of this tainted twentieth-century 'quick money.'"

The three Amory children — Robert, born in 1915; Cleveland, known as Clip, or Clippie, in 1917; and Leonore, 1921 — were brought up primarily by governesses and had a formal relationship with their parents. The Depression brought hard times for the textile industry and for the Amorys, at least compared with other families like them: they were "forced" to live full-time in their country mansion in Milton. Still, they were not so poor that the children could not attend the private, prestigious Milton Academy. The boys later went to Harvard, and Leonore attended Vassar. Both boys were excellent athletes, excelling in particular at sailing, golf, and tennis. The tall, strapping, curly-haired Cleveland was particularly athletic despite some health problems — including bad asthma, allergies, and eczema — that plagued him on and off for much of his life. The children may have been classic upper-crust New Englanders, but as Cleveland Amory relates in his autobiographical cat trilogy, they had a sense of humor and fun that sometime included playing tricks on their governesses, several of whom apparently did not appreciate the jokes and left the family after a short time. The two boys, in particular, often used their beloved sheepdog Brookie as a foil in these antics. Summers in Nahant, though, were uncomplicated. As Amory told journalist Edward R. Murrow in 1959, they were filled with street picnics and croquet in the early evening.

Like many insular subgroups, upper-class Bostonians had their own unique language, used in part to identify outsiders or to pinpoint those not of their stature. Amory believed it no accident that many New England cities have short names with difficult pronunciations. For instance, the "correct" way to pronounce "Nahant" is "the way a Bostonian refers to the wife of his uncle" (Nahaunt) and "not the small bug" (Nahant), Amory once said. And even his own surname was a topic of discussion among the Boston Brahmins. Shortly after *The Proper Bostonians* was published and its candor had duly annoyed some of its subjects, a sign was posted outside the exclusive Somerset Club in Boston: "What would you expect from an Amory who pronounces it A-mory," the sign said. The "correct" pronunciation by the original and true Amorys is "Emory," based on the English pronunciation. Early on in *The Proper Bostonians*, Amory pointed out the subtleties of pronunciation: "The broad 'a' and the stern omission of the 'r,' generally regarded as typically Bostonian, is not an invariable rule," he wrote. "Actually the Proper Bostonian is more inclined to speak with a clipped 'a.' He says not Haa-vaad . . . but Hah-vud. He may leave out the 'r' in a word like marbles, but he doesn't say maa-bles; he says mabbles."

Like others of their ilk, the Amorys were Episcopalian (although Leonore had been Unitarian), but they were not religious in the conventional spiritual sense of the word. Much of their religion had implications of class. Those with their status had Anglican backgrounds. And while the family had some money and had inherited a country home in Bar Harbor, they were not fabulously rich. By the time Robert Amory's mill was failing financially, when the boys were teenagers, the family had relatively little money by upper-crust New England standards. It was instilled in the children that ultimately they were expected to work, preferably at jobs that would contribute to society or "fulfill some sense of responsibility," Rob Amory said. This sense of duty to society and culture — noblesse oblige — was a hallmark of New England families of their class. Ironically, families like the Amorys practiced what Rob Amory called an "inverse snobbery" that says clothes and physical possessions, while of high quality, should not be ostentatious, and one should not purchase material goods one does not need.

This philosophy of deep-seated frugality and inverse snobbery was discussed at length in 2004 in a humorous article by writer William Zinsser, a self-described WASP and onetime doppelgänger of Amory's. Zinsser's light article in *Town and Country* describes how in 1936, when Zinsser was thirteen, his parents, whom he describes as conventional Long Island WASPs, were seeking a suitably WASPy young man to spend part of the summer with young William and serve as his tutor. They found a young Harvard student named Cleveland Amory. The name alone signified that he was a Boston Brahmin, Zinsser wrote, and the older boy took young William under his wing. The two played tennis and golf, and Amory taught him the intricacies of one of his favorite pastimes — chess. Most important, they indulged in a passion unknown to their parents: they spent much of the summer at Yankee Stadium. Amory was a die-hard Boston Red Sox fan for his entire life, and young Zinsser loved the New York Giants. Zinsser told the story to illustrate the insularity of Northeast WASPs of that era. "The [WASP] laws were coded into my metabolism at an early age," he wrote. "Gaudy clothes and flashy cars were out. Understatement was in. A sweater the color of oatmeal was as attractive as you could get. I was careful never to be seen in a green jacket or tan shoes, or to use the wrong language. I said 'curtains' not 'drapes'; I said 'rich,' not 'wealthy.'" And, as Amory wrote many years later, the frugality of New Englanders was ingrained in them so deeply that they never got over it. After he became famous as a writer and social critic, Amory and his wife appeared in a live broadcast of Edward R. Murrow's interview show *Person to Person*. The Amorys, like other subjects of the show, were interviewed in their own home. Amory recalled how a CBS technician, while setting up the cameras for the interview, whispered to another technician that "he [Amory] may be a celebrity but I'll tell you one thing — *I've* got more clothes than he has!"

In the third book of his cat trilogy, Amory wrote about his summer with Zinsser. It made quite an impression on him for several reasons. He was eighteen at the time, and it was his first paying job (he earned one hundred dollars a month and the promise of a fifty-dollar bonus, plus free room and board). And he remembered being amused by the vague title of the job: tutor-companion, which sounded suspiciously like an automobile — a "two-door companion." (In fact, he got figurative mileage out of the term for much of the rest of his career in articles he wrote and in speeches.) What stood out in Amory's mind was the baseball game he and Zinsser invented and played on a tennis court. It was elaborate and detailed and involved only the two of them—and a series of major league teams that played each other. As if daily games were not enough, the two played doubleheaders on Sundays.

It is interesting that both Zinsser and Amory would grow up to become writers, because writing was not seen as a suitable profession for young men of their social stature. (Both would start out as newspaper reporters—Zinsser on the *New York Herald Tribune* and Amory at several newspapers in Arizona. Zinsser also wrote books, including the well-known *On Writing Well*, which has been used for decades as a resource in newsrooms.) There was some expectation that both Zinsser and Amory would become businessmen or follow in their fathers' footsteps; Zinsser wrote that after he returned from the army, he—his parents' only son—was expected take over his family's one-hundred-year-old business. Instead, he got a job with the *Herald Tribune*: "At that time, newspapermen were still slightly disreputable; nobody actually knew any newspapermen," he wrote. Like his onetime summer mentor, Zinsser noted that he enjoyed being an outsider and unconventional—that was part of the *Herald Tribune*'s appeal.

Perhaps Amory's love of writing stemmed in part from his image of himself as an outsider looking in. His father shared with the Zinssers the view that writing was not necessarily an appropriate field for an upper-class young Bostonian. But Amory did not became a writer to rebel against his father. Zinsser recalled that he and Amory frequently talked about journalism during their summer together. As adults, Zinsser and Amory saw each other only occasionally—usually it was at a yearly New York Marathon party Amory hosted each year at his apartment on Central Park South and West Fifty-seventh Street. The marathon route ended on West Fifty-ninth, allowing Amory's guests to catch the final portion of the race.

In his own biographical material, Amory recalled that his first "literary effort" was undertaken when he was twelve. In collaboration with a Milton classmate, he wrote sixty-five single-spaced pages of a novel they called "Greater Love Hath No Man Than This." The boys apparently learned early the dangers of putting down one's writing before it is finished: "At the end of the summer, having killed off their hero in a society duel on the Island of Corsica, they paused to reorganize the manuscript and never returned to it." Nonetheless, Amory was never one who suffered from writer's block during his career.

In *The Best Cat Ever*, the third in the cat trilogy, Amory wrote at length about a visit he, his cat, and his friend and assistant Marian Probst made to Milton Academy for a reunion. The visit jogged memories of the school's strict atmosphere and austerity, which rivaled that of military academies. One topic that was never mentioned at Milton was sex, an ironic omission, Amory wrote decades later: "Milton . . . was one of the oldest of a distinguished group of New England prep schools including Groton, St. Paul's, St. Mark's and others which, taken together, became known as the St. Grottlesexers. This was an odd sobriquet because if there was one thing these schools were not long on, it was sex."

Amory's grades at Milton Academy were not stellar, although it was a competitive atmosphere where grades of Bs and Cs were not necessarily considered low. A copy of his grade card for the 1929–30 school year, when he was twelve, indicates that he earned mostly Bs and some Cs during the first half of the year, but that his grades dropped slightly during the second half. Courses he took included English, Latin, arithmetic, geography, history, music, and physical education. Comments by teachers indicate that while his effort fluctuated during the year, some of his work was careless or done too quickly. (Grades were apparently given six times or "periods" a year.) During the first period, he was given a B+ in English: "Has unusual ability in expressing himself in writing," the teacher wrote. "Occasional weaknesses in grammar. Consistent in effort and attitude." He was given a C− in Latin. ("Cleveland's test was disappointing. His effort is good," the teacher wrote.) Both his history and geography teachers indicated that he was underachieving in those subjects and each gave him a C−. ("Capable of honor work. Must guard against carelessness and too rapid preparation," the history teacher wrote. "Has ability to do better work," his geography teacher wrote.)

During most of his life, Cleveland Amory was not one to suffer from low self-esteem, but some of his teachers recognized that confidence was not always a virtue. He once received a C in history. "Overconfidence caused this slump," the teacher wrote. Others wrote that the student did well — if he was interested in the subject. During the fourth period, his C+ in geography represented an improvement, one teacher wrote. "When interested is a good worker, but frequently careless and inattentive." His arithmetic teachers gave him a C−. "Seems to have lost interest in attaining a high mark," the teacher wrote.

It is not known how the Amorys responded to their son's grades. But there is little question that all three Amory children had brilliant minds and tremendous intellectual curiosity. Leonore set high intellectual standards for her children and stressed integrity and achievement. This was emphasized not just to the two boys but also to Leonore. Shortly after she graduated from Vassar, she married Thomas Sawyers, a surgeon, and moved with him to California, where she has lived her entire life.

It was natural that the relationship between Robert Amory Jr. and his brother, Cleveland, was somewhat competitive: they were only two years apart in age, both attended the same schools, and both were reared in a background that stressed success and contribution to society. And certainly Robert Amory Jr. must have lived up to his parents' expectations. After graduating from Harvard Law School and practicing law for a few years, he entered the army in 1941. He eventually rose to the rank of colonel, commanding an amphibious regiment in the New Guinea and Philippines campaigns in World War II. He was awarded the Silver Star, the Bronze Star, and the Legion of Merit. In 1946, he was asked to teach law at Harvard, becoming the youngest law professor in its history. In 1952, he was asked to join the CIA, where he served as deputy director until 1962. As his son, Robert III, explained, Robert Amory Jr. was called to the CIA when the Cold War was raging; it was a call to service to his country. "They wanted bright people who were motivated to answer the call. That was my father's path," he said. After working at the CIA, Robert Amory Jr. headed the international division of the federal Bureau of the Budget and later became general counsel of the National Gallery of Art. He died in 1989 at the age of seventy-four.

While there was a certain amount of competition between the brothers for much of their lives, they were never estranged and kept in contact with each other; Cleveland Amory mentions his brother in an affectionate and humorous way in the first of his cat books, *The Cat Who Came for Christmas*, where he describes Robert Jr.'s visit to Cleveland's New York apartment as the two search for a cat in hiding. And nothing in Cleveland's writings indicates he was ever at odds with his brother. But the two men "pursued different paths," according to Rob Amory: "[Robert Amory Jr.] was trying to fight the battle for the Cold War and my uncle is writing books about socialites, the media, culture." Robert Amory Jr. also had a more conventional family life than his brother. He was married for more than forty years to the former Mary Armstrong, and they had two sons, Daniel and Robert. Cleveland was married and divorced twice and had a stepdaughter and stepgrand-daughter. Also, Cleveland spent much of his adult life traveling — primarily for business reasons, although his personal and business interests were frequently the same. Clearly, his home life was not as established as that of his brother.

▷ ▷ ▷ It was expected that boys like the Amorys would attend Harvard and thrive there — and Robert and Cleveland did not disappoint their parents. For families like theirs, money was not an issue when it came to selecting a college; one simply sent one's children to the "right" schools. But Amory claims in his writings that money may have been an issue when it was time for him to attend college. The textile business was at its lowest point when he was ready for college, he wrote in *The Cat and the Curmudgeon*, so most of his education was paid for by a beloved aunt named Lucy Creshore. But Cleveland's great affection toward his Aunt Lu did not come only because of her financial generosity. Aunt Lu was a soft touch when it came to rescuing stray cats and dogs, and young Cleveland loved visiting his aunt and indulging in what she called "stray play" with the many animals. As a boy, Amory respected his aunt for an even more important reason: she was able to ignore what people thought of her. "Some people . . . made fun of her," he wrote. "They told stories about how dirty her house was and how many messes the animals made. . . . From the beginning, even at a very young age, I didn't like those people. I loved her and her house and all the animals." Like his Aunt Lu, he, too, would become oblivious to ridicule when he felt that what he was doing was right. Furthermore, Amory noted, Aunt Lu never favored one pet over another: "She seemed to love them all equally — the pretty ones and the not-so-pretty ones, the nice, easy-to-love ones and the not-so-nice, not-so-easy-to-love ones." Aunt Lu also played a pivotal role in securing for the Amory children a pet of their own. For years, Leonore Amory had insisted that her children had enough contact with animals when they visited their Aunt Lu and did not need a pet of their own. But thanks to Leonore's formidable and strong-willed mother, and to Aunt Lu, the three Amory children did get a dog of their own. The arrival of the family's first puppy was the most memorable moment of his childhood, Amory would write seventy years later, and would herald the dawn of a lifelong love of animals and an appreciation and respect for their innocence, their intelligence, and their unique personalities.

Amory remembered vividly his first meeting with Brookie, the Old English sheepdog pup who arrived at the Amory home in a crate on the back of a truck. When the truck stopped and the back of it was opened, the pup sprang out of the crate and jumped onto Amory: "As I lay on my back, gasping both with excitement and for breath, I thought about something Aunt Lu had read me about Olde English Sheepdogs — that whatever any other puppy does, an Olde English Sheepdog also does, only more so," he wrote. The eight-year-old Amory was intrigued by all aspects the furry bundle of energy, but two qualities about the dog particularly fascinated him: that his fur covered his eyes, impeding his vision, and that he had no tail. The Amory children were given a quick lesson on the history of sheepdogs by their aunt. She told them that while the dogs had limited vision, their hearing was the best of any animal but the eel. And, regarding their tails, they were cropped as part of a tradition born in England. A tax was levied on long-tailed hunting dogs, Aunt Lu explained, and owners of sheepdogs, which were herding dogs, cropped their tails so they would not be mistaken for hunting dogs. And so began the relationship between Brookie, the Old English sheepdog, and the three Amory children.

Aunt Lu made a lasting impression on her nephew in other ways, too. It was she who introduced him at an early age to his favorite book: *Black Beauty*, by the British author Anna Sewell. As Amory would write much later in his life, *Black Beauty*, the "autobiography" of a horse, affected him greatly. (As he added much later, he realized even as a boy that the horse did not actually write the book, but that didn't matter to him: "All right, so he had a ghost writer. You don't think Joe Namath writes all *his* stuff, do you?") Amory was intrigued not only by the book and its clear illustration of mankind's inhumanity to animals but also by the story of Sewell herself. A Quaker, Sewell wrote *Black Beauty* when she was in her fifties and very ill. It took her seven years to complete. Anna Sewell never lived to experience the phenomenal success of her only book; she died several months after it was published. Cleveland Amory memorized much of the book when he was young, and its message became a guiding force that would affect him for the rest of his life.

▷ ▷ ▷ It was more or less preordained that the two Amory boys would attend Harvard. Three-fourths or more of the students at Milton went to Harvard, and Cleveland's father insisted that the Amorys be no different. Parents like the Amorys sent their sons there not simply to get an education but also to meet others of their social and intellectual standing. They also sent them there so they would ultimately become part of the brotherhood that is the

Harvard alumni. By the time Amory graduated in 1939, his schoolmates included Joseph Kennedy Jr., who graduated in 1938, and his brother John F. Kennedy, a 1940 graduate. While Amory knew them both, they were not close friends. Many other graduates during Amory's tenure at Harvard ultimately became key leaders in business, government, communication, education, and other fields.

And Cleveland Amory did excel at Harvard. He said in speeches throughout his life that the high point of the lives of most Harvard graduates was their years at that university. It was downhill from there, he would say only half jokingly. Throughout his life, Amory would talk about his Harvard years in speeches and write about them extensively. His anecdotes may well have been exaggerated or romanticized, but there is no doubt about his profound affection for Harvard and for his fellow students. He also took a perverse pride in the fact that, unlike most of his classmates, he never donated money to his alma mater. The reason? The university participated in research that involved experiments on captive laboratory animals, an activity he loathed, and besides, Amory had formed a nonprofit charitable organization of his own later in his life, one that he believed had a much greater need for donations than Harvard. But Amory did take great pleasure in the creative effort he put into turning down Harvard's requests for funding, which included writing elaborate and flowery letters rejecting those appeals.

Amory recounted in detail his freshman year at Harvard in the third volume of his cat trilogy, *The Best Cat Ever*. His roommate during all four of his years there was a Bostonian named Bruce Foster; like Amory, Foster had attended Milton Academy, and, like Amory's father, his father had also attended the university. Foster and Amory became close friends, and like many who joined Amory's inner circle, Foster became a partner in crime in Amory's antics.

As Amory told it, he and Foster had one immediate goal as soon as they entered Harvard: to take easy classes. Amory recounted tongue in cheek that he had witnessed firsthand how his brother Robert had taken five courses instead of four during his freshman year and had received straight As. Further, Robert had finished Harvard in three years. Amory wrote that he had no intention of competing with his overachieving brother, so he decided early on to take another tack for success at Harvard: to join the prestigious *Harvard Crimson*. The reason, he added, was not necessarily a deep interest in journalism but the fact that the grind of daily publishing made it acceptable to give one's studies short shrift. In actuality, though, his reasons for joining the *Crimson* probably had little to do with an ambivalence about classes. He had written for Milton's newspaper, the *Orange and Blue*, and he had an interest in writing and expressing his opinions. Also, he relished the prestige attached to becoming the top dog—in this case, president (editor) of the newspaper. And Amory did rise to the occasion: he was president of the newspaper in 1939.

Still, Amory's work on the *Crimson* did give him license to be less than a serious student. Foster had no desire to join the *Crimson*, but he shared Amory's thoughts about easy classes because he had, as Amory put it, "a well-honed desire to have . . . a grand good time. . . . The hardest I think I ever saw Bruce work was in our quest to find those easy courses." He and Foster consequently were very selective about the courses they took, Amory would say years later. Because they were out late—Amory at the paper and Foster at parties—they made sure to take courses offered after 11:00 a.m., and ones that were on the ground floor of classroom buildings so they would not have to make a trek up flights of stairs. This limited their possibilities, of course, and they found themselves in classes like Introduction to Art and Military Science. Amory's favorite, though, was a graduate class called The Idea of Fate and the Gods, which was offered in the Divinity School. The two undergraduates had to get special permission to take the class, and in *The Best Cat Ever*, Amory writes hilariously of how they were surrounded in class by graduate students, priests, rabbis, and others who, unlike them, were serious about the subject. To make matters worse, the professor confused the two throughout the semester, calling Amory "Foster" and Foster "Amory," a phenomenon that concerned Amory more than it concerned Foster. The hapless Foster took advantage of the situation and would sit in class and chronically talk to Amory while the professor was trying to speak. The befuddled professor of course thought it was "Amory" who was disrupting class with his comments. This mistaken identity culminated in a who's-on-first episode where Amory decided he was tired of it all, stood up and began walking out of the classroom. "Foster," the professor yelled. "Where are you going?" (Although Amory wrote humorously of his exploits with Foster, he loved him as a friend, and both Marian Probst and Amory's stepdaughter Gaea Leinhardt said he was devastated on learning of Foster's death in the military shortly before the start of World War II; they believe he never fully recovered from the premature death of his friend.)

Amory's grades at Harvard never earned him a spot on the honor roll. The 988 students in Amory's freshman class were ranked as I, highest distinction; II, high distinction; III, distinction; IV, high pass; V, pass, and VI, low pass. Amory's rank, like that of 31 percent of the freshmen in his class, was a V. But he passed. Harvard also offered its students opportunities to excel in activities other than classes. Amory was elected to the social club Hasty Pudding, and he cultivated his love for chess. He also earned a pilot's license and was elected secretary of his senior class.

In February 1937, Amory attended the Harvard-Yale-Princeton Conference on Public Affairs, which was sponsored by the newspapers at those three universities. The topic of discussion was "the role of the government in the national economy." In an essay about the event, Amory indicated that he believed his fellow undergraduates were idealistic but naive. They had spirit but no solid plans, he wrote: "The undergraduates present . . . seemed to display all the virtues and most of the faults of youth . . . a fine spirit of idealism, coupled with a willingness to sweep everything that existed aside, hopeful of the future. . . . The undergraduate displayed all the impatience of the immature and uneducated politician in that seeing weaknesses, seeing people unsatisfied, he proposes no new law or a new method of making people happy." Throughout his life, Amory was always happy to give his opinion — in person and in his writing. And he did not feel constrained when airing his usually liberal political views. His favorite causes — other than animal rights — included vocal support for Israel, the rights of Native Americans, and, ultimately, opposition to the war in Vietnam.

The chief influences in Amory's life were people he felt he could emulate. One of those was President Franklin Delano Roosevelt, a fellow Harvard alumnus, whom Amory met as a college student when he was invited to the White House in 1937. More than fifty years after that visit, Amory summarized his views about Roosevelt in a letter to a young man who wrote Amory asking his advice about how to succeed. Roosevelt, Amory said, was successful because of certain personality traits — "his wit, his warmth and humor, his lack of bitterness, his courage in adversity and his generosity to opponents, but most of all his utter determination to get done what he believed had to be done." Even as an activist battling his opponents, Amory's friends and acquaintances say, Amory frequently used humor to persuade, and never personally attacked those with whom he disagreed. And while Amory knew he would persuade only a small group of people, he took great pleasure in small victories. Amory also wrote this young man that progress is rarely attained in a climate of harmony: "Don't be dismayed, in a good cause, at the prospect of having enemies," Amory wrote. "Unhappily, almost all the social advances which we take for granted today were made at the cost of great personal sacrifice to their advocates, and strident disaccord in society at large. None of this should deter you from proceeding down a path which you believe to be right." At Amory's memorial service in 1998, Paul Watson, an environmentalist who worked with Amory on several projects, including efforts to prevent the clubbing of baby seals, recalled how Amory stressed the same points to him. "He said, 'You must never be concerned what people think of you. You must do what you think is right,'" Watson said. "And because of that, I have a lot of enemies today, but I did the right thing."

In one of his often-told Harvard stories, Amory explained why he never graduated with honors: he gave a "wrong" answer to the panel of professors who judged his oral exams. The panel, he said, consisted of a few faculty members who knew he often missed class. "Tell me, Mr. Amory, do you like *Beowulf?*" one professor asked, certain that that he had not read it. Amory, always candid, replied: "Dr. Lowell, I can discuss *Beowulf.* I can quote you sources on *Beowulf.* I can talk about the spreading influence of *Beowulf.* But to tell you the truth, sir, I haven't had time to think whether or not I like *Beowulf.*" Amory was denied the designation of "graduate with honors," but he thought he should get points for honesty. "Who in their right mind likes *Beowulf?*" he asked his readers decades later.

As president of the *Harvard Crimson* during his senior year, Amory was in effect the editor and publisher of the paper. In the hierarchy of the *Crimson,* the managing editor ran the news operations, and the editorial chairman was in charge of the editorial page. Amory, like all *Crimson* presidents, held most of the key editorial spots before his ascension to the top spot.

The *Harvard Crimson* of the late 1930s published a variety of types of stories, from interviews with celebrities (including one in January 1937 with Katharine Hepburn, no doubt written by Amory, who knew the Hepburn family as he was growing up) to news about the university. Sports was frequently played on the front page. Whatever their subject, nearly all the stories on page one were written by *Crimson* reporters. Few news articles had bylines, but many carried the initials of the reporter at the end of the story. The *Crimson* was a four- or six-page broadsheet with severe graphics by today's standards — there were few photos other than head shots, a vertical design uninterrupted by many graphic elements, and headlines with subheadlines.

Amory joked throughout his adult life that his work with the *Crimson* gave him a license to avoid his studies. But the truth is that the *Crimson* was and is a highly respected newspaper, and only the best journalists rise to the top there. Many students who hold top editorships go on to prestigious jobs in the media, and there is little doubt that his *Crimson* work helped Amory get a job on the *Saturday Evening Post* shortly after graduation. As such, he was the youngest editor in the history of that magazine. Former *Crimson* staff members frequently form a brotherhood that they maintain throughout their lives. In Amory's case, one of his *Crimson* colleagues — Caspar Weinberger, who was managing editor in 1937 — would come to Amory's rescue many decades later in a project close to Amory's heart.

Chapter 3 ▷ ▷ ▷ A Pen as Sharp as a Stiletto

> The Proper Bostonian is not by nature a traveler. . . .
> Basically he remains adamant in his lack of geographical
> curiosity outside the suburbs of Boston. The Beacon
> Hill lady who, chided for her lack of travel, asked
> simply, "Why should I travel when I'm already here?"
> would seem to have put the matter in a nutshell.
>
> ▶ CLEVELAND AMORY, *The Proper Bostonians*

*W*hen Cleveland Amory graduated from Harvard in 1939, he was following the same path taken by thousands of young Boston men before him. Attending Harvard was simply what men in his socioeconomic group did. Eight years after he graduated, in his best-selling book *The Proper Bostonians,* Amory quoted nineteenth-century "Proper Bostonian" Edmund Quincy, who was once a president of Harvard: " 'If a man's there,' he used to say [about Harvard], tapping his Harvard Triennial Catalogue, containing a complete list of Harvard graduates, 'that's who he is. If he isn't, who is he?' "

Swimming upstream against nearly two hundred years of tradition could not have been easy, but Amory managed to do it when it came to his career. He certainly took a less orthodox path than his brother, Robert, who graduated two years earlier from Harvard and attended Harvard Law School. After graduating, Robert was soon practicing law at a New York firm. Cleveland's interest and experience was in writing, a field considered somewhat unconventional for someone of his social standing and education. His Boston-area upbringing had instilled in him the idea that young men of his social stature do not stay idle for long. Shortly after he graduated, as he wrote in biographical material throughout his life, he joined the staff of the *Nashua* (N.H.) *Telegraph.* But he wrote and spoke surprisingly little about his tenure there. After working there several months, he was offered a much more prestigious job — that of an associate editor on the *Saturday Evening Post.* Amory wrote briefly about how he got the job at the *Saturday Evening Post* in his book *The Best Cat Ever.* It came about, in part, through his connections from Harvard and in part through his family's friendship with the parents of actress Katharine Hepburn. Of course, part of the cachet of attending Harvard was the life-long personal and professional links one forged while there. In this case, it is likely that his Boston pedigree or his connections from Harvard — or some combination of both — helped him get a job at the *Saturday Evening Post*. It also came about because of prodding by Mrs. Hepburn during his final years at Harvard — she wanted to know what his plans were after graduation — that prompted Amory to apply at the publishing firm of Little, Brown and Company in Boston.

There was no job for him there, but the top editor suggested he apply at the *Saturday Evening Post*. It was an odd suggestion for two reasons. First, nearly all the editors at the magazine were men who had been at the magazine for decades; and second, the magazine's headquarters were in Philadelphia and not Boston. Armed with a letter from Mrs. Hepburn, who had a friend who worked at the *Post*, Amory interviewed there and was given the job.

In an unsigned letter on *Saturday Evening Post* stationery confirming the hiring, the writer notes that Roger Scaife, a Harvard graduate in the New York publishing business, suggested the *Post* hire twenty-two-year-old Amory — a move that even *Post* editors apparently thought was unusual because of Amory's young age: "This is the first time within the memory of anyone on the editorial staff of the *Post*, that we've taken on a young man fresh from college, but he seems a level-headed youngster and we feel the experiment has an excellent chance of succeeding. Thank you for introducing Amory to us."

Amory had long been intrigued by the Hepburn family. Katharine, of course, later became famous, and Amory maintained his friendship with her throughout his life. Amory spent several summers during college in Connecticut near the Saybrook home of the Hepburns and socialized with the family often. He wrote many years later that he was "in love" with Katharine's younger sister, Peggy, and intrigued by both Mr. and Mrs. Hepburn. Katharine's father was a well-known surgeon in the area, and her mother was ahead of her time in many ways, Amory always thought — particularly in her views about such issues as politics and women's rights. She was, in fact, a leader in the woman suffrage movement, and her progressive comments at dinner would sometimes scandalize guests, Amory recalled.

At the time Amory was hired, the *Saturday Evening Post* had established itself as one of the most prestigious of the "slick" magazines of the era —

expensive-looking magazines that offered both fiction and nonfiction. When Cyrus Curtis, publisher of *Ladies' Home Journal*, bought the *Post* for $6,933 in 1897, it had a circulation of 2,000 readers and was on its last legs. Thanks to Curtis's business acumen and his understanding of the changing nature of the magazine business, the magazine was revived; it had a circulation of nearly 2 million by 1912 and 2.2 million ten years after that. Curtis, like other publishers of the '20s, took advantage of the needs of an increasingly sophisticated population for reading material. By the time Amory joined the magazine in late 1939, it was considered a plum outlet for freelancers and had established a reputation that only the best writers were able to get their work into the magazine. By 1940, writers like James Thurber, William Faulkner, F. Scott Fitzgerald, McKinlay Kantor, and many others regularly had their work published in the *Post*, which was seen as a particularly impressive venue for fiction. As historian Ronald Weber wrote, for nearly forty years until the early 1960s, "to appear regularly on its pages as the author of either fiction or nonfiction was to reach a point of well-paid professional success midway between the syndicates, Sunday newspapers, and pulp magazines on the one hand and the sober literary and intellectual journals on the other. . . . Competition was fierce."

Amory was hired initially to edit a standing page called Postscripts and to select cartoons for the magazine, but he soon began writing for the magazine occasionally. In fact, impressed as he was that he was the youngest editor at the magazine — and the youngest editor ever hired there — he still preferred writing to editing. Always one to take advantage of a situation, Amory jumped at an invitation to all *Post* editors by its chief editor, Wesley Winans Stout, to write a profile of the headmaster of the prestigious Groton School in Massachusetts. Stout sent a memo to all editors asking, "What would you think of an article on Groton School?" All the editors but Amory wrote a resounding no on the memo, Amory recalled. But he saw it as an opportunity to write, wrote yes on the memo, and shipped it back. "I had hardly returned to my desk when my buzzer sounded and Mr. Stout announced that he wished to see me," Amory wrote decades later. " 'Why,' he said, 'did you put yes on my suggestion for the article on Groton?' " Ever the proper Bostonian, Amory felt compelled to correct Stout's pronunciation of the school before responding: "He pronounced it Growton. Groton, I corrected him, pronouncing it Grotten." Stout, meanwhile, suggested that the story focus on the school's remarkable headmaster, a Dr. Peabody. "He pronounced it

Peabody," Amory recalled. "Once again I corrected him. Peabody . . . is pronounced in Boston by saying the consonants as rapidly as possible and ignoring all the vowels. It's Pbd, Pbd, I said, doing it a second time so he would get the hang of it."

Amory remembered the Endicott Peabody story as his first major published work and a landmark in his life. But that did not stop the young writer from being brutally honest. The Peabody story caused its share of controversy, and offered a glimpse into the future when it came to Amory's candid and detail-laden writing style. The "hook" of the story is the retirement of the eighty-three-year-old Peabody, the much-beloved head of the prestigious prep school. As Amory writes, though, this conventional image unravels. The young men at Groton are not simply taught the values of hard work and good manners. The *Post* article portrays Groton as a prison of sorts, where the punishments for minor infractions far exceeded the crimes and where the students served hard time. The story begins innocently enough: "[While] there are fifteen hundred private schools of all kinds, there is just one Groton," Amory gushes, adding that during the school's fifty-six-year history it graduated boys who became ambassadors, government leaders, and even, in one case, president: Franklin D. Roosevelt.

But the narrative quickly takes a sharp and brutal turn. Amory notes that Groton is a "church school," and "life revolves around Protestant and Episcopal services . . . weekdays ten minutes of morning services before classes, and Sundays two services. There are also prayers each evening." Of course, this follows the wake-up bell at 6:50 each morning. With the exception of a nineteen-day break at Christmas and a seventeen-day break at Easter, the boys must stay at Groton throughout the school year. And the living accommodations are hardly commodious, consisting of "a six-by-ten cubicle, containing a bed, a bureau, a chair and six hooks; and nothing may be exchanged or moved. In the lavatory, [the student] will find a small space reserved for him in front of a back soapstone watering trough, his own basin and three more hooks."

If a young man is "fresh" in class, he must work off the infraction by walking in circles for an hour, raking faculty members' leaves, or walking their dogs. "One master has an Old English sheep dog which is kept in show condition," the story notes. For rare offenses deemed "capital," the boy is put in "solitary" — kept confined in a room for two days. "Boys claim that the only solaces are bread and water and a Bible."

According to Rob Amory, Cleveland's nephew, the article caused quite an uproar when it was published. Although the living conditions at Groton were far from secret, it was the first time they were revealed to the world at large. And it was one of the first times Cleveland Amory would shed light on a group or organization's dirty little secrets — a talent he cultivated in his writing. If the New England upper crust who sent their children to Groton were upset by Amory's story, they had not seen anything yet: seven years after the Groton piece was published, Amory's *Proper Bostonians* brought truth-telling about the upper crust in New England to a new level.

Amory's career at the *Saturday Evening Post* was short-lived, thanks to World War II. He, like his brother, had been in ROTC in college, and later began serving in army intelligence. Throughout his life, Cleveland Amory would joke in speeches and in his writings about the "competition" that took place between him and his brother (including his refusal to compete with Robert's high grades at Harvard). In the army, however, Lieutenant Cleveland Amory had a formidable opponent in his older brother. Robert, like Cleveland, joined the army in 1941 as a private. But, as the *New York Times* noted many years later in his obituary, "he emerged six years later as a colonel." Robert Amory commanded an amphibious regiment in the New Guinea and Philippines campaigns and was given a Silver Star for gallantry in action and the Bronze Star and the Legion of Merit. Cleveland Amory emerged only with scars, but not from combat. He talked little about his army days, other than saying in biographical material that he served in Washington as a lieutenant in the Military Intelligence Division of the General Staff. These circumstances clearly kept him from achieving the same success in the military that his brother had. Shortly before the end of the war, Cleveland was given an honorable discharge for medical reasons. According to Marian Probst, Amory, who had long suffered from eczema and other skin ailments, had developed skin problems so severe that they required he be hospitalized at a clinic in Phoenix. The severe but temporary disfigurement had a dramatic effect on his outlook, Probst said. "He told me, 'I couldn't stand to look at myself in the mirror.'" Amory eventually recovered, although some remnants of the skin disease remained the rest of his life.

Amory quipped later in his life that his entry into the military did expedite one change of status that he normally might have delayed: marriage. Strange as it seems for someone who later wrote at length about most aspects of his life, Amory said very little about his short marriage to Cora Craddock, other than to note that the war was a factor in the decision of the two to marry in 1941. Little is known about Craddock, who came from a well-to-do Lynchburg, Virginia, family, and how the two met, other than information in wedding announcements. The two were married on September 13, 1941, in St. John's Episcopal Church in Lynchburg. The wedding party consisted of best man Robert Amory, the bridegroom's brother; maid of honor Ellie Craddock, the bride's sister; two attendants; and five ushers. The marriage was short-lived, and the two did not even live together for long; they were separated physically when Amory was in the army and working in Washington, and also after he was discharged and being treated in a hospital near Phoenix in 1943. In 1947, they were officially divorced.

Phoenix, Arizona, may not have been the first choice of residence for a man like Amory; after all, he had been raised and educated in the East and prided himself on his New England taste, manners, and lifestyle. Even if he had not needed medical treatment and had freely decided to move west, with his interest in the arts he might have chosen Los Angeles as his home. As he was wont to do, though, Amory took advantage of adversity, and his few years in Arizona would have a tremendous influence on the dyed-in-the-wool New Englander. When he recovered from his illness, he took a job as a reporter for the *Arizona Daily Star* in Phoenix and, shortly thereafter, the *Tucson Star*. In 1944, he became managing editor of the *Prescott Daily Courier*. Although he did not work full-time for the *Saturday Evening Post* when he was in Arizona, he still wrote articles for it on a freelance basis.

If Amory felt like a stranger in a strange land in Arizona, westerners who lived there may not have been ready for anything like the tall, handsome, and charismatic Bostonian who took great pleasure in shaking up the status quo. In 1944, he wrote a hilarious article for the *Saturday Evening Post* that gently took Arizona to task for a turnaround in its longtime publicity campaign marketing the state as a cure-all for most diseases. Until World War II, Amory wrote, sunshine was Arizona's ace in the hole in attracting easterners with respiratory problems, arthritis, and a host of other ailments. But after the war, Arizona had had enough. Too many expatriates from the East were causing overpopulation and ruining things for everyone. "Don't look now, but the boosters of Tucson sunshine are now saying maybe the climate isn't good for your health, so why don't you just stay home?" he wrote. Amory wrote — with a straight face — about a concerted effort by Tucson Chamber of Commerce employees and Arizona residents alike to discourage people from moving to Arizona. When prospective residents from the East called the chambers of commerce, they were told that there was no indication that a warm, sunny climate helped any illness. Further, those easterners who had already moved to Arizona were quick to tell friends, relatives, and others contemplating a move there that they were now sicker than when they had first arrived. They felt it was their duty to "deprecate the effects of climate on whatever ailed them."

According to Amory's remembrances, state officials were none too pleased about his take on their marketing approach to repel prospective residents. But Amory long believed that despite their criticism, the Tucson Chamber of Commerce loved the publicity. On the other hand, after Amory moved to Prescott, in the mountains, he wrote that this tiny town — which did not boast about its climate — *was* truly a haven for those with respiratory problems. But Prescott residents, he wrote, rarely talked about that. They did not want the positive publicity to lure outsiders to their town. "Tucson loved him," one of Amory's publishers bragged in promotional material about him many years later. "They just plain loved the publicity, good or bad. Prescott, however . . . is still gunning for him."

Amory always managed to capture the color and atmosphere of the places he visited. He noted long after leaving Arizona that one of the best stories he had ever written there focused on a Tombstone dentist named John Henry Holliday, a.k.a. "Doc" Holliday. At the time it was published in 1944, Holliday was notorious as a gunslinger who had killed twenty-three men in duels, but few people knew that he was a dentist or that he had tuberculosis. (The disease made him painfully thin, so he used to say that it would take "some might good shooting to hit him," Amory wrote). Years later, Amory would say, tongue in cheek, that he received thank-you notes from dentists "grateful that one of their number was recognized as a glamorous character."

Arizona received much free publicity when Amory lived there as a young man — he had an eye for a good story and offered many on a freelance basis to several national magazines. Editors at the *Saturday Evening Post*, of course, were familiar with his work and happy to publish it. In 1944, for example, Amory wrote a lengthy article about a charismatic thirty-three-year-old juvenile court judge, who, on hearing that juvenile crime in Phoenix was skyrocketing, found an obscure law on the books stating that parents could be found guilty of a misdemeanor if their children were accused of crimes. So he instituted a "night court" where unaccompanied juveniles were rounded up at eleven at night and forced to face the judge at midnight. Their parents were then called and summoned to court, too. As a result, the Phoenix City Council established a curfew law that was considered one of the strictest in the country, and juvenile crime declined.

Amory established himself as a successful freelance writer during his years in Arizona as a newspaperman. In addition to the *Saturday Evening Post*, he also wrote for the California-based *Coronet*, a popular magazine that often featured personality profiles. Amory soon established a reputation that allowed him to write about subjects he enjoyed, because editors had confidence in his writing talent and his ability to come up with solid ideas. He also wrote a few personality profiles focusing on one of his favorite hobbies. Baseball — and in particular the Boston Red Sox — was a lifelong passion for Amory, and it must have pleased him to pursue this hobby as part of a paying a job. During his time in Arizona, he wrote personality profiles of Joe DiMaggio and Ted Williams.

Amory claimed over the years that his time in Arizona was a life-altering experience. As he told Marian Probst many years later, he made a pledge to himself while recovering in the clinic from his skin ailment: "If I get out of this, I'll be hard to stop." Amory's assignment to cover a bullfight across the Arizona border in Mexico also dramatically affected his career and his personal life. He said in speeches throughout his life that the chilling brutality of that bullfight ended his complacency and jolted him to take action against cruelty to animals; he was so angry when the matador cut off the bull's ear that he threw a cushion at the man. (It hit the matador and he fell over, Amory reported, but he also acknowledged that the man may have simply tipped over out of surprise.) Amory immediately began joining anticruelty organizations. "I got as high as honorary vice president of the National Catholic Society for Animal Welfare, and that's as high as a Boston Episcopalian can go," he used to say. And the analogy may have been appropriate: animal rights soon became a religion to him. His fledgling interest in it was paradoxical, though, considering that upper-class New Englanders — with their furs, fox hunts, and attachment to certain animal-based gourmet foods — were particularly dependent on what Amory considered the exploitation of animals.

In another favorite story, Amory claimed it was a childhood experience that helped stir his feelings about animal protection. According to this account, he was shooting into trees with a new Sears BB gun he was given as a boy. After a bird was hit by an errant BB, it fell to the ground, squirming and writhing, while a bewildered Cleveland screamed at his father. "You shot him, you kill him," his father responded. Amory stamped on the bird to put it out of its misery, but the nightmarish experience stuck with him. That story may or may not be apocryphal; it is evident, though, that Cleveland Amory probably would have been destined to fight on the front lines of the animal-protection movement, bullfight or no bullfight, bird or no bird. Whether it was an inborn desire to help society in some way, a need to swim against the tide, or the simple love of a challenge, it seems unlikely that any one event would trigger such a lifelong passion. After all, as he claimed half jokingly, it was part of his ancestry. Amory told people that his paternal grandfather's second wife was a Thorndike — a relative of George Thorndike Angell, who founded the Massachusetts Society for the Prevention of Cruelty to Animals.

▷ ▷ ▷ Living in the West must have been an eye-opening experience for Amory, and he enjoyed his few years in Arizona. But the state was not a social or cultural capital, so it was unlikely he would stay there for long. Amory was in an advantageous position regarding his career: his jobs on newspapers allowed him to write freelance articles for national publications, and the doors opened for him on those publications in part because of his tenure at the *Saturday Evening Post* and in part because of the connections in publishing that he had through his birth and education. After spending a brief time in Hollywood in the mid-1940s, he returned to New York after an uncle died and left him a house in Bedford Hills. (Amory wrote little about his days in Hollywood, and his silence is unusual, since he either wrote or spoke publicly at length about most eras in his life.) He moved into the house to write the book that would become his signature work: *The Proper Bostonians*, published in 1947 by E. P. Dutton. When it was published, its author was twenty-nine. The book was dedicated "to Cora," although the two divorced the year it came out.

It is unlikely Amory could have guessed what a sensation his first book would become. It reached the *New York Times* best-seller list almost immediately and created what in today's parlance would be called "buzz." *The Proper Bostonians* hit a nerve — especially in Boston — and put Amory on the map in literary circles. Amory claimed much later that he wrote the book at the request of the publisher, who believed that the bulk of the country simply did not understand the Bostonian culture. "I decided I better educate them," he said in interviews.

And educate them he did. Throughout his life, even decades after it was written, Amory would get questions about the book at his speeches and gatherings. He was often asked what made him decide to write the book that, in its own way, was a tell-all about the quirks and idiosyncrasies of a certain closed caste of people. Now, in the age of advanced communications and tell-all memoirs, it is hard to believe that the Boston upper crust was able to remain a closed society whose habits and way of living were unknown to people outside of it. But Amory was privy to the lifestyles of his subjects and suspected that the general public would love to read about them. *The Proper Bostonians* was in some ways a social history that examined a subgroup, much in the same way aborigine subgroups were examined by sociologists. And, of course, being put under the microscope did not necessarily please the subjects of the book. What made it enjoyable, though, was Amory's dry humor and distinctive readable and sardonic style, which was based on anecdote.

Amory had a lot of raw material for *The Proper Bostonians*; part of its appeal lay in the fact that he was the one of the first to point out that the emperor had no clothes. It helped, too, that he had a sharp eye for detail, and those details spoke volumes. Recurring themes of the book are the absolute importance of family name and breeding (the best families—such as the Lodges, the Lowells, the Bowditches, the Quincys, and many others—disdained adoption and preferred to give birth to boys); the provincialism of Bostonians, with their ingrained belief that the world was a small place consisting mainly of Boston; and the vital role of the family matriarch, who was energetic, domineering, and uncompromising.

Mostly, Amory tells hilarious story after hilarious story with a straight face. For example, as he writes, "The dynastic proportions of Boston's First Families are staggering. One way of measuring these proportions is in the class lists of Harvard, to which most sons of First Families have naturally gravitated." The problem, though, is that the sons of many of the First Families have the same first names (i.e., Nathaniel, Richard, Josiah, Samuel) and the same professions (physician, judge, chemist, lawyer), causing great confusion for everyone. "A present member of the Homans family declares that when she says Dr. John Homans, she may mean her great-grandfather, her grandfather, her brother, her nephew or her cousin—all of that name and all physicians." Still, the name is of utmost importance. "Everywhere the Proper

Bostonian goes in his city he is likely to find that the magic of the Family Name pronounced will open virtually all doors, admit to the best clubs, and even see to a variety of special attentions," Amory writes. "Trains have changed schedules, stores have changed hours, and courts have changed statutes — all for the First Families."

A good portion of *The Proper Bostonians* is devoted to the vitality of the woman of the house, who in many ways is responsible for maintaining the rules and continuity of the families. One of these inviolate rules is the insistence of the First Families that they never get publicity or media attention for their activities. With the possible exception of charitable activities, no true Bostonian would talk to a reporter, nor would any want to do so. At the time the book was published, gossip columns like the ones in other newspapers nationwide did not exist in the Boston newspapers, Amory noted.

Amory created in the book an amusing picture of the formidable Boston matron who, with her low-heeled shoes and modest dress, is a whirlwind of energy and health. She is a puzzle to doctors and psychologists, who have tried for years to pinpoint the source of her vitality and longevity. "Few . . . mind giving their exact ages and many take great pride in their advancing years," Amory wrote. "Gray hair is not something to be delayed by cheap artifice; it is something to be looked forward to. Life for the Proper Boston women begins at no mere forty; it is more likely to be sixty."

Amory's book is nothing if not readable. As the *New York Times* wrote in the headline of its review, it presents Boston as seen through "a state of mind": "[Amory] collects all the ancient stories and some new ones, all the ancient legends and some modern tales, all the old personalities and some recent additions to the canon." The *New York Times* gave the book a favorable review, as did most other reviews in national publications. It continued: "*The Proper Bostonians* was based primarily on anecdotes, and relied heavily on the author's considerable ability to tell a story, and retold tales that many insiders had been telling for years." Like many other reviews, it also noted that Amory may be the first to snitch on his peers when it comes to the Boston aristocracy. "*The Proper Bostonians* is written with enough impudence, accuracy, affection, and respect to make the First Families anxious lest there be a second volume," wrote *Atlantic*. "This book may be banned in Boston, but not for the usual reasons, " wrote *Commonweal*. "Mr. Amory is guilty of *lèse-majesté* toward the Proper Bostonians and names names." The reviewer for the *Nation* may have summed up what would be Amory's style — and tone — for many years to come: "It is weak on history but rich in anecdote and written *con amore*." Interestingly, some of the reviews, like the one in the *Nation*, noted that while Amory's book may mock convention in many ways, it is not cruel or biting. As the reviewer for the *New York Herald Tribune Book Review* noted, "Many there are in the elder generation who will chuckle over his pages, for here are the stories they have been telling one another for half a century, but behind closed doors." And that sums up Amory's writing style and his personality: for years to come, even when he was engaged in serious debates with those he thought hurt animals, he never resorted to mean or petty comments. It was a technique that served him well in both his writing and his life.

The Proper Bostonians was a sensation, and it propelled Amory into the literary big leagues. He already had written for national magazines, and of course his family and social ties already had helped him professionally. But publication of the book made him a legitimate player socially and in the publishing world. The book sold well and remained on the *New York Times* bestseller list for eight months but, beyond that, people were talking about it. The response to the book by Bostonians provided even more material for its author. The reaction to it was typified by a member of the prestigious Somerset Club, previously quoted, who put up a sign on the bulletin board that read, "What would you expect from an Amory who pronounces it A-mory?" The Somerset Club itself, a Boston institution, was always a great target of his since all proper Bostonians were members. Amory liked to recount the story — supposedly true — about what happened when a fire broke out in the kitchen of the club: the firemen, as they rushed in, were rerouted so they could enter through the servants' entrance.

By the time *The Proper Bostonians* was published, Amory had returned to New York. Certainly his tenure out west had offered him an opportunity to experience a part of the country with which he was unfamiliar, permitted him to expand his freelance career, and given him material for speeches and articles for much of the rest of his life. Within a few years, he had another book under his belt — this time, it was fiction. No matter what he wrote, Amory could never stray far from his own life.

▷ ▷ ▷ Three years after the 1947 publication of *The Proper Bostonians*, Cleveland Amory was again on the book-lecture circuit. Again, he had written about something with which he had firsthand experience: the book-publishing industry. His novel, *Home Town*, tells the story of Mitchell Hickok, a young newspaper reporter from Copper City, Arizona. Hickok has just published his first book, and it has become an unlikely best seller. The young man is summoned to New York and, in a fish-out-of-water story, learns the hard way about the vagaries of the publishing world. Amory may not have been quite the babe in the woods that his fictional counterpart is — Mitchell is wide-eyed at cocktail parties and nightclubs — but it would be difficult to presume that *Home Town* is not autobiographical. As syndicated columnist John Crosby wrote, "After writing a book which brought him quite a large measure of fame, Cleveland Amory couldn't resist the temptation to write a book about an author who had written a book which had brought him a large measure of fame." It is a lighthearted satire on the publishing industry and, like the nonfiction *Proper Bostonians*, is heavy on anecdotes and written with a light touch. Along with the usual world-weary publishers and jaded press agents who promote Mitchell's book, there is the obligatory beautiful blonde, Gin, who falls in love with the protagonist. And it is unlikely Amory had to invent some of the minor characters the reader encounters, like the female autograph hound who tells the author that she always wanted to write a book, "but I can't think of anything to write about."

Overall, *Home Town* received mixed reviews. Some critics thought it was an effective and funny parody, while others thought it was superficial. Some thought it a bit too "inside" for the average reader. "Mr. Amory's novel, which includes a few lively scenes and several funny parodies, is more likely to amuse publishers, their clients, and his own friends than the rest of us," according to the *New Yorker*.

A few critics compared *Home Town* unfavorably to its author's previous effort: "This very slight story is a satire on publishing promotion, which carries more sting than humor. A disappointment to those who enjoyed *The Proper Bostonians*," *Booklist* wrote. The *Chicago Sun-Times* was more brutal: "This is an astonishingly poor performance," the critic noted, adding that he had given less severe reviews to worse books because "I did not consider their authors to be of the caliber of Cleveland Amory, who ought to know better." But not all the reviews were negative. The *Chicago Tribune* critic thought anyone who ever read a book could identify with the protagonist: "All any reader needs in ways of preparation for its hilarious enjoyment is just to be able to read." The *New York Herald Tribune* and the *New York Times* gave the book positive reviews. ("A light, bright satire, as fresh as a newborn author and as true as the words of jest," the *Herald Tribune* wrote. "A genial if somewhat oversimplified lampoon of the ruses and devices and skepticism of book publishers.... Mr. Amory has written his expose tersely, humorously and with muffled malice," according to the *Times*.)

Home Town was reviewed by all the "right" publications, and it became a *Reader's Digest* condensed book, which no doubt increased its readership. It also earned a television-writing credit for Amory: it had been adapted as an episode of the *Robert Montgomery Presents* show in 1954. The episode starred Montgomery's daughter, Elizabeth, who later became a popular television actress. The show, one of several others like it at the time, presented each week a drama or comedy in the form of a play.

Ironically, *Home Town* also gave Amory the opportunity to go on yet another book tour. Such tours themselves are ripe events for satire, with authors visiting many cities in short periods, often having to endure unruly or rude fans and last-minute changes in schedules. Throughout his life, Amory took full advantage of exploiting them for the absurd situations they were. In *The Cat and the Curmudgeon* he tells the story about how, when visiting Phoenix as part of his *Home Town* book tour, he was invited to the home of Nancy Davis (later Nancy Reagan), whom he had once dated. Davis had been living on the estate of her father, a well-known neurologist who was immediately skeptical of the visiting author. During dinner, "I had the distinct impression that . . . to interest Dr. Davis for very long, I was neither bright enough, successful enough, famous enough, rich enough nor Republican enough," Amory wrote. Things did not improve when, sitting by himself, his pipe accidentally burned a hole in Dr. Davis's prized desk, which had once been owned by Alexander Hamilton. The doctor, he feared, would take him out and shoot him if he knew, and the tale ended with Amory arranging for repairs for the desk with neither Dr. Davis nor his daughter ever knowing. Decades later, after Ms. Davis married her famous husband and then became First Lady, "I've watched the career of Miss Davis with great interest, " Amory wrote. "I'm always saddened when a woman I once dated sees fit to be so unwise as to settle for a secondary choice as a marriage partner rather than me."

Ultimately, *Home Town* did not make the splash of *The Proper Bostonians*, and it was the only full-length novel Amory would write (although he would later dabble in the writing of a television series and other less conventional forms of fiction). But he was not by any means finished with book-length projects. Within five years of the publication of *The Proper Bostonians,* Cleveland Amory had another best-selling book.

▷ ▷ ▷ By the time he returned to Boston in the early 1950s, Amory had become a sought-after man-about-town: because of the success of *The Proper Bostonians,* he was seen as a wit and social commentator, although many within the closed circle of Boston society were not too pleased with him by that point. Still, he was invited to all the right parties and, in part because of his pedigree in Boston and his years at Harvard, he knew all the right people. This status was solidified in 1952 when he began working as a periodic commentator for the fledgling *Today* show.

NBC broke new ground in January 1952 when it aired the first *Today* show, a combination news-entertainment broadcast from 7:00 to 9:00 a.m. The show was the brainchild of then-NBC vice president Sylvester L. Weaver, and he was taking a chance. "Breakfast television," as it was called, had proven popular in a few local television markets but had no established track record nationally. When it debuted, *Today* featured Dave Garroway, Jim Fleming, and Jack Lescoulie. Interestingly, the first episode of *Today,* novel as the show was, earned a thumbs-down from television critic Jack Gould of the *New York Times,* who labeled it a "self-conscious" effort that was "pretentious" and "unreasonably confusing." Gould called the show "a challenging experiment for which Mr. Weaver deserves real credit , and no doubt he will soon have an answer as to how many persons are going to look at TV first thing in the morning." As television history has shown, the answer to Gould's question was "millions," and *Today* became a fixture in the history of broadcasting. (Interestingly, Gould remembered his *Today* review as one of the most oft-quoted reviews of his career.) Amory had been hired on a freelance basis — he was paid $300 per appearance, and offered a three- or four-minute commentary every few weeks. He had the leeway to discuss anything he wanted, as long as it was light and humorous. While Amory may not have been a full-time anchor or commentator on *Today,* his job there made him a familiar face to millions of viewers.

Late in 1952, Amory's second "history" of high society, titled *The Last Resorts,* was published. In the vein of *The Proper Bostonians,* this book relied on anecdote and history to describe the rise and fall of the great resorts frequented by the nation's richest families. Amory admitted, much later, that after the publication of *The Proper Bostonians,* getting people to talk to him was not all that easy. He liked to tell the story on the lecture circuit about the Bar Harbor teenager who poked him in the stomach with her finger and told him that he probably did not realize what people were saying about him. " 'No,' I told her. 'What are they saying?' " The girl replied, 'I won't tell Mr. Amory about your family if you don't tell Mr. Amory about my family.' "

Amory managed, however, to ferret out information about his topic. In the book, he treats the resorts in Palm Springs, Southampton, Saratoga, Palm Beach, Newport, Bar Harbor, White Sulphur Springs, and Tuxedo Park almost as people with distinctive personalities; and the very rich and often oblivious residents of these resorts provide much fodder for examination. For example, he writes that those who live in the huge mansions in Newport, Bar Harbor, and the like have always referred, sans irony, to their sumptuous homes as "cottages":

> Looking back on the great American resort extravaganza, it is quite possible that its most outstanding single feature may be the use of the simple word "cottage." Through the years this word has been used with remarkable aplomb to denote the million-dollar mansions, marble palaces and chateau castles. . . . It is a curious fact that originally, in the early days of resorts, the word "cottage" was used humbly. . . . Their patrons [were] known as "cottagers" or the "cottage colony."

While the book is amusing and written in Amory's smooth and quick style, it does not have the zest and wry tone of his previous social history. Nonetheless, it also became a best seller and earned respectable reviews from many major publications. The *New Yorker* noted while *The Last Resorts* was "a diverting piece of work," it was "not nearly as well constructed" as *The Proper Bostonians*. The critic for the *New York Herald Tribune Book Review*, though, liked it: "There is a chuckle in every paragraph and a hearty laugh on every page." The most interesting reviews did not discuss simply this book but Amory's overall style and tone in general: "Mr. Amory has a quick eye for the bizarre, a quick ear for the apt riposte to the nasty thrust, and a pen as sharp as a stiletto," wrote Fanny Butcher of the *Chicago Tribune*. John McNulty, a critic for the *New York Times*, noted that Amory had a fine sense of the absurd but no feelings of malice: "Mr. Amory has the great gift of being able to enjoy the daffiness and the grotesqueries of this class of Americans of a generation or two ago — and to do so without manifesting any socially conscious anger." *The Last Resorts* apparently caught the attention of the rich and famous. Amory recalled, thirty years later, that as he walked into a cocktail party one evening shortly after the book was published, he heard that *The Last Resorts* had been one of the topics of Walter Winchell's gossip column. Winchell reported that composer Irving Berlin had planned to write a musical based on the book. The play would feature Broadway star Ethel Merman, he wrote. It would not be the only time Amory flirted with converting one of his books into a play, and it would not be the only time the plans were thwarted. The rights to the book were later optioned by eleven different producers, but because of various temperamental stars and political infighting in the theater, it was never converted into a play.

More important, though, was the fact that the publication of *The Last Resorts* cemented Amory's reputation as a shrewd social commentator and historian, and it literally earned him good tables in nightclubs. In a letter to his mother from Chicago, Amory in early 1953 gave her a quick review of a road company presentation of *Call Me Madam*. "The music and dancing is awfully good and the girl who plays the Ethel Merman part has a great deal of charm," he wrote. "I got an exceptionally good table in a crowded spot — the Pump Room — last night and I had to leave for a moment and when I came back the girl I was with said, 'The headwaiter came over and said he put you here because his wife heard your talk and thought you were very, very good.'" Amory had learned by then that celebrity status did not necessarily guarantee financial success. As he added in his letter, "Undoubtedly the head waiter makes several times what I make even in a good year, but still the book must be getting around."

The early 1950s were pivotal for Amory. In addition to making his debut as a *Today* commentator and publishing his second best-selling book about society, he was married for the second time. On New Year's Eve in 1953, Amory married the former Martha Hodge, who had been a stage actress, primarily in musicals and comedies. Hodge had a daughter, Gaea, who was about eight when her mother married Amory. Martha had been married to Broadway and film actor Myron McCormick, a Tony Award–winning stage and film actor who was best known for his 1950 supporting role in Broadway's *South Pacific*. Martha grew up in Greenwich, Connecticut, in a theatrical environment. Her father, William Hodge, was a stage actor and prolific playwright in the 1920s and 1930s. Amory apparently met the beautiful redheaded Martha at a book party for *The Proper Bostonians*, and the two kept the marriage a secret for a few months, until it became a "Marriage Revealed" item in the Milestones section of *Time* magazine. Amory was thirty-six and Martha forty-one at the time they were married. Martha and Cleveland Amory spend nearly their entire married life in Manhattan, but correspondence from Amory to his mother indicates that they planned at some point early in their marriage to live in Southern California. A note from Amory to his mother on MGM Pictures stationery thanks her for a $300 wedding gift and notes that he was working for a movie studio, at least temporarily: "The work has been very interesting if very indefinite toward the future, but it has also been very time consuming. There are many fascinating things about the movie business, particularly the technical side, and I do not think I shall regret having taken the job." He added that the film studios were suffering financially and nearly closing but that they were coming back, with "Metro" (presumably MGM) making about twenty-five films that year, compared with none two years before that. The details of that job are unknown, as is the reason the Amorys left Los Angeles. But Amory may have assumed that he could make a good living by involving himself in some aspect of the movies.

In some ways, Martha Hodge was a perfect companion for her husband: the two enjoyed traveling and attending social events. Cleveland loved Martha's daughter, Gaea, and vice versa. The two would grow close over the years. But being the wife of Cleveland Amory was a full-time job, and Martha soon gave up her acting career. Gaea Leinhardt, who is now a professor of education at the University of Pittsburgh, remembered that her mother played a major role in the writing of *Home Town* and that in fact the book was cowritten by Amory and Martha. But Amory alone is listed as the author, although the dedication reads, "For Martha Hodge who helped write it." Amory had great respect for his wife's intellect, Leinhardt remembered, and would routinely give her drafts of his articles and other writings to read, asking for her suggestions and hoping for her approval.

By virtue of his celebrity, Cleveland Amory was *the* person to have at cocktail parties, and he and Martha seemed to have it all — good looks, celebrity, and the ability to travel around the country while Amory gave lectures and wrote magazine articles. It was a great life, and many who met him were quick to flatter Amory and compliment his versatility. But Amory would soon learn that his dual role as social historian and raconteur did not always mix.

chapter 4 ▷▷▷ His Last Duchess

> I remember suggesting to [the Duchess of Windsor]
> that if she were going to write a book, it might be
> helpful if she would also read one.
>
> ▶ CLEVELAND AMORY, on his role in writing the
>   "autobiography" of the Duchess of Windsor

*F*ive years into his marriage to Martha Hodge, Cleveland Amory had established a reputation as an astute observer of American society. By this time, he had written two of what would become a trilogy of books about aspects of American high society, and his book tours, lectures, and writings had further cemented this reputation.

He and Martha enjoyed the trappings of their celebrity — both the social and material aspects of it. And they certainly must have known they had made it when, on April 17, 1959, they were interviewed by Edward R. Murrow on his show *Person to Person*. Murrow conducted fifteen-minute interviews as he sat in the CBS studios in New York, but subjects were seen in their "natural" environment — usually their homes. And he often focused on their personal lives, their hobbies, and their families rather than their jobs. Martha and Cleveland Amory were seen at 10:45 p.m. Sunday night inside their East Side Manhattan apartment. Their interview aired after Murrow's segment with Mrs. Babe Ruth.

The short segment portrayed the family as the genteel unit it was. (Gaea was fourteen years old at the time.) It gave Cleveland an opportunity to repeat, tongue in cheek, what he had said many times in his writings and in lectures about the insularity and frugality of those raised in Boston and its environs. (In Nahant, where he grew up, "everything was simple," Amory said. "But across the way we used to hear tales of a simply terrible place aptly enough called Newport. It was really frightful. I don't think this would be any place to repeat those tales. Ed, they spent their money.") Martha told Murrow that she was born in New York and raised in Greenwich, Connecticut, a fortunate happenstance since "Bostonians never marry Bostonians." "We can't, Ed," Amory piped in. "We have to spread the culture."

The spot also gave Amory the chance to bring up his unfortunate lot as a Boston Red Sox fan, "but I'm bringing up my daughter to be a Yankee fan. It's a happier life," he said. Amory also shared one of his other passions: his love of chess and his many chess sets, which he showed to Murrow and the television audience.

Clearly, though, it was a recent episode in the Amorys' life that must have triggered the interest in having Amory appear on *Person to Person*—an incident that Amory would talk about for decades to come, and one that Murrow asked about immediately, albeit in his low-key manner: the Amorys' adventures with the Duke and Duchess of Windsor.

▷ ▷ ▷ It would be difficult to overestimate the impact of Amory's two society books—*The Proper Bostonians* and *The Last Resorts*—on his career and reputation. The fact that they were both best sellers certainly established his celebrity status. But beyond that, the two books were read by the "right" people: celebrities and people with money. So it was not unusual that a pair with no less stature than the Duke and Duchess of Windsor would seek out Amory—not just as a party guest but to ghostwrite an "autobiography" of the duchess. A magazine writer named Charles Murphy, who had worked for *Life* and *Fortune*, had ghostwritten a successful autobiography of the duke in the early 1950s, and the duke had asked him to write an autobiography of his wife. Murphy began an extended visit in Paris with the Windsors in October of 1954, but after writing several hundred pages, he was unceremoniously fired by the duchess, who did not like what she had read. In *The Best Cat Ever*, thirty years after the fact, Amory recalls in detail how the duke, after reading *The Last Resorts*, called him and requested a meeting with him about the possibility of Amory ghostwriting an "autobiography" of the duchess.

As Amory fully reveals in *The Best Cat Ever*, the arrangement from the start was an accident waiting to happen. He implies in his retelling that, from his first meeting with the couple, he should have been able to predict disaster. Ever the optimist, though, he decided to take on the assignment (in part, he admits, because he was flattered by the invitation). Amory describes his first face-to-face meeting with the couple during tea at the Waldorf Astoria in Manhattan. He expected only the duke, but also in attendance were the duchess and the couple's three pugs. The animals snored through much of the meeting. They looked suspiciously like their mistress: "People who like a certain kind of dog and have them all their life often grow, in later life, to look more and more like them," he wrote years later. "The Duchess liked Pugs, and there was something about the way she did her hair — parted down the middle — or indeed the whole shape of the her face, particularly the jaw, that made her seem to resemble a Pug."

By 1955, when the Amorys left New York for Paris, the story of Prince Edward, Duke of Windsor, and his wife Bessie Wallis Warfield of Blue Ridge Summit, Pennsylvania, could accurately be described as a sensation; it was one of the biggest society/celebrity stories in the world. It had begun with the romance between Wallis Simpson, as she was then known, and King Edward VIII, as he was crowned in 1936. The objections of Edward's government, his family, and many of his subjects to the prospect of her becoming the queen ultimately caused a crisis in the United Kingdom. Edward was forced to abdicate his throne before he could marry the twice-divorced American in 1937, after which he was awarded the Duke of Windsor title. No members of the British royal family attended the wedding, nor did they ever accept Wallis Simpson as part of the family. The world, meanwhile, had a schizophrenic attitude about the whole episode: on one hand, many found it tremendously romantic that the King of England would abdicate this throne for the purpose of true love. Others viewed Wallis Simpson as a gold digger whose sole purpose was to gain the celebrity and wealth that came with marrying a royal. And the duke's visit in 1937 to Germany branded him in the eyes of many as a Nazi sympathizer. More than seventy years later, the story of the Duke and Duchess of Windsor remains a controversial one in British royal history. Even now, the private life of the couple remains a mystery: they traveled around the world, apparently with little to do.

Amory's stepdaughter, Gaea, believes that even though Amory was initially wary of the invitation to ghostwrite the duchess's life, he believed it was possible that the British public had given her a bum rap — that British royalty had purposely smeared her name. But Cleveland and Martha were both Francophiles who loved the French culture and way of life, and they may have seen the invitation as a chance to live there for an extended period of time. The couple soon learned, however, that Amory's optimistic view of the Windsors was very misguided.

There were other harbingers of disaster. Amory explained to the couple that he did not want to be a ghostwriter but would rather have the book written by the duchess, "as told to" him. The duchess said nothing in response, although the duke seemed to indicate that would be all right, Amory wrote. And Amory was already thinking of a title. It could be, simply, *Untitled*, a play on words referring to the fact that the duchess, much to her chagrin, was prohibited from using the term "Her Royal Highness." The suggestion, he wrote, was met with "dead silence." And it was the first of many indications to Amory that the duke and duchess had absolutely no sense of humor or irony — a quality that would manifest itself repeatedly in his dealings with them. Amory would say later that he found it ironic the duchess would "write" her autobiography, since she admitted to Amory that she doubted she had ever read a book all the way through.

Still, Amory agreed to the arrangement and signed a $25,000 contract with the royals, which included a five-month stint with the couple in Paris and churning out a draft of the manuscript at the same time. Meanwhile, the royal couple was guaranteed more than $500,000 by the publisher, David McKay Co., and from *McCall's* and the *London Daily Express* for reprint rights.

Amory apparently left for Paris to meet the royal couple in early May 1955, and Martha followed about a month later. Amory was given a hotel suite as a home base, but he spent most of his time with the Windsors, their thirty or so servants, periodic guests, and the rest of their circle. Martha stayed at the Normandy Hotel while he was working. At first Martha's letters home to Amory's parents were breezy and light, as she described plays the couple had seen and people they met. But she acknowledged early on that her husband was earning every penny of his salary: "It's excruciating work for Clip . . . . There is little time for Clip to see or do. . . . It's all work and pressure now," she wrote. And early on signs emerged that all was not well in the relationship between subject and writer: "Although she [the duchess] is warm and informal to the hilt, the atmosphere of formality and protocol around is nerve-racking." Still, Martha Hodge Amory, who grew up in upscale Greenwich, was impressed by her surroundings: "It's like a Greenwich estate — trees, lawns high ceilings, crystal chandeliers like mushrooms — elegant Louis XV furniture — fabulous porcelain crystal."

Amory began writing almost immediately, completing three hundred pages in about three months. Martha noted periodically in letters home that the Windsors' representatives liked the initial portions of the manuscript. But things went downhill, quickly and dramatically. By the third week of September, Amory had announced he had quit as the duchess's ghostwriter. Immediately, the Windsors' staff told the world this was not true: he actually was fired, they said. Amory began telling his friends and relatives that the Windsors wanted him to change the story of the duchess's life and, in essence, become her press agent. While the sophisticated Amory clearly knew that he had been hired to write a favorable portrait of the duchess, he claimed that he could not, morally, substantially change the facts of her life. In addition, he did not want to write the book in first person, nor would he approve of the duchess's title for the book, *Wistful Thinking*. The Windsors' publicity machine began spinning wildly, announcing that the ghostwriter had done an inferior job and therefore had to be fired.

Within a week or two, the story of the Duchess of Windsor and her ghostwriter became international news. Walter Winchell wrote briefly about it in his widely read column, as did many of the other New York columnists. *Newsweek* reported briefly on the debacle in its Press section, quoting headlines of some of the New York papers: "Wally's Ghost Explains Why He's an Ex-ghost," the *Daily News* wrote." Can't Make Her into a Rebecca of Sunnybrook Farm," according to the *Journal-American*. "Writer Throws Her Book Back at the Duchess," proclaimed the *Mirror*. Amory's comment that you "can't turn the Duchess into Rebecca of Sunnybrook Farm—the facts of life are very stubborn things" was widely quoted then and for years afterward. *Newsweek* tried to summarize Amory's side of the story: "According to Amory, the break had been the duchess's fault. She was trying, he told all the papers, to prove that she was 'born on the right side of the tracks' and to demonstrate that she and the duke were 'happy and busy.'" Amory also was saying that he took issue with the duchess's title for the autobiography, *Wistful Thinking*. That, Amory implied, was simply too ironic. "Strongly implying that he thought the duchess anything but wistful, Amory said that he had told her, 'I am willing to omit facts, but not to distort them,'" *Newsweek* wrote.

According to letters from Martha Amory to her in-laws, the job had been a stressful one for Amory all along—and one he was happy to abandon. She wrote this the day of her husband's resignation: "An hour ago, Clip severed all connections with the Duchess and Duke. The changes [in the manuscript] that the lawyers tried to make are pretty laughable in regard to the story. Clip said he could not be connected in any way with a dishonest book." Martha noted that her husband would get the salary he was promised, although she predicted—wrongly, as it turned out—that the royals would permanently give up on the book. But the chilly manner of the royals was shocking even to the cosmopolitan Martha Hodge Amory. "It's all coolly amicable. . . . The casual way they can be dishonest makes you know that ice runs through their veins," she wrote. The good news, she noted, was that a tremendous burden had been lifted from Amory, and now the two could enjoy Paris. "What a relief. . . . Clip and I have five delicious days to play and see Paris. We feel so free and Clip is like a different person in just the last few hours. . . . It has been quite an experience. One emerges from it stronger and wiser and rich with material."

"Rich with material" was certainly an accurate phrase — for Amory, the Windsors, and all the journalists who wrote about the story. The Windsors and their inner circle immediately rehired ghostwriter Charles Murphy, who had written the duke's autobiography, and the book, titled *The Heart Has Its Reasons*, was published a year later. Amory, meanwhile, realized the Windsors had intended his role to be as one of their many servants: "I abdicated — and never regretted the decision," he would say when retelling the story.

As he reflected on his months with the Windsors in *The Best Cat Ever*, Amory saw them as a bored couple who could barely find enough diversions to fill their days; he also painted them as stingy, even though their lavish lifestyle was paid for in full by the British government. And their income did not include the millions they had in the form of jewels, furnishings, and stocks. As for activities, their days — which usually began after they woke up at about ten thirty — were filled with giving orders to their many servants; playing a variety of games, including golf and bridge; meeting with hairdressers and masseuses and the like; and having elaborate meals with friends and acquaintances.

When he left Paris, Amory was hardly done with the Windsors. After he and Martha sailed from Paris back to the United States that October of 1955, he gave countless interviews and speeches about his experience, noting that he planned within the next few years to write a book about his months with the couple. And the Windsors were not about to ignore what they apparently considered an unpleasant experience with Cleveland Amory. It was clear, Amory noted, that the duchess ran the show; all the servants took orders from her, virtually ignoring the duke, and the duchess was known to order the duke out of the room if he annoyed her. Despite the fact that she was "untitled," Amory noted, the butler, when announcing dinner, said in a voice audible to everyone, "Your Royal Highness, dinner is served."

Meals were a complex and intriguing event at the Windsor homes, Amory wrote. When he and the duchess had lunch alone one time, no fewer than nine courses were served. The duchess, though, had only a tiny taste of each one, as if to illustrate her oft-quoted statement, "A woman can never be too rich or too thin."

More unnerving to Amory than the Windsors' lifestyle, though, was their duplicity and narcissism. The duchess had decided she did not want any dates in her "autobiography" (ostensibly because they could, indirectly, reveal her age), forcing Amory to "write around" important people and events in her life — including two ex-husbands. Further, her "remembrances," particularly of her childhood, were often contradictory, further perplexing her (auto)biographer. Amory recalled that the Windsors' publisher had sent her a tape recorder with which to dictate her thoughts and remembrances for Amory. At one point, Amory told her that she told two differing versions of the same story from her childhood, based on the tapes. She told him, essentially, to reconcile the differences himself: "They told me the tape recorder was not for me, it was for you," she said.

Most disconcerting for Amory, though, was what he determined to be several anti-Semitic remarks by the duke, most of them made at gatherings after the duke had had many drinks. In one case, Amory noted, the duke "amazed an English friend when the subject of Hitler came up. 'I have never thought,' the Duke said to this man, 'Hitler was such a bad chap.'" Amory was horrified at what he perceived were the duke's Nazi sympathies.

Cleveland Amory did, many decades later, tell his side of the Amory-Windsor story. Why he did not write about it sooner is unclear, although the Windsors may have played a part in the delay. In the Cholly Knickerbocker gossip column in the *New York Journal-American*, on June 13, 1956, the duchess is quoted as saying she would sue Amory if he published details of his extended visit with the Windsors. At some point, Amory apparently agreed to do a piece on the Windsors for the CBS *Twentieth Century* documentary series. After paying him for the segment, network officials told Amory they did not want it and would not run it. Network officials gave no reason, but Amory declared it was pressure from the royal family that influenced the network's decision.

When he and Martha returned to New York that fall on the *Queen Mary*, they were greeted by reporters who wanted to know the "true" story. Certainly he and members of the press knew that if he had written the Duchess of Windsor's "autobiography" as she wanted it written, he would be a wealthy man, based on income from sales and excerpts in magazines. But, as Amory noted, he did not have the stomach for it. "By the time the summer was up I had had all of the Windsors I could take," he recalled. Still, in what is distinctly uncharacteristic of his philosophy of life, he admitted that the entire episode was a mistake and that his decision to enter into it was a bad one. "[It] was a major error in my life and . . . a plentiful waste of time."

▷ ▷ ▷ Cleveland Amory talked about his experience with the Duke and Duchess of Windsor for much of his life. During his interview with Murrow in 1959, Murrow broached the subject — briefly. "You've been asked to ghost-write books," he remarked. After Amory established that his brief ghostwriting career consisted only of his adventures with the duchess, he revealed that it was Martha, not he, who had coined the phrase that came to characterize his view of the debacle: "My wife said, 'You can't make the Duchess of Windsor into Rebecca of Sunnybrook Farm.'" Amory added that he had wanted to write about the lives of several people — including Marlene Dietrich, Billy Rose, Aga Khan, Zsa Zsa Gabor, and others — but he implied he preferred no constraints on the content. "I sometimes wonder what happened to the plain old biography without the 'auto,'" he said. While Amory never did write a biography, with or without the "auto," he did some biographical writing decades later when he wrote personality profiles in the 1980s and 1990s for *Parade* magazine. Those profiles, mostly of celebrities, were hardly unflattering, but they were candid. Amory did not shy away, for instance, from revealing that Cary Grant had used LSD or that Gregory Peck's son had committed suicide.

The Amorys' appearance on Murrow's *Person to Person* was typical for the show. Amory, Martha, and Gaea appeared to the audience to be a "conventionally" attractive, upper-crust Manhattan family living on the Upper East Side. In some ways that was true; in other ways, looks were deceiving. Gaea remembers growing up in an intellectually stimulating environment where her mother and stepfather encouraged her to read the *New York Times* even before she went off to school. "He would have long letters in the margins of the *Times* saying, 'read this before you go to school.' Then he would quiz me in the evening to see if I remembered." Gaea said Amory also took her to Central Park and taught her the intricacies of baseball. "He took me to see the Giants and to see the Yankees, although we didn't like the Yankees. We rooted for the Red Sox passionately."

The Amory family always had dogs — usually big dogs, even though they lived in a Manhattan apartment. Gaea remembers a series of dogs when she was growing up — usually poodles, including her first dog, Biff, a standard poodle; a small white poodle, Elf, that the Amorys brought back from their trip to France with the Windsors; and, finally, a small gray poodle named Tiger, who lived to a ripe old age. After Gaea went to college at the University of Chicago, the Amorys adopted two Siberian huskies, which Martha walked several times a day. "They weren't suited for an apartment," Gaea remembered. "It was tough keeping them." Her stepfather liked the theory of the owning such large, exuberant dogs, but "he wasn't much on the practice," Gaea said.

Gaea and her stepfather were very close, but she remembers him as complex and mercurial, particularly with his wife. "He was a lot of fun when he was in the mood to be fun," she recalled. He adopted a paternal attitude toward her, she said, like the attitude he took toward animals — that they were, ultimately, defenseless and guileless, and needed someone to look after them and represent their interests. But the relationship between Cleveland Amory and Martha Hodge was far more complicated.

Gaea remembered that the two were very much in love when they first met and married. When Amory traveled and was away from Hodge, he would write her four or five times a day. With his accomplishments and energy, it was perhaps predictable that Cleveland Amory would fall in love with someone who could keep up with him intellectually. And, indeed, Martha Hodge was brilliant and talented. But these were qualities that did not necessarily serve her well when it came to her marriage. She was instrumental in critiquing Amory's work and even contributed to his writings, as was evident in the dedication to *Home Town*. Hodge, who had a successful acting career, stopped working when she collaborated with him on *Home Town*, Gaea said. Further, when Amory later wrote columns for *TV Guide* and *Saturday Review*, "he never sent one in without my mother going over it in great detail. He'd go up and down the hall reading it," Gaea said. Martha also shared her husband's interests in animal protection, and, later in their marriage, she spent much time working with him and traveling with him to promote that cause. Early in the marriage, Martha had planned to return to the stage, but she never did. Amory, Gaea said, did not specifically discourage her, but as Martha learned, being the wife of Cleveland Amory was a full-time job. "He didn't stop her from returning, but he also had a very high demand of her." Although Martha intended to return to her acting career, "eventually she fell into that stage of being the 'former actress,'" Gaea said, a status that did not necessarily please her mother.

The couple's living and sleeping schedules also were out of sync. Amory often went to bed about midnight, but he required only about five or six hours of sleep, and was up by 6:00 a.m. Martha required much more sleep, her daughter recalled — although she enjoyed staying up much of the night, she could not rise early the next day, nor could she work an eighteen-hour day.

Gaea described her mother as a "fiery, intense" person who was not necessarily easy to live with. "She was a tough women to be with. . . . She had a fiery temper. . . . They had tumultuous fights and tumultuous makeups." Gaea remembered that her stepfather's natural tendency to nurture extended to his wife, but Martha Hodge did not necessarily seek stability in a partner. "I don't think she was necessarily looking for reliability," her daughter said.

Despite his nurturing tendencies, there was one area in which Cleveland Amory was, indeed, unreliable: he was notoriously unfaithful during the marriage, Gaea recalled, and certainly, with his fame and all the invitations he received, meeting interesting women was not difficult. Her mother ultimately grew tired of the behavior, Gaea said. "He had lots of other relationships. He had lots of other women."

Cleveland Amory and Martha Hodge were married nearly twenty-two years when they divorced in 1975, although the marriage had been over long before the divorce was final. In a brief *New York Times* announcement of the divorce, a flippant Amory is quoted about custody: "Mr. Amory . . . said yesterday that his wife will have custody of their 9-year-old Siberian huskies, Peter the Greatest and Ivan the Terrific, 'because she has done a great job on them,' but that he has been awarded visitation rights."

▷ ▷ ▷ Amory's experiences with the Windsors gave him more than just fodder for anecdotes. He insisted throughout his life that it also helped to change his thinking about society and the definition of "society" and "celebrity." His unhappy time with the duchess became deeply ingrained in his psyche for a long time, perhaps because he felt he had been deceived by her. After all, he was willing to give her the benefit of the doubt regarding her lifestyle and her personality. Before he took the assignment as ghostwriter, part of him truly believed that she and the duke may have been getting a bum rap from the public and the press. But he had been wrong, as he soon realized.

By the time Murrow interviewed him on *Person to Person* in 1959, Amory apparently was observing that his favorite topic of discussion — American society — was changing. But he was changing, too. Although he had expanded his area of expertise beyond that of social observer, he was getting tired of serving as the public's favorite social arbiter. He wanted to move beyond that.

As he would do for the rest of his life (and as he had already done), Amory in the early 1960s began to reinvent himself and his career. In late 1960, the third of what would be known as his trilogy of books on American blue-blood society was published with the apt title *Who Killed Society?* Three years later, he edited a book that could be considered a companion piece to that: *The Celebrity Register.*

As he spelled out many years later in *The Best Cat Ever,* Amory had a eureka moment when he was surrounded by the sycophants and yes-men who comprised the Windsors' inner circle. While the duke and duchess certainly could be considered the quintessential high-society couple, they really were not, he concluded on the long ride back to the States aboard the *Queen Mary*: "Having seen, almost nauseatingly firsthand, what passed for Society in the form of the . . . fawners and hangers-on around the Windsors, I became more and more convinced that the word 'Society' itself was suspect — that whatever it once was, it certainly was not anymore, and that something new might not be any better but it could hardly be, at worst, worse." Through his readings and discussions with those he met at social gatherings, Amory concluded that the new society of the early 1960s was actually a society of "celebrity" — that is, based increasingly on media coverage that focused less on lineage and breeding and more on the activities and quirks of the rich and famous, which turned "socialites" into "celebrities." And, he concluded, Americans' respect and idolatry, once reserved for blue bloods, now went to these celebrities. While celebrities were of course known for their accomplishments in a specific field — often entertainment — their real fame stemmed from itself. They were famous for being famous, he believed.

Resulting from this epiphany was the 599-page *Who Killed Society?* — part humorous essay, part social history, and part rumination on the changing cultural scene of the United States. The book was black with stark red lettering, in a parody of the cover of the long-established *Society Register.* By the time it was published, in 1960, many in society already had bemoaned the gradual watering down and decay of "society" in the United States. Amory implied in the book, though, that the last nail had been pounded into the coffin. Ever the punster, he even coined the word "publi-ciety" to indicate that popular consumption of celebrity news in the mass media is what makes or breaks celebrities — and that the barometer of fame and social status is the amount of publicity one receives.

Of course, the success of Amory's two other books about society, *The Proper Bostonians* and *The Last Resorts*, ensured that this third book would sell well. And it did. Almost immediately, it earned a spot on the *New York Times* best-seller list (at a time when *The Proper Bostonians* was in its sixteenth printing). Overall, critics liked *Who Killed Society?* and, as they had in the past, praised Amory for his engaging and witty writing style and his meticulous research into social customs. This latest book has all those characteristics and more — it is heavy on gossip and name-dropping, with the author offering his own theories about who really helped "kill" society. The suspects abound, he proclaims, but some — including his favorites, the Duke and Duchess of Windsor — are particularly culpable. Also at fault is another of Amory's least favorite people, the party giver and society maven Elsa Maxwell, who takes somewhat of a battering in other parts of *Who Killed Society?* Early in the first chapter, Amory lists people, concepts, and institutions that he believes are responsible for the "murder" of society. The list is printed in descending order, with those who are guilty of "Murder in the First Degree" listed first. These include the Windsors, powerful newspaper columnist Walter Winchell, Franklin Delano Roosevelt, Hollywood, the Bureau of Internal Revenue, and a few others. Other culprits guilty of a slightly lesser charge include Harry Truman, talk show host Jack Paar, both world wars, the Cold War, and Prohibition. Others on the list — those who committed various degrees of "manslaughter" or "negligence" resulting in the death of society — include Gloria Vanderbilt, Aristotle Onassis, the Kennedy family, all the Gabors except Magda, the Newport Jazz Festival, and Bermuda shorts. (Numerous gossip columnists are included on the list, presumably because they provided the needed publicity.)

Who Killed Society? launched a public feud between Amory and Maxwell, who was a regular fixture in newspaper society columns. Maxwell had been an outspoken critic of the Duchess of Windsor and wrote and talked extensively about what she thought was her greed and social climbing. In one article, after reciting a laundry list of what she felt were the duchess's faults,

Maxwell noted, plainly, "I don't like her." (But after the duchess's "autobiography" was published, the two women apparently resolved their differences, much to the chagrin of Amory.)

This mutual resentment toward the Windsors apparently did not forge a bond between Maxwell and Amory, though. Maxwell's name appears several times in *Who Killed Society?* and the author is hardly subtle in his distaste for her and his resentment of her role as social arbiter: "When it comes to what might be loosely described as her writing, Miss Maxwell is one of the few authors who has literally written more than she has read," he writes. "She averages close to an autobiography a year, some of them in styles amazingly different from her columns." More interesting than her literary "change of pace," Amory continues, is her "change of face" regarding her opinion of the Windsors.

Amory's mentions of Maxwell may have proven his own premise: that when it comes to celebrity, there is no such thing as bad publicity. After *Who Killed Society?* was published, Maxwell was continually asked about the negative comments about her. "When asked what she thought of Amory's book, she brushed it off," a reporter for the *Miami Herald* wrote. "'If Mr. Amory says that I murdered what he called society, I should be crowned, not hanged. I make my own society. We all do. I consider myself something of a goodwill ambassador throughout the world.'"

For years, Amory would use his rivalry with Maxwell in his writings and speeches. In 1961, he wrote in the *Saturday Evening Post* that he was seated next to her at a luncheon not long after he had reviewed, and panned, her latest book in the *New York Times*. In a loud voice, and in front of others at the table, Maxwell pointed at Amory: "You," she said, "seem to have absolutely no idea how important I am." Amory replied: "I don't. But I guess I'm going to, all right." Maxwell then reached into a large handbag and produced clippings and letters that were all laudatory of her. She read from them throughout the meal. "What have you got to say?" she demanded of Amory after lunch. "I told her that I had nothing at all to say—that somehow I had stupidly left my clippings at home."

The spat between Maxwell and Amory also provided fodder for conversation during his book tour in 1960 and, indirectly, made its way even into Maxwell's *New York Times* obituary three years later. In it, the writer notes that Maxwell "never could explain why she remained such a durable figure in the changing world of international society." But, the obituary continues,

Amory's *Who Killed Society?* says it was because she had mastered the art of getting—and giving—publicity.

In general, though, most critics who reviewed *Who Killed Society?* seemed to think that fascinating as it was, it did not quite live up to the brilliant—and original—*Proper Bostonians*. But, overall, they gave it points for its unique premise and its lively tone: "Being himself to the manor born, or, to use one of his felicitously coined words, 'an upper crustacean,' this proper Bostonian who, on occasion, can be gloriously improper, is inclined to regard New England's old order with amused indulgence not unmixed with a definite hierarchic admiration," according to the *Saturday Review*. Or, as Charles Rolo wrote in the *Atlantic Monthly*, "I found the book almost consistently entertaining. Amory combines a huge zest for his subject with an astringently ironic perspective, and he does a devastating job of sticking pins into highly inflated balloons—social arbiters, party givers, and the like."

The *Christian Science Monitor*'s review was lukewarm but somewhat complimentary: "For the reader the prospects are mixed. . . . When Mr. Amory is at his keen-eyed and keen-eared best, he records social history with zest, and human foibles with a deceptively ingratiating air. On the other hand . . . the excesses of conspicuous consumption . . . cannot comfortably be played for laughs these days, if they ever could. . . . *Who Killed Society* offers sociologists material for a new wave of we-are-going-to-the-dogs-in-a-limousine books."

The *Chicago Tribune* called the book "much more than a book of anecdotes, more than a series of sketches of well-known persons and America's wealthiest families. . . . It is a lightly written but seriously researched history of American manners and morals."

Amory continued his research by looking into the roots of the words "socialite" and "celebrity," and he tried to learn how the definition of each had evolved. Eventually he found the irony he sought. The word "celebrity," he reported much later in *The Best Cat Ever*, was used in the nineteenth century to describe no less a blue blood than John Jacob Astor: as the *American Quarterly Review* described Astor in 1836, "from an obscure stranger he had made himself into one of the 'celebrities' of the country." Amory wrote much later in *The Best Cat Ever*, that "society" started as "celebrity" and later evolved into "aristocracy." But Amory never wrote in a vacuum, and he did not do so in *Who Killed Society?* He realized early on, when he wrote that book, that changes in culture, politics, and technology all contributed to the declining status of socialites in the United States, and as the country became more democratized and egalitarian in the mid–twentieth century, so did the definition of high society. As Amory himself described it in a speech he gave in 1962, "This country was founded on a disbelief in the hereditary title system. Money is not so much looked up to but standard among empire builders. Also, morals and manners are reputedly on the decline — anything goes."

Amory expanded on these notions in his lengthy promotional tour for *Who Killed Society?* When he went to Palm Beach, he learned from columnist Tanya Brooks of the *Palm Beach Post* that his book was "causing more than a few murmurs." And many who met him believed the man himself was as impressive as his books. Amory, she wrote, looks like "a great big Newfoundland dog — a little on the shaggy side and quite handsome." Mrs. Amory, she wrote, resembled actress Arlene Dahl.

Amory's visits around the country were clearly big events. Most of those who attended his talks had never seen or met him. Many were impressed by his bearing. "Amory has an interesting style of speaking which, as the saying goes, loses a lot in translation," wrote one reporter in 1962 for the *Sacramento Bee*. "A lot of his humor depends on his pronunciation, lightly 'Bahston,' and his emphasis on the last syllable. This puts the reader at a distinct disadvantage."

The publication of *Who Killed Society?* launched a new career for Amory, and a new interest. While he was hardly through lecturing and joking about American society — his anecdotes and musings about the subject would be staples in his speeches for the rest of his life — Cleveland Amory would now immerse himself in the world of celebrity, entertainment, and the media. A few years after the debacle with the Windsors, he subtly implied in a freelance article for the *Saturday Evening Post* that he was done with writing about society. He was repeatedly asked, he noted, if he liked his "chosen profession" chronicling members of America's high society. For the most part, he did, he said, but "the field doesn't seem to be something that a grown man would want to devote a lifetime to."

In writing and talking about celebrity, though, he became a member of the group he subtly mocked. By the early 1960s, Amory certainly could be considered a member of the celebrity club, just as he was a member of America's upper-crust society. And he wrote about celebrity just as he wrote about society — with the same mixture of awe, amusement, and light contempt.

Chapter 5 ▷▷▷ From Mrs. Astor to Her Horse

> He [Amory] always rooted for the underdog. He said
> that's what being a Boston Red Sox fan did for you.
> ▸ EDWARD NEY at the memorial service
> for Cleveland Amory

*B*y 1963, when Cleveland Amory and his assistant Marian Probst tried to persuade the residents of Harmony, North Carolina, of the cruelty of their annual "bunny bop" — in which residents chased bunnies and, on catching them, clubbed them — Amory had quite a pulpit. He gave periodic commentary to millions of *Today* viewers every few weeks and was in the third year of writing a weekend syndicated newspaper column for the Sun-Times/Daily News syndicate. The column consisted of a series of short (three- to four-inch) items about a variety of topics, from culture and celebrity to politics and his personal life. As the syndicate noted in publicity for the column, it was "a . . . weekly review of the general American scene." Before Amory came to Harmony, a tiny town in the foothills of the Blue Ridge Mountains, the bunny bop was a popular and well-attended local American Legion event. After Amory left town, even more people knew about it — including the millions who watched the *Today* show.

▷▷▷ Despite his busy schedule as a *Today* show commentator, syndicated columnist, and popular lecturer, Amory by the early 1960s was not content to be considered a dilettante. For much of his career, he had worked on longer, book-length projects, and by the early 1960s his interest in American society had morphed into an interest in celebrity. As he told Edward R. Murrow, this stemmed from his observations that, owing to changes in American culture, "celebrities" were the new socialites, and it was these celebrities who were held in awe by the American public. Accordingly, Amory and press agent Earl Blackwell thought it appropriate that the long-standing *Social Register* should give way to a new compendium that reflected these changes in society. The result was the *Celebrity Register*, which editors Amory and Blackwell subtitled *An Irreverent Compendium of American Notable Quotables*. The 677-page *Celebrity Register* was an immediate hit when it was published in the fall of 1963 — in part because of Amory's ambitious publicity tour and his inside comments about celebrities and their quirks, and in part because reporters and columnists who wrote about Amory knew they would get instant readership by the dropping of celebrity names.

When he gave interviews about the book, Amory focused on the idea that unlike the socialites who were listed in the *Social Register*, the 2,800 people who made the pages of his book were judged on what they did, not on their breeding. He and Blackwell also claimed that the people mentioned in their book came from all over the country, not just from the nation's largest cities. And, unlike the real *Social Register*, their version contained people who were not white Anglo-Saxon Protestants. Amory tried to explain "celebrity" to the *New York Times*: "My definition of celebrity is a name which, once made by news, now makes news itself," he said. Amory also explained what the book was not: "This is not a Blue Book," he said. "It's not a Who book, either. 'Who's Who' is a rank list. You have to be a full professor or a major general to get in and each man has control over his own biography. He can forget an old marriage. We don't allow that. . . . We feel that a little social worker may have more worthwhile-ness than many of the 'Who's.'" As Amory noted years later, his and Blackwell's definition of a celebrity was someone who, ultimately, became well known outside his or her area of expertise.

With two best sellers under his belt, Amory knew what sells: the *Celebrity Register*, as several reviewers noted, may not have been "serious," but, with its gossipy tidbits, puns, and tiny photos of its subjects, it was fun. As the *Saturday Review* wrote, "Tidbits of scandal, quotations dragged in to zip up the prose and nurture the sentence structure, and some marvelous puns make this the wackiest biographical dictionary ever."

Vogue's widely read People Are Talking column described the book as "some 2,800 small biographies that are in the main relevant, occasionally inaccurate on facts, opinionated, and definitely amusing."

As *Book Week* noted, the *Celebrity Register* was fun but not to be taken seriously: "[It] is a dubious reference for anyone in search of more than juicy quotes, colorful quotes and an insight into who — and for what reasons — was considered notable in this country at this particular time."

Amory, always the punster, does not hold back in this volume. Of Richard Nixon (who by the 1963 publishing date of the book had run for president unsuccessfully against John F. Kennedy), he writes: "His career reads like a combination of an Horatio Alger Hiss–story and Poor Richard's Almanac." Of Marlon Brando: "a tempest in a t-shirt." And southerner Truman Capote is "quick on the drawl."

Interestingly, when Amory wrote about high society, his subjects rarely protested — at least in public. They may have complained within their own ranks, but the wealthy New Englanders who were the subjects of his previous books kept their complaints to members of their own social circle for the most part. When Amory entered the world of celebrity, he found his subjects bit back. The columnist Walter Winchell, for instance, was not pleased about Blackwell and Amory's book, and with his clout as a newspaper columnist and regular television and radio commentator, Winchell was a powerful force to be reckoned with. Amory recalled how Winchell called him at 3:00 a.m. the night before the book's publication, demanding that Amory not include Josephine Baker in the *Register*. If Baker's name appeared, Winchell hissed through the phone, "it would not only be the end of the *Register*, it would be the end of me," Amory wrote. Amory surmised that Winchell's strong feelings about Baker were generated by the fact that she was black — and that she had had the nerve to enter the Stork Club, a famous nightclub owned by Winchell's friend Sherman Billingsly. Billingsly had refused to serve her. Amory, of course, did not honor Winchell's request, and the *Celebrity Register* was published with an item about Baker. Winchell never followed through on the threat.

Although it received substantial publicity in several major publications, including the *New York Times*, *Celebrity Register* did not sell well. As Amory noted decades later in *The Best Cat Ever*, its audience may have been limited: many of those who were not included wanted to be in, and many of those who were in it were not pleased by the flip way their entry was written.

Despite its reputation as a somewhat light and lightweight publication, Blackwell and Amory's *Celebrity Register* helped Amory establish himself as a commentator about the current celebrity scene and helped him distance himself from his reputation as a social historian whose commentary was limited to the nation's blue bloods. At age forty-six, he had successfully reinvented himself — as he would do several more times in his life and career.

▷ ▷ ▷ By the mid-1950s, the animal-protection movement in the United States was experiencing great growth. Anticruelty efforts in the country before this time were scattershot and to some degree unorganized. As James M. Jasper and Dorothy Nelkin describe in their history of the movement, *The Animal Rights Crusade: A Growth of a Moral Protest*, differing philosophies and priorities hindered efforts of anticruelty groups until the mid-1950s. One disagreement centered on whether the use of animals for medical experiments was acceptable, a dispute that would continue for many years. But the number of organized animal-rights activities grew dramatically by midcentury, in part because of the growth of big cities. Heads of anticruelty organizations — most of which were based in large urban areas — began to focus more attention on such issues as animal shelters, rescue leagues, and education on the proper care of animals. As Jasper and Nelkin write, "If we are right in linking animal protection with bourgeois domesticity, its reemergence at this time is understandable." The Animal Welfare Institute was founded in Washington, D.C., in 1951. In a move that would have ramifications for decades, some members left the American Humane Society in 1954 to form the Humane Society of the United States (HSUS). A third group, Friends of Animals, was formed in New York in 1957. As Jasper and Nelkin write in their history, the scope of these newly formed groups was much larger than that of the original group. In addition to attempting to change individual behavior, these groups sought institutional change, and their tactics were more aggressive.

Amory became a part of this environment when he joined the HSUS board in the mid-1950s. Amory, of course, had long had an interest in animal protection, but this was the first time he became active in a meaningful way. From the start of his activism, Amory was an advocate of the more aggressive school of change; he believed in change from the grassroots level, and he did not suffer fools gladly when it came to those he thought violated his principles.

Indeed, the early 1960s was the perfect era for Amory and the animal-rights movement. The effort was gaining momentum, and in Amory the movement found the perfect activist: he was single-minded, obstinate, charismatic, and he had friends — celebrities and editors — in high places. By this time, Amory also felt that the movement focused too much on endangered species and cruelty to pets while neglecting wildlife. Amory believed that most people did not think of wild animals as intelligent creatures that experienced fear, pain, and other emotions. With animal rights, Amory found a way to channel his brilliance, his passion, and his tendency to help the underdog.

And it did not hurt that he had access to the right people who could help him get publicity for the movement. Most important, though, was Amory's deep understanding not of animal behavior but of people.

As is the case with most charismatic leaders, Amory was instilled with a deep confidence that led him to either ignore or challenge those who criticized him. For example, in late 1960, shortly after his first syndicated column appeared, he was forwarded a scathing letter from the vice president/managing editor of the *New York Herald Tribune*. The letter said the column was "another column of chit-chat instead of the glossy, sophisticated, witty and intelligent item about people in the social scheme of things that we had expected." The news executive went on to say that "the first part of the column is devoted to a combination of politics and celebrities peppered with quotations, many of which have already appeared in the news." The reaction to this deep and detailed criticism? Apparently no reaction: Amory kept writing the column as he always had. And Amory the lecturer did not always take kindly to what he felt was unfair criticism. In 1973, for example, he was forwarded a lengthy letter from the lecture bureau that scheduled his talk. The letter came from a woman belonging to the Tuckahoe Women's Club in Richmond, Virginia, who complained that during a recent speech Amory strayed from the topic of television (he was then television critic for *TV Guide*) and spoke too much about himself and animals. She wanted a refund.

Amory responded with a very long and detailed letter in his defense, stating that he did, indeed, speak for forty-five minutes about television, and that his comments about himself related to how he became a critic. Amory also quoted at length clips from the local Richmond newspapers stating that "the audience laughed until it cried. . . . Too bad you were not there," he said in the letter. After he explained that many people in Richmond had asked him about his animal-rights activities, he chastised the letter writer: "I understand . . . that you want a refund. I am astonished at this, having had no similar experience in twenty-five years of lecturing. I do not know how to answer except to say that you most assuredly *will not get one*." And he included one more sentence in his response: "I would, however, like an apology." He apparently received none.

Another of Amory's most marked qualities was loyalty — particularly to those who he felt were committed to the cause. By the early 1960s, two people in his life had become pivotal in shaping his work as a writer and activist: Marian Probst and Norman Cousins.

It is not surprising that Norman Cousins and Cleveland Amory were great friends: they were two of a kind in many ways. On the surface, they were both writers and editors, both avid chess players, and both fans of a good — or bad — practical joke. But on a deeper level, both were brilliant and mercurial idealists who thought one person could change the world.

Cousins was the legendary editor of the *Saturday Review* from 1942 until 1971, and again from 1973 to 1977, and he was responsible for establishing the magazine as an eclectic combination of reporting, essays, and criticism. As the *New York Times* noted in Cousins's obituary, his greatest strength as an editor was "his deep and lasting rapport with hundreds of thousands of prosperous, educated middle- and upper-middle-brow people around the country." It is unclear how Cousins, a Columbia University graduate, met Amory, although Gaea Leinhardt believes they may have met when Amory worked at the *Saturday Evening Post*. However they met, they forged a fast friendship that spanned many decades and, ultimately, a continent. (Cousins wrote a best-selling book, *Anatomy of an Illness*, when he was in his midsixties. The book posited that, based on his or her personal experience, a patient's attitude can have a deep effect on his or her health; he then became an adjunct professor in the Department of Psychiatry and Biobehavioral Science at the University of California at Los Angeles.) Leinhardt remembers Cousins and his relationship with Amory when she was growing up in New York: "They shared in different ways intense idealism about things. Norman worried about peace. He was also at a local level very idealistic. And Clip was, too." She recalled how the men's families spent parts of summers together in Tarrytown, New York — the Amorys, with Gaea, and the Cousinses, with Norman's wife, Ellen, and their five daughters. The two men were virtually inseparable, Gaea Leinhardt recalled. Their wives maintained a cordial and friendly relationship, but they had different personalities. Ellen Cousins was socially conscious and concerned herself with promoting organic food and working to ban and control chemicals in the environment, causes that were not top priorities for Martha Hodge Amory: "My mother didn't think about that," she said. "She lived on coffee." But Leinhardt said she greatly enjoyed the time she spent with the Cousins family.

As smart and accomplished as they were, Amory and Cousins were naturally competitive in a benign way. "They would play endless jokes on each other — Norman would call the Connecticut Turnpike Authority and give them Clip's license plate number, and they would stop him," Gaea said. "They would spend weeks trying to determine who could do a more ridiculous practical joke."

Considering the close relationship of the men and their similar outlooks on life and society, it is natural that Cousins would offer his friend a monthly freewheeling column in the *Saturday Review*. Amory's column, First of the Month, which was carried near the front of the magazine, was a rumination about politics, celebrity, books, education, or whatever its author deemed appropriate. About fifteen hundred words, it usually consisted of several small items of several paragraphs each. The column was perfect for Amory in several ways. First, it allowed him to write about whatever he wanted. Second, and most important, Cousins never interfered with the subject matter. Amory, who disliked being edited, was in heaven. And unlike many editors, Cousins was not afraid of controversy and, indeed, may have courted it. Cousins had always been a peace activist and, by the mid-1960s, had voiced extreme opposition to the war in Vietnam. Amory also opposed the war and occasionally commented on it in his column. By 1967 and 1968, though, Amory's open resistance to the war had intensified: nearly all his monthly columns included items about the war — all with an antiwar stance. But Amory had his own pet causes, too; by the early 1960s, animal rights and sympathy for Israel were two of them. It was natural he would mention both in his column, with no opposition from his editor.

By 1963, though, Amory had plenty of bully pulpits from which to broadcast his views — and the *Today* show was one of them. He worked on a freelance basis for the show, providing commentary every three weeks. But *Today* executives were content to let Amory be Amory, and they did not ask him to give them a transcript of his comments before air time, although it was an informal policy that someone in management read the comments before they aired.

By 1963, Amory and Martha Hodge had been married nearly ten years. But one other woman had became pivotal in Amory's life at this time: Marian Probst, who met him in 1961 and became his assistant, friend, travel partner, doppelgänger, and right-hand woman for the rest of his life. Probst, like many of Amory's close friends, worked with him for many decades for little compensation; she, like the others, was drawn to him by the sheer force of his personality. Probst, who grew up in Salem, Ohio, worked for Amory from the day after she met him on May 24, 1961, until the day before he died. She met him through a mutual friend at the *Saturday Review*. Amory, knowing Probst was a big Cleveland Indians fan, asked her to an Indians-Yankees game. She was amazed and impressed by his outrageous enthusiasm. "He stood up and exuberantly yelled throughout the game," she recalled. Amory never officially hired Probst but just naturally assumed she would come in the day after the game to begin work for him. She did come to work for him the next day — and nearly every day after that for thirty-seven years. It was Probst who typed Amory's handwritten scribbles on yellow legal pads and turned them into neatly typed magazine stories, speeches, and manuscripts; Probst who maintained all his personal and professional records; Probst who frequently traveled with Amory on business for the Fund for Animals, which Amory founded in 1967; and Probst who helped Amory establish, promote, and maintain the fund. In short, it was Marian Probst who helped Cleveland Amory *be* Cleveland Amory — in many ways, she was the woman behind the man.

Nearly forty years after the event, Marian Probst recalled in detail the trip to Harmony, North Carolina, and the birth of Amory's "Hunt-the-Hunters Hunt Club." Amory wrote at length about the Hunt Club in his book *Man Kind?* and spoke for much of the rest of his life about his journey to Harmony to meet the group that sponsored the annual "bunny bop." Supposedly to combat rabbit overpopulation, participants would chase rabbits, catch them, and club them to death. It was one of the town's most popular annual events, and the fact that killing was a social event further enraged Amory. Little did the residents of Harmony know that, in the spring of 1963, their little gathering would receive particularly wide publicity — details of it were beamed into the homes of millions of *Today* show viewers, courtesy of Cleveland Amory.

After learning about the bunny bop, which was sponsored by the American Legion, Amory and Probst traveled to Harmony and engaged in a debate with its planners to try to dissuade them from holding the event. Many years later, Probst remembered vividly that most Harmony residents were not overly enthusiastic about a visit from this tall — and apparently overeducated — Yankee. At the debate, the mayor introduced him, Probst recalled, but it was hardly a friendly endorsement. "'We have this fellow who has come down from New York and he doesn't like the way we do things,'" the mayor said. "'He's a graduate of Harvard and many other colleges.'" After the debate — in which Amory stressed that beating rabbits to death was inhumane — the group took a vote to determine if the bop should take place the next day. Not unsurprisingly, Amory and Probst were the only two who voted against the event, which was ultimately held as scheduled.

Today show management expected Amory to offer lighthearted commentary about the trip when he returned; what they and millions of viewers heard may have been humorous, but it was hardly lighthearted. Amory delivered a version of an essay he wrote for several magazines called the "Hunt-the-Hunters Hunt Club." He proposed the formation of a hunt club where hunters themselves would be tracked down and killed — for sport, of course. Mimicking arguments he had heard many times, he proposed that the killing of hunters would be, at its core, humane. After all, he noted, because of the hunters' overpopulation, killing them in cold blood would actually be kind. And how would these hunters be lured out of the brush? With the sound of a cocktail shaker, of course. Still, once the deed was done, there was no need to be ostentatious, Amory added. "After you have bagged your hunter, do not drape him on the automobile or mount him after you get home. Merely the cap or the jacket will suffice."

Many viewers did not see the humor in this satiric commentary, and some felt personally affronted. Amory would come to learn firsthand about the power of the hunting lobby in the United States, and NBC officials got a taste of it after they aired the hunt-the-hunters commentary. The reaction to it was swift, severe, and mostly negative. Probst remembered that NBC president Julian Goodman literally called Amory upstairs and reprimanded him.

Officials of the show no longer waived their rule about preapproving commentary when it came to Amory. They now wanted to know what he would say before he said it. "This is a rigid NBC policy that we have occasionally breached, particularly in your case," *Today* producer Al Morgan wrote in a memo to Amory shortly after the bunny commentary. "We have been reminded that the policy does exist. . . . I must have a written script from you at least two days before air."

But Amory achieved his goal, despite the angry reaction from *Today* show management: the unwanted publicity did force the American Legion to end its sponsorship of the rabbit hunt. And Amory did for a while return to his usual wry, relatively harmless commentary — until he decided once again, in the fall of that year, that some animals needed his help.

By this time in his life, when he was in his middle forties, Amory had become a true believer. He was convinced that animal abusers — and his definition of the term included hunters, some scientists, and many self-described "naturalists"—were able to get away with their actions because the public was not fully aware of them. With his platform and access to the media, he believed he could help change that, by informing people and by initiating animal-protection legislation. Within a few months of his hunt-the-hunters commentary, he was taking up the cause of animal rights in a more serious way.

Shortly after his bunny-bop satire aired on *Today*, Amory raised a brouhaha nationally when he expressed his opinions in the *Saturday Review* and the *Saturday Evening Post* about vivisection—the abuse of animals in laboratory research. Amory did not unilaterally oppose the use of animals in laboratories. He opposed what he said was the cruelty and mistreatment of those animals in many labs. The controversy was launched in the *Saturday Review*, when Amory wrote about what he felt was the cruelty of some animal experimentation for medical purposes in his First of the Month column. Editor Norman Cousins, of course, did not edit his friend Amory, and the column ran precisely as Amory had written it.

Amory's activism was turning him into an expert in public relations. The Harmony bunny bop was perfect for him from a marketing point of view—the wholesale bloodshed inflicted on such furry and innocent-looking creatures provided him with a dramatic way to illustrate the plight of abused animals. And that, combined with the fact that he was able to use humor and satire to illustrate the event, provided a perfect opportunity for Amory. Throughout his decades as an animal-rights activist, Amory became adept at making the most of opportunities available to him. (Years later, he guessed—accurately—that the soon-to-be-canceled *Dick Cavett* morning show on ABC was one of the few television programs that would show brutal video clips of seals being clubbed. With cancellation imminent, the producers, he surmised, had nothing to lose.) Amory was also very aware of another public relations precept: if one major news outlet ran an interesting or compelling item, other news outlets would almost certainly follow.

In June of 1963 Amory wrote in his *Saturday Review* column that his previous mention in that column of pending bills advocating more humane treatment of lab animals drew nearly a thousand letters from readers. And with the exception of two letters from two doctors at Johns Hopkins University, all were supportive of the legislation, he wrote. Amory's columns were almost always about a variety of topics, but this particular column dealt solely with the pending legislation and details related to it. And he focused much of it on gruesome testimony that detailed cruelty to laboratory animals including, among other things, animals being beaten, starved, blinded, and burned for purposes of research. The numbers, he said, were staggering: up to 300 million animals of all kinds died annually in laboratories.

The June column drew even more mail. He wrote in a later column that he received ten thousand letters — nine thousand of them agreeing with his contentions. There appears to be no record of what the other thousand letters said, or a way to verify whether Amory's numbers were accurate, although the *Saturday Review* did publish several letters sympathetic to Amory. Among Amory's personal papers, though, is a letter forwarded to him by Cousins from a doctor and medical professor in Los Angeles who took offense at a 1964 column in which Amory discussed animal rights. "To put up with his snide accusations about the cruelty to laboratory animals is hardly more that can be borne," the letter writer said. "I enjoy reading your magazine, but to be faced at every turn with these comments is distressing." The writer, Dr. Josiah Brown, said that with Amory's comments, *Saturday Review* "[is] in the medical far right — anti-vivisection, anti-fluoridation, even anti-vaccination."

In the 1963 incident, though, Amory was relentless. The reaction to the *Saturday Review* columns prompted him to submit a Speaking Out column to the *Saturday Evening Post* titled "Science Is Needlessly Cruel to Animals." He noted that six bills were pending in Congress to regulate use and treatment of animals in scientific laboratories, and that such bills were being proposed because of widespread abuse of animals in labs nationwide. Amory cited several examples of animal mistreatment, including inducement of slow death by freezing to see how animals adapted to the cold, and instances of burning. Amory became more specific about who was doing what to animals in specific laboratories: "At Creighton University, for example, researchers starved dogs to death. It took [them] 65 days to die," he wrote. At Harvard (his alma mater), "scientists forced dogs to inhale flame and then did not kill them until five days afterward." Using tactics of the champion debater that he was, Amory quoted a doctor who acknowledged the existence of cruelty in research laboratories. He also criticized the American Society for the Prevention of Cruelty to Animals (ASPCA) for what he called its ineffectiveness and its sales of some homeless animals to laboratories.

Amory might as well have lobbed a grenade onto the medical and scientific community, and he soon learned that *Saturday Evening Post* editors were not as unflappable or permissive as Cousins. Within days, the *Post* was inundated with reaction letters to Amory's column, and its editors indicated in the magazine that the reaction was far from positive.

Three weeks after the column appeared, the *Saturday Evening Post* published seven letters — six from scientists and doctors — claiming that Amory distorted facts and painted an inaccurate picture of laboratory activities. "We protest, as a God-centered institution, what is grossly unfair and inaccurate concerning the work we have done to help people have healthier, longer and better lives," wrote Richard L. Egan, M.D., dean of Creighton University's School of Medicine. People who are motivated to go into medical research "do not become transformed into sadists when they enter their laboratories," wrote James V. Warren, president of the American Heart Association. Another letter came from William Rockefeller, president of the ASPCA, who stated the group did not routinely supply laboratories with homeless animals but, by law, had to supply them with such animals if repeated efforts to find other homes were unsuccessful. He added that few animals were given to laboratories.

It is impossible to determine how many unpublished letters the *Saturday Evening Post* received that voiced support for Amory's points, if any. In early September, though, the magazine published an editorial that stated some of Amory's accusations were without merit, and that many lifesaving medical findings and procedures stemmed from animal research. The editorial noted that "Mr. Amory accused scientists of needlessly inflicting pain on animals, but he did not explain the purpose of their investigations, which is to find ways of alleviating pain and staving off death in humans. . . . Lifesaving results have stemmed from . . . experiments attacked by Mr. Amory."

To Amory, though, there was no such thing as bad publicity — the reaction to his *Saturday Evening Post* column kept the debate alive. *Newsweek* magazine told readers of the war between Amory and the medical and scientific community. A reporter wrote, naively perhaps, "Cleveland Amory, the affable chronicler of society . . . would seem the last person to be leading a flaming medical crusade." The article noted that while it was unlikely that scientists were deliberately abusing animals in their efforts, it was also possible that their smugness about the subject could enrage the nation's 25 million dog owners and 28 million cat owners, who would then in turn pressure Congress to enact laws preventing such abuse.

Amory was far from finished, however. In response to the *Saturday Evening Post* editorial and the letters to the editor from doctors, he wrote his own letter to the editor of the magazine. "You cannot imagine my surprise to see your letters column on my article. I had no idea that of your 22 million readers not a single one would like my article and that every single fact I wrote was totally incorrect," he wrote sarcastically. "I was also touched by their sense of humor." (Amory was responding to one Utah scientist who had suggested that perhaps Amory would have preferred that he and his friends be used for experiments in the laboratory instead of animals.)

The widespread reaction to the issue no doubt prompted Amory to keep the debate going. A good way to do this, he must have assumed, was to speak about it to *Today* viewers during his periodic commentary on that program. And one day that fall of 1963, he spoke on *Today* about the evils of vivisection. He did not get approval from NBC beforehand to speak on the topic.

Once again, the switchboard at NBC lit up, not with gun owners and hunters but with scientists and doctors on the other end. This time, NBC officials did not reprimand Amory. They fired him immediately.

Oddly, the firing by NBC apparently came as a surprise to Amory. "He was upset," said Probst. The fact that scientists and doctors had now joined hunters in their criticism of Amory led to his firing, Probst believes, although Amory was stunned that NBC would take such drastic measures. Like most clever and successful people, though, Amory had an ability to interpret and adjust to the environment in which he operated. If the *Today* incident taught him anything, it was perhaps that some occasions call for the use of subtlety. By the mid-1960s, his fanaticism about animal rights had grown even stronger, but he was careful not to abuse the platform he had been given as a social and cultural critic. For the most part, he did not use his *TV Guide* column to write at length about animal rights, but he did talk about his favorite cause on the lecture circuit.

Three years after Amory brought up vivisection in his magazine column and on the *Today* show, Congress passed the Animal Welfare Act of 1966, the first federal law spelling out guidelines for the treatment and care of certain species of laboratory animals. The act was amended four years later to include all warm-blooded animals. Meanwhile, Amory had managed to make a lifetime of enemies in the science and medical communities, a group that joined hunters in monitoring his activities and speaking out against him whenever they could. He was not oblivious to the fact he was hated by many people, but the fight was worth it to him. As he said many times in his life — and as he constantly reminded those who worked with him — one is judged not only by one's friends but also by the quality, and quantity, of one's enemies.

Leonore Amory with her children Robert Jr.
(*left*); Cleveland (*right*), and baby Leonore, 1921.
From the estate of Cleveland Amory.

Young Cleveland Amory
with a feline friend.
*From the estate of
Cleveland Amory.*

Siblings, *from left*, Robert Amory, 12, Leonore
Amory, 6, and Cleveland Amory, 10, in 1927.
From the personal collection of Gaea Leinhardt.

Amory at age 12 or 13.
From the estate of Cleveland Amory.

Marian Probst, who was Amory's
assistant for more than 35 years.
From the estate of Cleveland Amory.

Amory's wife, Martha Hodge Amory, in 1942 at age 30.
From the personal collection of Gaea Leinhardt.

Amory on the balcony of the Normandy Hotel, Paris, 1954, with Elf, a dog he adopted in France while working on the life story of the Duchess of Windsor. *From the personal collection of Gaea Leinhardt.*

Martha Hodge Amory with Elf, 1954, at the Normandy Hotel, Paris.
From the personal collection of Gaea Leinhardt.

Martha and Amory's beloved Siberian Huskies Ivan the Great and Peter the Terrible in Central Park, 1969. *From the personal collection of Gaea Leinhardt.*

Martha and Amory's pet poodle, Tiger, 1959.
From the personal collection of Gaea Leinhardt.

Amory at a rally.
From the estate of Cleveland Amory.

Chapter 6 ▷ ▷ ▷ New Directions

> If you take a good look at what Mark Twain and
> Will Rogers said and wrote, there is a lot of sharp-edged
> humor to it. It's the same with Cleveland. He's a
> true humorist. They were geniuses and so was he.
>
> ► Editor and publisher WALTER ANDERSON

*L*ike many true believers, Amory was vaguely aware that others did not always feel as strongly as he did about some issues regarding animal rights, but the movement was far more important to him than making or keeping friends. As he grew increasingly active in anticruelty efforts, he began living in a bubble, surrounding himself with people who were active in the movement. Certainly his readers and his editor at the *Saturday Review* had sympathy for the cause, and for at least two other causes in which Amory strongly believed.

Since he began his monthly *Saturday Review* column in 1952, Amory wrote about a variety of topics, including societal trends, books, television and Broadway shows, and even a little gossip. But he also had some potentially controversial items, and by the mid- to late 1960s his column was a forum for his stance against the war in Vietnam. The target audience of the *Saturday Review*—high- and middle-income, well-read liberals—did not disagree with Amory on this issue, and wrote to tell him. Editor Norman Cousins, who was vehemently antiwar and who worked for world-peace organizations much later in his life, was not going to edit his friend when it came to items about the war, or anything else. For example, at the height of antiwar protests in July of 1965, Amory opened his column with an item about President Lyndon Johnson's Festival of the Arts (which he described with a characteristic pun as a "post-Easter egghead roll on the White House lawn"). The event, Amory was quick to point out, was marred first by poet Robert Lowell's refusal to attend, owing to his antiwar stand, after he had previously said he would be there: "as if this weren't enough, half a dozen others also declined—many of whom, interestingly, hadn't been invited in the first place," Amory wrote. He injected his own opinion of the protests: "While we can't agree with Mr. Lowell that an invitation to the White House involves a 'subtle public commitment' to the President's foreign policy, we do feel that a foreign policy that involves making the Vietcong the greatest underdog since Robin Hood is, at the very least, unstable."

Amory often wrote about the war in his column with not-so-veiled sarcasm. For instance, in June of 1965, he noted how actor Raymond Burr, who starred in the popular *Perry Mason* television show, traveled to Saigon to meet with generals and ambassadors there. "Mr. Burr is . . . a defense attorney, and while frankly, we think the government, judging by its actions, would have preferred a prosecuting type, judging by its actions, we still think the idea is wonderful. Foreign policy . . . is too important to be trusted to foreign politicians." Further, Amory notes, other actors — including Robert Reed, who played Sherlock Holmes in a series called *Baker Street*, and E. G. Marshall, who played a detective — should also travel there: "If there's one thing we need in Vietnam, it's a real sleuth — to find out what's going on. And he can come back and tell the rest of us all about it." Later that year, Amory wrote in his column about antiwar protestors at some college campuses. The protests, he wrote, "brought violent response. But the fact remained that, call the paraders 'Vietniks' or what you will, they will be among the ones fighting a war which . . . is as yet undeclared by Congress."

As the scope of the war escalated, he wrote repeatedly and sympathetically in his columns about antiwar protests all over the country, and was always quick to note the famous actors and writers who opposed the war. Amory was particularly critical of what was known as the "military-industrial complex" — the concept that businesses in the United States would always profit from war, and that this profit motivated government officials to embark on the war in Vietnam. In one column, he quoted writer I. F. Stone: "'It is the Machine,' Mr. Stone wrote, 'that is at stake in Vietnam. It is Boeing and General Electric and Goodyear and General Dynamics. It is the electronic range-finder and the amphibious truck and the night-piercing radar. It is the defoliant, and the herbicide and the deodorant and the depilatory.'"

When it came to marshaling followers to a cause, Amory understood well the power of celebrity. In mid-1967, he devoted almost one full column to the comments of actor Robert Vaughn, who was then a star of the popular television show *Man from U.N.C.L.E.* Vaughn, he wrote, spoke at Harvard in what Amory labeled one of the most carefully reasoned yet strongest statements yet against the war in Vietnam. Vaughn asked: Will the United States, in pursuit of its stated goal to halt communism, routinely "oppose inevitably emerging popular revolutions when they don't meet with our fancy, and by our opposition, totally ignore the will of the people involved? Are we to prevent the spread of Communism by sacrificing the principles of our democracy? . . . If we think our methods are righteous, we are fooling no one but ourselves. Certainly not the rest of the world! Certainly not ourselves!"

Amory noted that Vaughn's speech had been interrupted several times with applause and was followed by a five-minute standing ovation. Amory wrote that Vaughn personally sent letters to twenty-five other Hollywood celebrities who had previously opposed the war publicly, urging them to speak up again. But Amory added that, until recently, few people in the public eye had been brave enough to take a stand against the war. "Now what I call my political fan mail runs 100 to 1 in favor of my stand," Amory wrote.

The tide was turning against the war by 1967, and Amory had little trouble finding war-related topics about which to write. He was also finding it easier to find celebrities who shared his views on the war. In the fall of 1967, he quoted at length a book called *Authors Take Sides on Vietnam* and made a detailed list of those authors who voiced opposition to the war, those who stated their support of it, and those who were undecided. (The list of those in opposition was more than twice the size of the list of supporters.) He also quoted playwright and humorist Jules Feiffer and author Susan Sontag. "I'm against it. Isn't everybody?" Feiffer asked. And Sontag: "America's war in Vietnam makes me, for the first time in my life, ashamed of being an American."

By 1968, the year of a presidential election, Amory could hardly contain himself when it came to his opposition to the war, and his support for liberal antiwar candidate Eugene McCarthy. Amory raved about McCarthy in his columns as the election grew near. Many famous people who opposed the war also voiced support for McCarthy, and Amory continued to use tactics in his column that he believed worked best to promote his cause: he quoted celebrities who spoke favorably and, he believed, eloquently about the candidate. Actor-writer Wyatt Cooper, husband of Gloria Vanderbilt, had started a National Committee of Arts and Letters for McCarthy. Amory quoted Cooper's introduction of the candidate before a speech: "We live in a time of chaos, a time of change, a time of great confusion. Many of the old values do not hold. Certainly the old slogans do not suffice. . . . Meanwhile, the bodies of dead boys pile higher, and the cries of homeless children grow louder. . . .

But there is a new spirit alive in the land . . . . How fortunate we are that our present crisis has brought forth a man for our times."

In mid-June, Amory devoted about half his column to an interview with McCarthy and his wife, noting that McCarthy wrote poetry and was very different from the typical superficial, fawning candidate. "Was it true, we asked sternly, that in the entire campaign so far he had not yet kissed a single baby? Not true, the candidate replied. He did try to kiss one recalcitrant baby boy."

As 1968 progressed, events made it impossible for Amory to avoid writing even more about politics: candidate Robert F. Kennedy was assassinated, the Democratic National Convention in Chicago turned chaotic as the mayor authorized police to break up massive antiwar protests in the streets and parks outside the convention center, and the chances of putting a Democrat in the White House grew increasingly dismal. After the convention, Amory wrote disparagingly about Chicago mayor Richard Daley, although he did not dwell on the convention. In one column, for instance, he takes a swipe at respected newsman Walter Cronkite for lobbing Daley softballs in an interview: "One of the many disappointments at Chicago was the undoing of many long hours of fine work on the part of one of our old favorites, Walter Cronkite. It is hard to speculate on what possessed Mr. Cronkite to interview Chicago's mayor in such fawning fashion — frankly, we prefer not to." Amory, as he generally did in his column, let others speak for him. After the death of Robert Kennedy, he opened his column with a quick summary of the month: "June was the awful month — of the late RFK, his gallant [wife] Ethel, and the stirring Ted [Kennedy]. Almost everything else seemed of such unimportance as not to have happened at all." He quoted sportswriter Jim Murray at length about the sadness that gripped the country: "Once again America the beautiful has taken a bullet to the groin. The country is in surgery. The Violent States of America. One bullet is mightier than one million voters. It is not a Democracy, it is a Lunacy. A country that shrinks from punishing its criminals, disciplining its children, locking up its mad. . . ." To Amory, however, the tragedies had a silver lining. He speculated in the column that the country's gun lobby could lose some of its clout: "One thing during the month was certain — the nation was up in unarms."

Amory also used his column to publicize his favorite causes: animal rights, of course, and his sympathy for the plight of Israel. He followed the activities of state legislatures regarding pending laws about animals and animal cruelty. In September 1965, Amory told his readers, the president "irritated us considerably during this month [with] . . . his cutbacks of four more wildlife refuges — after already cutting down completely on five." In the same column, he noted some good news: many states were beginning to pass anticruelty measures regarding rodeo animals. He was also able to publish in the *Saturday Review* references to other anticruelty activities and events. For instance, after the daytime *Dick Cavett* show aired what Amory called atrocities regarding the annual spring "harvest" of seals on the ice floes of the Canadian Magdalen Islands in the Gulf of St. Lawrence — where, he said, fifty thousand baby seals were clubbed to death — he mentioned in his column the mail he received from readers grateful that Cavett had aired the piece. He also advised readers to refuse to wear or buy any product made from seal fur; to write the prime minister of Canada; and to give to his newly founded charity, the Fund for Animals.

Throughout much of his adult life, and especially following the Six-Day War in the Middle East in June of 1967, Amory was very sympathetic to the Israelis and defended what he perceived as their ingenuity and intelligence. For decades, he wrote and spoke admiringly of them, and he visited Israel several times. In his *Saturday Review* column, he was direct in stating that he believed the Israelis acted in self defense against the Arabs in the Six-Day War, and he was critical of the United States because he felt it gave more aid money to Arab countries than to Israel. Further, Amory believed that the Israelis were for the most part outmatched in manpower in many of the battles of the war, but they still managed to win a quick and decisive victory: "Contrary . . . to what many people think, the war was not a small one," he wrote. "The Sinai battle, for example, in which the Israelis sent 325 tanks against 850 Egyptian tanks, was the largest tank battle in history. When the Egyptians did run, the Israelis could have killed thousands upon thousands of them. They not only didn't kill them, they didn't even take them prisoner."

Amory's *Saturday Review* column was in many ways a window into his beliefs and personality. It revealed his quirky nature and the odd things he thought important or interesting. For example, he occasionally wrote about events in the magazine-publishing world. In February of 1969, he noted in a brief item the demise of his literary alma mater: the *Saturday Evening Post*, "the ancient and honorable [magazine] . . . which many readers of this column will remember was never the same since an editor who shall be nameless handled 'Post Scripts.'" On the flip side of the closing, however, was the formation the previous year of a new magazine called *New York*. The new magazine, Amory noted, was to be edited by a *New Yorker* and *Saturday Review* alumnus named Clay Felker. Amory wrote that the magazine "rose from the ashes of the [New York] *Herald Tribune* supplement of the same name, and immediately earned well deserved plaudits. We wish it a fun life." Amory did not know at the time that nearly forty years after its launch, *New York* would still be in business.

He wrote briefly about what was new in books, on and off Broadway, and on television, although, from 1963 to 1976, he was the chief television critic for *TV Guide*. Some of the items in Amory's column were ironic considering his own lifestyle and beliefs. While it was not unusual for him to note interesting or unique happenings at college campuses, one item of academic research he noted may have personally, to him, hit home. Amory quoted an article in *McLean's* magazine on research at Ohio State University that found extramarital affairs do not necessarily cause guilt and can, in fact, "provide the vital part of life that is missing in the marriage" and help it, according to the study. "Considering man as he is, as a mammal, monogamous marriage is a bizarre and unnatural state," the researcher said. An interesting item, considering that monogamy had never been a priority for Amory during much of his two-decade marriage to Martha Hodge.

Throughout this part of Amory's writing career, it was not only Norman Cousins who let his copy appear primarily as it was written. Management at the *Today* show may have learned the hard way that Amory occasionally needed some editing. But it is likely that few editors — even at publications for which Amory wrote as a freelancer — edited him with a heavy hand or changed his sometimes caustic tone. An article he wrote for *Holiday* in 1957 drips with sarcasm and hardly treats its subjects with kid gloves, even though its author took to task a sacred cow of Americana: the Texas oilman. The magazine's subhead seemed innocent enough as it described the profile of four Texas oil millionaires: "Meet the rich-rich Texans — our open-handed fellow citizens with the world's biggest bank accounts. A witty study of the blessings and embarrassments of wealth, by America's sharpest observer of the social scene." What followed in the long article was for the most part a scathing indictment of the four men. Amory noted that, at best, they managed to skirt many laws to obtain their wealth and, at worst, they were self-centered narcissists who cared only about feathering their own nests. Amory, an astute student of dialect, opens the story by mocking the accent of one of his subjects, who declares he is donating money to an unknown charity:

Mah name . . . is James R. Robinson, and mah nickname is Jimmy. Ah have a ten-thousand-acre ranch in the Panhandle, and mah brand is JR. Ah run ten thousand barrels of oil a day and ah own outright the Robinson Oil and Gas Company. Ah have a ten-thousand-dollar baby-blue Cadillac outside, and on it, in gold, are mah initials, JRR. Ah like this charity and ah want to give ten thousand dollars — *ah-nony-mously!*"

Briefly, and almost as asides, Amory nonchalantly recounts the stories of the millionaire oilman who led a double life and had two wives in two different cities; of the wife of another oilman who left her millionaire husband for the decorator who helped design one of her houses; and other gossipy tales. But the backbone of the story outlines how the oilmen — most of them newly rich — acquired their wealth through questionable transactions regarding federal tax codes and the circumventing of other laws. What these men lacked in formal education, they made up for in chutzpah, Amory implies. One, Hugh Roy Cullen of Houston, may have had humble beginnings, but he was far from humble: "He gave the University of Houston some $100,000,000 not including one extra check for $2,250,000. This tip was given for an upset football victory over Baylor." Of Fort Worth's Sid Richardson — a bachelor and arguably the richest oilman in Texas, whose net worth was more than a billion dollars — Amory writes:

Much of the time he spends in seclusion on his own island in the Gulf of Mexico where, like so many oilmen, he likes to indulge in shooting, hunting and fishing. He is not without a sense of humor and believes in teaching people the hard way. Once a niece of his, a small child, came to him with a pat-ball racket and bet him a dollar he couldn't hit the ball sixteen times without missing. He put the ball on a bed, hit it sixteen times, then took her dollar.

And Amory was not afraid to point out the oilmen's lack of, well, sophistication. Clint Murchison of Athens, Texas, east of Dallas, owned several spectacular homes, including one 75,000-acre ranch in the Sierra Madre Mountains in Mexico. So grand and rich were the Murchisons that they once entertained one of Amory's favorite pairs, the Duke and Duchess of Windsor. " 'From the beginning,' Mrs. Murchison says, 'my husband told me there would be no curtsying or backing out of the room or any of that sort of thing. There wasn't.'"

Murchison's empire, like that of many of the oilmen, extended far beyond Texas and far beyond oil. He owned "all the taxicabs and buses in Dallas to all the water in Indianapolis" as well as a pipeline that ran through much of western Canada, a candy company in Chicago, and a steamship line in Washington," Amory wrote. Curiously, Murchison owned the Henry Holt & Co. publishing firm, but he was hardly a patron of the arts. "'Wal,' he says, 'I got it right after the war. I figgered with the Government givin' all the money to send veterans to college, somebody sure was gonna use a lot of textbooks. I found out Holt made a lot of 'em so I bought 'em.'"

It is not known if *Holiday* received complaints about the profile of the four Texas oilmen, and in fact the subjects of the story may have felt that all publicity was good. Interestingly, Amory would become reacquainted with the name of Murchison much later in his life. In 1980, when he was about to realize a lifelong dream of founding a sanctuary for abused animals, he was seeking a large plot of inexpensive land. Amory's pride and joy, Black Beauty Ranch, was located in eastern Texas, adjacent to the small town of Athens. The city that housed the Black Beauty Ranch was Murchison, Texas, named after Clint Murchison.

▷ ▷ ▷ Like many talented writers, Amory was particular about his writing and did not always enjoy being edited. But one of his longtime editors said that Amory welcomed comments from editors whom he respected — and he believed that talented editors could improve his work. But the ranks of those editors whom he deemed "talented" were slim.

Walter Anderson, editor and publisher of *Parade* magazine, the Sunday newspaper supplement for which Amory wrote during the last fifteen years of his life, said that Amory's copy required little editing. "I would say that probably nine times of out ten, when he wrote an article for *Parade,* it was fairly close to the length that we would publish," he said. "Nine times out of ten, if I told him we needed two thousand words, he would get close to it." As the years passed and Anderson and Amory became friends, Amory would sometimes send Anderson comments from editors who were editing one of his books. "He would get angry at book editors sometimes. . . . With Cleveland, if you're going to make a criticism you better have a suggestion," Anderson said. As Anderson learned throughout his decades-long association with Amory, Amory had a wonderful memory — a quality that cut both ways when it came to friendships. At Amory's memorial service, Anderson recalled a phone call he received one day from an angry Amory, who railed on and on about how a certain book editor made what he considered unnecessary editing suggestions to his manuscript. Anderson listened patiently, and calmly suggested that Amory write a short but carefully worded letter to the editor, telling her that he appreciated the suggestions and that he had incorporated every one of them (even though in reality he had taken none of them). Amory followed Anderson's advice, and the book was published as he wrote it. Anderson was pleased he could help Amory — until years later, when, in response to a few of Anderson's editing suggestions, Anderson received the same carefully worded letter from Amory — and no changes to the article.

Anderson said that Amory was the consummate professional who valued suggestions that improved his work. If he had a problem writing a piece for *Parade*, he would write a draft and send it to Anderson, who would edit it and return it. This occasional back-and-forth was the heaviest editing he ever had to do on Amory's work, he said.

Amory was a natural writer who understood story structure. "He was as much an editor as a writer," Anderson said. "He had an innate sense of structure, of the architecture of an article. He was a great storyteller. He knew how to lead you into an article and how to conclude it." To Anderson, Amory's forte was humor in the vein of Will Rogers or Mark Twain. "If you take a good look at what Mark Twain and Will Rogers said and wrote, there is a lot of sharp-edged humor to it. It's the same with Cleveland. He's a true humorist. They were geniuses and so was he." Editing writers like Amory was difficult, Anderson said, because of their talent and organization. "[Writers like that] are hard to edit. It's like undoing a spider's web."

Despite the onetime wealth of his family, Amory was not a rich man during his adult life; he certainly did not earn much from his freelance magazine writing or from his regular column for *Saturday Review*, for which he was paid a flat amount per column. Even with his high-profile position at the *Today* show, he was paid only $300 per broadcast and was not part of the *Today* staff. Much of his income was patched together, with royalties from his books contributing. But most of his travel — as well as the social events associated with his job — was paid for when he was on the lecture circuit or on assignment for a magazine article.

Amory's livelihood was dependent in many ways on word of mouth. That is, his visibility on television, on the lecture circuit, and in the print media led to more work in those areas. In that way, his firing from *Today* hurt him — not because of the lost income, but because the wide audience of the show was a tremendous launching pad for more jobs and speaking engagements.

By the time his tenure at *Today* ended, however, Amory was about to embark on a new chapter in his life — and one that would give him more fame and celebrity. He was hired as the chief television critic of *TV Guide*.

▷ ▷ ▷ One of Amory's theses in his book *Who Killed Society?* was that an increasing lack of civility, including foul language and bad manners, helped destroy polite society. By the time he entered middle age, Amory further marketed this contention by labeling himself a curmudgeon — in other words, he was able to be critical of some people and institutions because of this status. But while this label worked effectively from a marketing point of view, it was paradoxical in some ways. As his friends attest, Amory was oddly guileless, and his humor never stemmed from cynicism or hatred. Yet he did not suffer fools gladly, and he targeted many of his writings and speeches at what he considered absurd behavior or customs.

What was particularly perplexing to Amory as he grew older was a creeping immorality in American daily life — the daily and offhand mentioning and describing of sex. In a 1960 *Washington Post* article, for example, he bemoaned a new candor when it came to previously unmentioned topics. "Altogether, our moral slips would indeed appear to be showing," he wrote. "The once-whispered Facts of Life are shouted from the housetops, and the good authors who once knew better words now not only use four-letter words but also seem to have taught virtually nothing else to a whole new generation."

By the early 1960s his work was ubiquitous. In addition to his extensive freelance writing in many major publications, his column in the *Saturday Review*, and his syndicated newspaper column, he was a fixture on television talk shows, had a syndicated radio show where he offered brief commentary, and was a tireless and popular lecturer. And although his topics varied depending on the times and the venue, he invariably addressed one general issue: American culture and its quirks. In one freelance *New York Times Magazine* piece, Amory bit the hand that fed him — he lampooned the ironies and absurdities of the lecture circuit. In his piece "Fee Speech: Lecture on

Lecturing," Amory writes, tongue in cheek, that the "industry" of lecturing may benefit the three or four key lecture bureaus that get paid handsomely to arrange lectures — the bureaus often take half or more of the total fee paid to the lecturer — but that lecturing itself is usually boring to most audiences and not lucrative for the speakers. And, in an odd twist of fate, the lecturing business actually benefits from bad or hard times (when audiences want to hear remedies or insights into why times are bad) and from television. Although the growing medium of television allows audiences to remain in their own homes and hear speakers at no cost, the medium only contributes to the popularity of people seen on television, making them even more sought after as paid speakers. The whole phenomenon, Amory writes in this hilarious essay, is absurd.

In some ways, Amory had a knack for being in the right place at the right time. But it is also true that his talent, his versatility, his drive, and his enthusiasm for life led him to those right places. In 1963, the popular magazine *TV Guide* was seeking its first full-time television critic. By 1963, Amory had been fired from *Today*, and he sought a large venue that would allow him to provide regular commentary. It is perhaps inevitable that Amory and the editors of *TV Guide*, then the largest-circulation magazine in the country, would form a relationship.

By 1963, *TV Guide* was ten years old and tremendously popular. Founded in 1953 by publisher Walter Annenberg (who remained in that position until 1988) and editorial director Merrill Panitt, it sold 1.5 million copies of its first edition. By 1960, its circulation had climbed to more than 7 million copies a week, and by the late 1970s it would be selling about 20 million copies per week. In their extensive history of the magazine, Glenn C. Altschuler and David I. Grossvogel note that while television viewers could read television logs in their daily newspapers, there was something about *TV Guide* that attracted them — perhaps it was the magazine's compact size, perhaps it was the fact that they could get some news and interviews with the logs, or perhaps it was the magazine's simple format. At first, the researchers note, Annenberg and Panitt designed their magazine as a booster for television, but gradually that goal changed. The two men employed full-time writers in bureaus all over the country as well as an eclectic stable of well-respected freelance writers that included, among others, William Saroyan, Margaret Mead, and Ronald Reagan. By the 1960s, the magazine was achieving a maturity that overcame its initial boosterism. It was a magazine that "was more skeptical, cynical, and adversarial, yet ready to accept television for what it was," according to the two researchers.

By the fall of 1963, TV *Guide* editors had decided to hire a critic whose job would be simply to review television shows. That person would be free from the constraints imposed on some television critics who wrote for newspapers: usually they had to review programming, write profiles or feature stories, and offer criticism and information about the state of the industry. The TV *Guide* editors selected author and commentator Cleveland Amory. Amory did know Walter Annenberg, the publisher of TV *Guide*, and this no doubt helped open the door for him. But it is more likely that the idea of television as an increasingly pervasive force in society was what led to the selection of Amory as TV *Guide*'s chief critic.

Amory was paid per column and worked nine months a year. Because the networks ran reruns in the summer, his column was suspended during the latter part of June, and in July and August. His columns were usually about five hundred to seven hundred words in length, and during his first few years as reviewer they were published at the very front of the magazine. Later on, after the magazine was redesigned, they appeared after the television logs near the back of the magazine.

Amory's column often became a form of cultural criticism. The mass nature of television itself made it a natural cultural force, and by the time Amory started reviewing, it was well on its way to becoming ingrained in the fabric of American society. Amory's TV *Guide* column also was a great forum for his humor and irreverence. Although he liked many of the television shows he viewed, Amory was no fan of television overall in the mid-1960s. In lectures, he harshly criticized much programming and called television a "fried-potatoes medium" that gave viewers a quick fix of what they wanted rather than what they needed: "What the public wants isn't always good for it," he said. "We should all eat nutritious food, but we want fried potatoes. We should all go to church, but we want to play golf." He laid the blame on the Nielsen ratings, the Federal Communications Commission, and lazy television writers who continually turned in unoriginal scripts and who underestimated viewers' intelligence. "In Hollywood, there is a group of scriptwriters who know their own little world. They know story lines but they don't get around much," he said. "They don't know anything about relationships of people except in their peer group." Many writers, he maintained, were guilty of "copycattiness"—they either were not original or felt they would make more money by mimicking others. In speeches around the country, Amory was particularly critical of the Nielsen ratings, which he said did not accurately gauge who was watching what on television. Further, he said, the FCC, which regulated television, was dominated by "friends" of the television industry: "The presidents of NBC, CBS, ABC all employ the same lures—crime, violence and sex."

Yet Amory was careful to note in his first column for *TV Guide*, titled "On Being a Critic," that he did not enter the job with preconceived notions of television: "We object strongly to the 'in' intellectual approach—the idea that if it's television it can't be good," he wrote. "But at the same time we're right far from the 'all-out' Madison Avenue or network-executive approach—the idea that 'everything we're doing is great!'" He added that he realized that the world of television programming was a huge and complicated one: "We realize we are entering a jungle," he wrote. "The television world, make no mistake about it, has few ground rules and no foul lines." But Amory was somewhat of a reluctant critic. Over the years, he had written book reviews for various national magazines and newspapers, but he never had the job on a regular basis. He reminisced that when he first agreed to take the job, he could not help but remember a sign on the desk of his *Saturday Review* editor Norman Cousins: "The Critic Judges Himself in His Criticism."

Indeed, Amory hit the ground running. In the second half of his first *TV Guide* column was a stinging indictment of an American institution: the Miss America pageant, which was broadcast live from Atlantic City. Amory noted that while the show always had high ratings, it left a lot to be desired—unless, he said, viewers thought that it was so bad it was good. Because it is so highly rated, he wrote, "[there is] no reason for it to be so appallingly bad. . . . We have long harbored a suspicion that one of the reasons for the large audience is that it is actually so bad that it is all the way round to the other side of good and is, in its horrible way, actually fascinating." The show, Amory explained, is "phony" and a "pseudo-event."

In a brief essay that was published in the same edition as Amory's first review, Panitt explained why the magazine hired Amory. First, he said, Amory's guest appearances and experience as a guest on talk and news shows like *Today* gave him an insight into television that other critics did not have. In addition, Amory's best-selling books about society showed he was "witty, discerning, and sometimes shocking." Finally, Panitt wrote, *TV Guide* editors did not expect readers to agree with Amory all the time. But, he added, "we do ... hope you will agree with us that what Mr. Amory has to say, he does say it well." Amory said in a separate interview that the main reason he was hired was that the editor was impressed by his *New York Times* book reviews.

Amory began reviewing for TV *Guide* during a pivotal time in the history of television. Some Americans today can still remember television in its infancy. RCA, a company that owned two radio networks, began broadcasting television shows in the late 1930s, and its chief rival in radio, CBS, broadcast two fifteen-minute newscasts a day on its New York television station in 1941. But the advent of World War II slowed the progress and development of television with the country's focus on military production, and it was not until the late 1940s that the new medium began experiencing serious growth. Comedian Milton Berle in 1948 guest-hosted the first four installments of *Texaco Star Theater* to rave reviews in *Variety*, and by the next year Berle's show was seen each week, and he was on the cover of both *Time* and *Newsweek*. Jack Benny took his radio show to television in 1950, and George Burns and Gracie Allen, Frank Sinatra, and Bob Hope all hosted their own shows. Television then branched out to game shows—including Groucho Marx's *You Bet Your Life*—and, by 1951, to innovative programming such as *I Love Lucy* and *The Ernie Kovacs Show*.

Television historians refer to the early and mid-1950s as the medium's "golden age," owing in large part to programming that borrowed heavily from live theater. Program staples included dramatic anthologies such as *Kraft Television Theater*, which debuted in 1947, *The U.S Steel Hour* in 1953, *Playhouse 90* in 1956, and other dramas that were televised live. In the 1955–56 season, fourteen of these anthology series aired. These early shows featured the work of many directors and actors who would later become well known for their work in film, including directors Sidney Lumet, John Frankenheimer, and Arthur Penn, and actors Ernest Borgnine, Paul Newman, Eva Marie Saint, and Charlton Heston. It was also during this era that television became involved in current affairs; television first covered the presidential nominating conventions of the two major political parties in 1952, and the medium began providing serious competition to newspapers in news coverage. In 1963, the three networks expanded their evening network news shows from fifteen to thirty minutes.

But according to many historians chronicling the rise of television, the true heyday of the medium came in the late 1950s and 1960s. A combination of technological innovations, creative strides, and increasing profits for the three networks turned television into a true mass medium. A wide variety of types of programming — from *The Nat King Cole Show*, which debuted in 1956, to *Perry Mason* and the *Real McCoys* (both in 1957) to Leonard Bernstein's first Young People's Concert in 1958 — demonstrated the true diversity of what could be beamed into American homes. On September 26, 1960, presidential candidates Richard Nixon and John F. Kennedy squared off for what was to become the first of several "Great Debates" — three days before the airing of the first show of the series *My Three Sons*.

As the audience for television grew and the diversity of programming expanded, newspapers, magazines, and television itself were faced with the dilemma of how to chronicle and assess the content of this new medium. By the late 1940s and early 1950s, newspapers, in particular, found it impossible to ignore the explosive growth of television, and many large newspapers assigned a full-time critic to the task of reviewing the medium. Two of the most well-known and influential were Jack Gould of the *New York Times* — who wrote about television from 1946 to 1972 — and Lawrence Laurent of the *Washington Post*, who was that newspaper's television critic in the 1960s and 1970s. Other large metropolitan newspapers also employed full-time television critics, including John Crosby of the *New York Herald Tribune*, Hal Humphrey and Cecil Smith of the *Los Angeles Times*, and Larry Wolters of the *Chicago Tribune*. But the task of these early television critics was a daunting one; their job was not just reviewing shows but also explaining to readers the business side of the television industry while at the same time keeping track of television logs and programming. As his son, Lewis, noted in a compilation of his columns, Jack Gould's job as television critic also focused on the minutiae of setting up television logs in the paper. Further, these pioneering critics had to decide how much of their newspaper's limited space should be divided among reviews of entertainment programming, news, hour-long dramas, and specials.

In addition to reviewing programming and writing stories about the status of the growing television medium, Gould's columns occasionally dealt with deeper issues, including the role of the critic and his or her influence. In some ways, during the era of the live television drama, the critic's influence was limited; he or she had to air opinions about these live shows "after a show has disappeared for all time," as Gould wrote. Gould discussed at length the responsibility of television critics in two columns, both written in May of 1957. "Critics are in a sense proxies of the viewers," he wrote. "This does not mean that viewers necessarily will agree with their reviewers. But it does mean that there is the common bond of an independent opinion independently reached. The TV set owner in deciding whether he likes a show or not invokes only his own standards. . . . The critic is his stand-in."

Although researchers, critics, television programmers, and others could argue endlessly about the quality of television in the 1950s, 1960s, and 1970s, one of the most famous and often-quoted assessments of early television came from the head of the Federal Communications Commission in 1961. During a May 8 address to the National Association of Broadcasters, newly appointed FCC chairman Newton Minow called television "a vast wasteland," a phrase that endured long after Minow left the chairmanship after two years. But as television critic and researcher David Bianculli noted thirty-one years after the speech, Minow also praised some television during that speech — particularly the anthology dramas of the 1950s, the broadcasts of the 1960 Kennedy-Nixon debates, and Edward R. Murrow's *See It Now*.

The year Minow made his now-famous comment about television content, series such as *Doctor Kildare, Hazel, Mister Ed*, and many others that are now considered classic debuted, and the anthology series were fading. Although color had not been perfected — only about 600,000 of the 47 million televisions in U.S. households beamed color images — the technology was improving rapidly.

But the wide reach of the medium, combined with its variety, was making television a cultural phenomenon that could be greater than theater, radio, and even film, critics were beginning to believe. Jack Gould began to realize this in 1957, when he wrote about the power of television: "Television . . . must be weighed in light of contemporary life as a whole, just as the theatre, movies and books are. Television quite properly should be hailed in many ways for widening the horizons of the public. But it also must be mindful of the reality of its narcotic ability to deaden the national awareness of important standards and serious issues. . . . With its enormous power television can take much of the country along with it, either way. That is everybody's concern." Gilbert Seldes, a critic, novelist, and playwright who wrote about the arts for several national publications including TV *Guide* and the *Saturday Review*, also saw television as a unique art form because it brought the same programming to millions of homes at the same time. Therefore, he considered early television not as one of the lively arts but more as a mass medium. But the result was not necessarily positive; many of Seldes's television reviews criticized content, and he accused network managers of producing programs that appealed to the lowest common denominator.

Into this environment—the phenomenal growth of television along with the realization by many that it had tremendous power in influencing culture and thought—came Cleveland Amory. In Amory, *TV Guide* editors hired someone who would not mince words or curry favor with anyone. And Amory was candid in his reviews, although at times it hurt him to be critical, his assistant, Marian Probst, recalled. He was never mean-spirited or unfair, she believed, although sometimes he could not rein in his tendency to turn a phrase. One of her favorite Amory lines came from a negative review that focused on author Harold Robbins, who had written a miniseries called *The Survivors*. "Mr. Robbins is a writer only in the sense that a woodpecker is a carpenter," Amory wrote. The result? When Robbins saw Amory at the Beverly Hills Hotel, he conspicuously turned his back on Amory and walked away.

With his job at *TV Guide*, Amory all but abandoned his role as commentator and critic of high society. He was now the official voice of American television criticism.

Chapter 7 ▷ ▷ ▷ Critiquing the Vast Wasteland

The thing that bothers us about [critic]
Cleveland Amory's editorial "we" is that it
may mean there is more than one of him.

▶ Letter to TV Guide from reader

A. PETER HOLLIS, 1973

*I*f Amory thought writing about the topic of high society had been too limiting, he had to be pleased that his editors at TV Guide gave him a free hand to expand his reviewing into the realm of cultural criticism. And this was probably why they offered him the job in the first place: they wanted someone who could stretch the definition of television criticism.

In 1960, three years before he started at TV Guide, Amory let the world know his definition of the perfect editor and writer. He or she should be someone who is sophisticated yet down-to-earth; someone who never underestimates his or her audience; and, most of all, someone who does not take himself or herself too seriously. That was the definition he established in an anthology he coedited that year. The anthology was an homage to the magazine Vanity Fair, which was published from 1914 to 1936. Amory thought that magazine — which was a compilation of fiction, reporting, and literary nonfiction centering on current issues in politics, culture, society, and celebrity — had a common touch while at the same time appealing to an educated and cosmopolitan audience.

Amory edited the Vanity Fair anthology with Frederic Bradlee, a grand-nephew of the magazine's legendary editor Frank Crowninshield. The anthology focused on the era that Amory considered the glory years of the magazine: the 1920s and 1930s. The magazine was, indeed, a beautifully glossy compilation of reporting, essays, poetry, and fiction from the nation's most respected writers, including Robert Benchley, Lillian Hellman, Dorothy Parker, Alexander Woollcott, D. H. Lawrence, Thomas Wolfe, and many, many others. Its contributors also included some of the top photographers and artists in the country.

In a glowing four-thousand-word introduction, Amory sings the praises of Crowninshield, whom he adored, and writes that the then-defunct *Vanity Fair* was elegantly ageless: "There never was, nor in all probability ever will be again, a magazine like her. . . . And today, as we look back at her from out of the shadowy sixties, she seems, all in all and all at once, behind her time, ahead of her time, and yet, unmistakably, of her time."

But Amory's greatest platitudes are reserved for Crowninshield, whose tremendous talent for editing and whose personal warmth and sophistication made the magazine what it was, Amory believed. And one cannot help but think that Amory's admiration for the editor stemmed in part from his own identification with him. Crowninshield, he writes, was a genteel observer of the social scene who respected his audience and never underestimated his readers. He also was a pioneer who was not afraid to go against the grain. And while he worked hard and always gave his best, he never took himself or others too seriously. Most of all, he ran the magazine with a gentle humor and playfulness. Amory wrote that when publisher Condé Nast first thought of the idea for such a magazine, he asked his friend Crowninshield, then art editor for a magazine called *Century*, his opinion about what it should be. Crowninshield replied that no magazine in the United States currently "covers the things people talk about at parties — the arts, sports, humor and so forth."

But it was Crowninshield, Amory notes, who insisted that the magazine not write down to its readers. "The magazine was pleased to take for granted the fact that its readers were cultured people, or at least people susceptible to so being — and to prove the point, published modern art as if people were already initiated to it . . . and was also not averse to publishing a piece entirely in French." Furthermore, he notes Crowninshield's wit was evident within the magazine and outside it. One of Amory's favorite Crowninshield aphorisms was his comment that "married men make very poor husbands" (Crowninshield never married).

The introduction to the *Vanity Fair* anthology is filled with anecdotes about the editor and the quirks of the magazine's staff members and contributors. In it, Amory describes the first caption written by fledgling writer Dorothy Parker, who was paid ten dollars a week to write brief explanations underneath the magazine's photos. Her first caption accompanied a series of photos of women's underwear: "Brevity is the soul of lingerie, as the Petticoat said to the Chemise," she wrote, paraphrasing Shakespeare.

Amory also reminds readers of the anthology that Crowninshield was one of the first editors to recognize black cultural and literary figures and included in the magazine articles about and photos of singer Florence Mills, actors Paul Robeson and Ethel Waters, Joe Louis, Louis Armstrong, and Jesse Owens.

In retrospect, Amory concludes, the magazine was ageless under Crowninshield: "Looking back at the issues of any magazine published a quarter of a century or more ago, one expects to find much that is dated and little that is still refreshingly alive," he writes. "But the batting average of *Vanity Fair* is superlatively high. Furthermore, so much of the other material that might be termed 'dated' is so pleasantly and mistily nostalgic that it cries out to be seen again."

Amory did not supervise or work with other writers when he became chief television critic for *TV Guide*, but he of course did respond to readers of the magazine, who frequently commented on what he had to say. (And he also, at times, dealt with actors, writers, and television executives who were, directly or indirectly, the subjects of his reviews.) Despite his many connections in show business — including many in Hollywood — he did not play favorites. If he did not like a program, the fact that he knew someone responsible for it did not influence his review. The magazine's editors also let Amory do what he wanted without mandates — Amory's opinion was Amory's opinion, and editors freely admitted that they sometimes disagreed with him. In one 1968 column, editorial director Merrill Panitt half jokingly noted that the editors frequently disagreed with their television critic "violently." "But he is our critic and we respect him and we print what he writes," Panitt wrote in the magazine. "This does not mean we endorse what he writes."

As Marian Probst remembered, writing a negative review about a show was sometimes difficult for Amory, particularly if he felt the staff of the show worked hard. And negative reviews may have made life a little awkward for him when, during his travels in New York and occasionally in Hollywood, he would meet those about whom he wrote. Probst remembered in particular a negative review Amory wrote about a new television series called M *A *S *H, which was based on the film of the same name. (Probst believed that Amory's disdain for the series stemmed from the fact that it centered on the topic of war — a distasteful topic for Amory.) But Amory would occasionally see one of the show's stars, Alan Alda, at social and cultural events. Alda, she remembered, was always friendly and gracious to Amory despite the review. (The phenomenal success of that show, though, may have eased any pain felt about the review.)

In a question-and-answer column, Amory was once asked if actors took his reviews personally. He responded that Monty Hall, who starred in the popular game show *Let's Make a Deal*, apparently was not pleased by Amory's negative review. Hall, Amory wrote, "cornered us at a hockey game in Los Angeles and went through our review of *Let's Make a Deal*, line by line. He was against it." On the other hand, "Robert Stack, whom we had criticized in the *Untouchables*, the *American Sportsman* and *The Name of the Game*, wrote us a card which we admire. 'Thanks,' he wrote, 'for your continuing support.'"

Amory apparently received many notes from celebrities thanking him for his reviews. Some may have been written partly with tongue in cheek, such as one typewritten note from Quinn Martin, head of Quinn Martin Productions, which produced several television shows of the era: "I want to thank you for the very nice review you gave our show 'The Fugitive.' It is very pleasant not only to get that kind of review, but to see in print the things articulated that one is trying to do with the show. By the way, I am a fan of your column and read it every week in TV Guide and think your analyses of shows are excellent — mainly because I happen to agree with them, I suppose. Thanks again."

Those in Hollywood certainly must have appreciated Amory's clout as a reviewer; with 24 million readers, *TV Guide* was the largest-circulation magazine in the country in the 1960s, and Amory was one of only a handful of critics who was virtually a household name. Still, some of the notes he received — such as one from Patty Duke — were no doubt sincere expressions of gratitude. Duke was the star of a popular situation comedy in the 1960s called *The Patty Duke Show*. Her handwritten note, on pink paper, said in part, "[Thank you] for the very kind review you wrote about our show. I really appreciate your generosity. I love doing the show and it's an extra bonus to know it is appreciated. . . . I am looking forward to meeting you sometime in the future."

Even Bing Crosby — who already was a big star by the time he appeared in an ill-fated television show in 1964—seemed oddly candid in a letter to Amory:

We were gratified recently to read the flattering review in TV Guide concerning our show, "Breaking Point." In a business whose vagaries are immense, it's nice to know that what we have done appears to have some merit. Your opinion confirms me in the belief that [we have] done some things that are first class. We're unhappily tottering on the brink of cancellation for next year, but there is a small chance we will be renewed. It seems rather sad to realize that you've achieved the quality you sought at the beginning only to find that it hasn't been proved successful.

Amory's TV Guide columns were generally seven hundred to eight hundred words in length, and during the first few years of his tenure they were usually placed near the beginning of the magazine. At first his column was accompanied by a small, photographic head shot of him, complete with ubiquitous pipe. After several years, the photo was converted to a more modern-looking line drawing, and many of the reviews appeared near the end of the magazine. (This prompted one reader to ask in a letter to the editor, "You put Cleveland Amory on the next to last page of your magazine. Why don't you put him two pages back?") The columns carried no headline, other than the name of the program being reviewed, with the tagline "Review."

Amory's reviews were rarely completely negative. Even if he did not like a show, he nearly always found qualities about it to praise. If the writing was poor — and good writing on television, he believed, could be hard to find — he often would praise the acting. His reviews were never cruel. But, as he was the first to admit in columns, he was a stickler for good writing, and a solid script and realistic dialogue were necessary to get a thumbs-up from him.

Many of his reviews had several characteristics in common. First, as was the case throughout his career, puns abounded — some were obvious plays on words, and others were subtle references to Shakespeare. (Of one poorly written show that featured stars Tony Curtis and Roger Moore, he wrote, "In this show, the fault, Dear Brutus, was not in the stars.") He made continual cultural references to current commercial jingles, best sellers, and even previous shows in which famous actors starred. For example, in a review of the detective show *Barnaby Jones*, which starred *Beverly Hillbillies* star Buddy Ebsen, he quoted a network news release that stated Ebsen's "quaint country charm masks a trigger wit." Amory's response? "The quaint country charm we'll buy — who could ever forget, even with utter determination, *The Bev-*

erly Hillbillies? But the trigger wit — ouch. If he has it, someone double-locked the safety." And he frequently quoted excerpts from a network's own news releases — usually to pan the show, or to show the irony of the quote.

Television history has shown, of course, that some of the programs that critics praise do not last a season, while others they criticize go on to become big hits. Some of Amory's favorites during the 1960s and 1970s included *The Waltons, Rhoda* (a big favorite of his), *Baretta, Kojak, Saturday Night Live, Good Times, Chico and the Man, Police Story,* and the miniseries *Rich Man, Poor Man.* He praised *Chico and the Man* for its acting and writing, and said each plot was like a miniature vaudeville routine. *Rhoda* was clever, fresh, and featured phenomenal comic acting, he thought.

Overall, his favorite shows were those that were creative, had good writing, or took a fresh look at an existing topic or category. His least favorite shows had what he considered an unoriginal premise, weak writing, or contained what he considered tasteless sex or violence.

His least favorite shows included *M*A*S*H, Happy Days, Monday Night Football, Young Dr. Kildare, SWAT, Monty Python's Flying Circus,* and *The Wild, Wild West.* Amory — normally a big sports fan — had little positive to say about *Monday Night Football* hosts Frank Gifford and Fred Williamson, and while he praised Alex Karras for his "infectious galoot quality," he criticized a tasteless comment Karras made about the Denver Broncos' defense holding hands during the huddle.

Throughout his tenure at *TV Guide,* Amory stressed the need for more originality in the premises of shows. In a summary column called "Second Thoughts," which was his last column for the 1965–66 television season, he noted that nearly all the new shows that year fell into one of three categories: spy spoofs like *Get Smart* and *The Avengers;* "fun-war" shows like *Hogan's Heroes* and *The Wackiest Ship in the Army;* or situation comedies, including what Amory thought were the hideous *My Mother the Car* and *Green Acres.* Amory believed *Hogan's Heroes* was funny and well written despite its setting in a prisoner-of-war camp.

In addition to *M*A*S*H,* Amory gave lukewarm reviews to several television shows that would become classics in decades to come. *The Dick Van Dyke Show,* he believed, was written with redundant situations and gags and was not very funny. (But Amory did praise the principal actors.) And shows like *Green Acres* and *Petticoat Junction* did have staying power, although they did not earn Amory's respect. *Green Acres* and *Petticoat Junction* were both spin-off shows — *Petticoat Junction* of the *Beverly Hillbillies*, and *Green Acres* of *Petticoat Junction* — and Amory usually hated spin-offs.

In his review of *Green Acres*, Amory warns of the "overbreeding" of some situation comedies: "If [the networks] are going to let these shows out at night, unchaperoned and in some cases even unattended, they're simply asking for trouble," he writes. "In fact, what all of us need, on the part of all networks, is a rigorous program — you will pardon the expression — of Planned Showhood. If these networks must breed these shows, let them be bred with love and care and understanding — with knowledge of blood lines and dominant features and character traits." After savaging *Green Acres* for trite writing and repetitive gags, he concludes that it "should be put out to pasture as rapidly as possible and — let me make this perfectly clear — by itself."

Amory dealt with *Green Acres*, however, in a kinder way than he dealt with *Let's Make a Deal* and *What's My Line?* The review that so angered *Deal* host Monty Hall notes that the show had already been on for four years (during the day and in the evening), and "there are several ways to avoid this show — but you have to be nimble." Amory goes on to say, "This is not the worst show in the history of television — there was you recall, *Queen for a Day*. . . . The immoderator for all this is Mr. Monty Hall. No other man living and a few dead could put up with what he does and still look like he's enjoying himself. Our theory is that he's not looking at it."

Amory had similar complaints against *What's My Line?* which he said should be put out to pasture after what seemed like decades on the air. And he was uncharacteristically brutal: "When the show first went on the air, it was, our late grandfather once told us, highly popular," Amory wrote. "Since we last heard a favorable opinion, though, a whole new generation has been bored." Amory had little positive to say about the show's regulars, which included Bennett Cerf, Arlene Francis, and Dorothy Kilgallen, although he noted somewhat grudgingly that they could be charming and fun. As he sometimes did when he was critical, Amory hoist the cast by its own petard. He noted that as Kilgallen was trying to guess the occupation of a man who made earmuffs, she asked, "Would a sensible person wear this product more in winter or in summer?" Amory answered the question as the last line of the review: "We just don't know, Dottie, we just don't know. Our theory is that, for this show, you should never be without them."

Amory did, however, like some game shows — if he considered them funny, like *Hollywood Squares*, where the humor lay in the clever retorts from the guest celebrities. Asked the difference between crude oil and regular oil, for instance, Paul Lynde replied, "Family background." Amory liked that reply enough to quote it in the review.

If readers were unsure of some of his dislikes or preferences — unlikely, since Amory was hardly subtle — or if they missed some of his columns, they were treated each year to a column called The Amory Awards, a spoof on the Emmy Awards in which Amory gave his "best of" in many categories, such as individual acting and various genres and categories of shows. As he noted before the awards were listed, "We vote just as you vote — but our vote is actually the only vote that counts."

Amory loved hearing from readers — so much that at the end of each television season he ran a letters column called Mail Bag, in which he selected a half dozen or so letters from readers and included his response. Amory said he received thousands of letters during his tenure as reviewer. As time went on, readers learned that humorous or cleverly worded questions were the ones most likely to find their way into Amory's column; he loved questions that enabled him to offer a humorous response. Amory's use of the first-person plural or third-person singular, referring to himself as "we" or "he" rather than "I," was a natural source of humor on its own. (For example, one reader wrote, "I think you are mellowing. Are you?" "Nonsense," was the reply. "We weigh the same as we weighed in college. It's just that with us writing each week, television could hardly fail to get better.") Another reader asked, point-blank, "Why do we use we?" "We is just me, we is more amusing than I is," was the reply. "We would not have laughed, for example, if Queen Victoria said, 'I am not amused.'" Another reader gave Amory a dose of his own medicine: "The thing that bothers us about Cleveland Amory's editorial 'we' is that it may mean there is more than one of him," he wrote.

Like many critics, Amory could be mercurial — it was sometimes difficult to predict what he would like or dislike based on previous reviews. And while he did dislike certain genres, he could surprise readers by writing a positive review of a new show in a genre he previously had criticized. For example, he noted that television in 1966 may not have needed yet another action-packed adventure series "involving undercover work in a 'fun war.'" But the show *Jericho* was enjoyable and the "best of its kind."

Still, Amory did not compromise his views of a show even in the name of political correctness. His review of the groundbreaking show *Julia*, the first half-hour situation comedy featuring a black family — and a single-parent family at that—was not positive. The show featured Diahann Carroll as a nurse and single mother. "This show deserves high marks for breaking the color barrier," he wrote. "Nonetheless, it is so self-conscious about doing so that a good part of the time, *Julia* will give you a fast pain. And without providing fast relief. . . . The pace is so slow that there are times when you are going to be convinced that the show has stopped entirely." The show, he added, was "soap-opera like," but featured fine acting by the principals, particularly Carroll.

One favorite of Amory's was the show *Sanford and Son*, about which he raved. The show—like the popular *All in the Family*, which Amory also loved—was based on a British comedy called *Steptoe and Son*, he wrote, and was written by the same team that wrote *All in the Family*. The writing and casting, he said, were brilliant: Redd Foxx, one of the stars, has "wonderful off-beat delivery with brilliant behind-beat timing." Amory wrote that he feared the show, which featured an all-black cast, would be open to accusation of racism. "People will say it's insulting to blacks and Amos-'n-Andy-ish," he wrote. "Won't it be nice when all characters can just be individuals and not 'represent' anyone—white, black, green or purple?" *Sanford and Son* did, of course, go on to become a wildly successful series.

A negative review of the special *Music Country USA* apparently angered many country music fans, based on letters to *TV Guide*: "[Amory's] review reeked of ethnocentrism," one reader wrote in Amory's Mail Bag column. "His comment that the singers sound 'similar' tells us more about his competence as a critic than it does about the performances." Another reader accused him of anti-American sentiments, commenting that Amory did not like the show because "maybe Amory doesn't like country music. Perhaps he doesn't realize the shows like *The Waltons, Apple's Way* and country music shows are about Americans and America. Can he tell us why he is against America?" Of course, nothing pleased Amory more than illogical arguments; he took great pleasure in attacking them. "Almost every show on television is about America and Americans," he replied in an editor's note. "Your viewpoint may be a bit narrow. Amory isn't against America. He's for good television programming."

Amory also paid great attention to the relationship between characters and insisted it be real. In a review of the drama *Harry O*, with David Janssen, Amory reminded readers of his "Critic's Creed": "That the most important single element in any show is the relationship between characters." (He added that this show, which featured a loner private eye, violated that rule but was still very watchable.)

Amory's combination of humor and cultural criticism made his reviews both enjoyable and meaty and set him apart from some television critics of the era who wrote for newspapers. For example, this imagined scenario — which dealt with the "birth" of the singing group the Monkees — was typical Amory. He began his 1966 column by describing how television programming managers must have been influenced by the phenomenal success of the Beatles:

> It had to happen sooner or later. Some big boy upstairs saw a Beatles film and he called a network meeting. "Get the Beatles," he snarled. Whereupon everybody agreed it was a terrific idea. . . . All except one little guy. "I don't think we're going to be able to get the Beatles, Boss," he said. "They're richer than we are."

The result? "The Beatles Next Door!" — the Monkees, Amory wrote. Still, Amory was enthusiastic about the Monkees' new television show, which he called "so fast-paced that even when they're over-milking the kind of comedy you outgrew in kindergarten, by the time you get mad at them, they're on to something else." As for their singing, he wrote, "once you've heard them sing "Last Train to Clarksville," with those beautiful lyrics — both of them — if you're a girl you'll just have to mother them, and if you're a boy, well, lots of luck."

Sometimes he would change his mind about a show, a luxury most television critics writing for daily newspapers did not have. Amory had the time and space in TV Guide to occasionally run a column he called Second Thoughts, in which he took another look at some programs and discussed the shows that generated the most reader comment. In June of 1973, for example, Amory noted that the largest number of disagreements between him and readers were generated by the shows M*A*S*H, The Little People, UFO, and Banacek: "We went back to all of them and found M*A*S*H a little better, The Little People a little worse, UFO a lot worse and Banacek better — (see, we can admit we were wrong)." Also, he noted, he was "too hard" on shows like McMillan & Wife and The Streets of San Francisco, which he admitted he had grown to like.

In the same column, Amory revisited his initial negative reaction to An American Family, a public-television documentary series that may have been the first reality show: it videotaped the lives of the Louds, an affluent California family, and aired portions of their unscripted activities and comments. On second thought, Amory noted, the show was innovative and a realistic dramatization of the decline and fall of the American dream, despite the fact that it was "technically mediocre, pointlessly overlong and poorly edited." Ironically, he continued, *An American Family* was the polar opposite of another show airing that season, *The Waltons*, one of Amory's all-time favorite shows. "Look at both these series," he writes. "A Depression family with nothing. An affluent family with everything. And then ask yourself: which one had everything and which one had nothing?"

Amory also occasionally re-reviewed a program if he felt it had changed. For instance, shortly after the 1973 debut of the CBS *Morning News*, he termed it a "qualified disaster. . . . Qualified because it was a good idea to give the *Today* show some new competition. It is a disaster because it has not come close to the high standard CBS News has set in other programs." Seventeen months later, however, Amory noted, the show had made some dramatic changes — including the dismissal of coanchor Sally Quinn and increased focus on hard news reporting, and the result made it worth watching.

Amory filled his reviews much of the time with puns and references to current events and social trends. For instance, of the situation comedy *Movin' On*, he wrote, "We have warned you before about shows that have an apostrophe in their title — it's a sure sign that something else has been left out, too. Like, for example, an idea. Not necessarily a good idea, mind you. Just an idea." He opened his review of the show *Kung Fu* with a reference to the activities of the president: "This show is a kind of combination of *The Fugitive, Run for Your Life* and President Nixon's trip to China." Or, in the case of the first nighttime soap opera parody, *Mary Hartman, Mary Hartman*, Amory noted, jokingly, that men were usually not tough enough to watch soap operas. He parodied arguments made in the then-fledgling feminist movement: "We men have come a long way in recent years — in freedom of dress, in being allowed to express our opinions, even in being given a taste of equality in minor decision-making. . . . One thing we are still not up to is the average soap opera — we do not have the emotional stamina." (But the review was a positive one.)

Amory was able to choose what he wanted to review, and his choices usually represented the diversity of television programming. He occasionally reviewed news programs or programs produced by the networks' news divisions, but, as illustrated by his initial review of CBS *Morning News*, his opinions were not always positive. Yet he did recommend to readers the series CBS *Reports*, another news show. "Television is still a pretty new trade to talk about tradition," he wrote. "If there is one show which is entitled to do so, however, that show is CBS *Reports*. This show has, season after season, come up with the finest documentaries this side of a good book."

Amory had eclectic tastes, but he could usually be counted on to praise a program that he considered sophisticated. *The Dean Martin Show*, for instance, earned his praise. Calling it the best variety show on television, he specified that it offered, as the genre implied, "genuine variety" and was interesting from start to finish. "With all this, Mr. Martin makes it seem like fun, and very funny, too."

The Jerry Lewis Show did not fare so well. Despite the host's tremendous popularity, and the fact that he signed the most lucrative contract in television history, Lewis and his show were clearly not among Amory's favorites. "The Jerry Lewis Show is live," he writes in the first sentence of the review. "But not by much." The show's target audience appears to be people "over 95" and those "yet unborn," he concludes later in the first paragraph. Furthermore, "this is one of the few shows . . . where fewer ideas from the writers might help."

About the police drama *Ironsides*, he wrote, "I like the relationship between [actors] Raymond Burr, Barbara Anderson, Don Mitchell and Don Galloway." Of the new spy-film spoof *Get Smart!* "You have many semi-spoofs of the James Bond cycle on your TV screen this season. . . . It's sometimes hard to tell the good spies from the bad spies. Credit the developers of *Get Smart!*, Mel Brooks and Buck Henry, with at least getting down to the serious business of being funny right from the start."

Although Amory did not routinely review children's shows, he did take the unusual step in 1969 of watching a children's show called *The Banana Splits*. His opinion of the show, and of its sponsors, was not a high one. "This is a fine program for the 1-and-under set," he wrote. "For the 2-and-older, we're doubtful. You might be better off with straight commercials." But even those ads and the resulting product placement drew his scorn. "The program is officially entitled Kellogg's Presents the Banana Splits Adventure Hour, and the commercials are so well integrated, it's almost impossible to tell where the serial ends and the cereal begins."

Amory's legacy as a television critic is also, in part, the legacy of *TV Guide*.

Its editors were among the first in the United States to allow a television critic to focus solely on reviewing without having to write other types of stories. Further, as television grew in scope and complexity in the 1960s and 1970s, so did the magazine. In their history of TV Guide, Glenn Altschuler and David Grossvogel write that since its founding in 1952, the magazine noted television's pervasive influence on American culture: "At its most basic level, TV Guide helped Americans define the possibilities and limitations of television and understand the entertainment industry as a business and an art form," they say. "In doing so, inevitably it has provided information and analysis of political issues and cultural trends." By the early 1960s, the magazine had achieved a level of sophistication that kept it from being solely a booster for the television industry. Editors reduced the number of personality profiles and ran articles about such diverse topics as Johann Sebastian Bach and Huckleberry Finn, Altschuler and Grossvogel write. "If television could be dismissed as a 'vast wasteland,' readers needed reasons to respect the magazine that covered it." Both Amory and the editors of TV Guide understood the power of television and its ability to engage viewers and shape the way they saw the world.

▷ ▷ ▷ As Amory covered television for TV Guide and watched countless shows, it may have been natural for him to think that he could come up with an idea that was more original than those of seasoned scriptwriters. And Amory did have an idea for a situation comedy that actually made it on the air — at least for a short time. But his brief experience as the creator of a television show was an eye-opening one even for the cosmopolitan and erudite Amory; he was the first to admit his naivete about the workings of network television and his innocence about the fact that what viewers ultimately see probably has no relation whatsoever to what was in the creator's mind. Amory relived the experience in a long and hilarious article in TV Guide. As he noted about his brief tenure with the Windsors, he concluded that his time as creator of a show called O.K. Crackerby! was a learning experience.

Throughout his life, most of what Amory wrote had autobiographical overtones — his fiction was taken from episodes from his life and experiences, and his nonfiction was based on his background and upbringing. After reviewing television for about two years, he had a discussion with Douglas Cramer, head of program development for ABC, about the idea of having a real magazine on the air — that is, a show focusing on the workings of a magazine not unlike the *Saturday Review*. In his tongue-in-cheek recounting of the event in *TV Guide*, he recalled that Cramer said he had a "similar" idea (which was not similar at all) — a show based on Amory's writings about society.

Using Cramer's idea, Amory was off and running: the show would focus on a crusty millionaire Oklahoma widower named O.K. Crackerby who had just moved east to fulfill a promise to his late wife: that he would make sure his three children would be "cultured" and learn the niceties of life. To accomplish this, he would hire a "tutor-companion" to teach the kids manners and the value of good sportsmanship and integrity. The series would, essentially, revolve around the tutor, whose name would be St. John Quincy, and would be set in several of the most exclusive eastern resorts.

The parallels to Amory's life and previous writings were obvious, harking back to his days with William Zinsser as a "tutor-companion" and his descriptions of the resorts he wrote about in *The Last Resorts*. Part fish-out-of-water story, *My Man St. John* would be a satire on the quirks of New England society with the focus on St. John and his attempts to educate Crackerby's three children. The millionaire Crackerby would, for once in his life, be out of his element in the East.

In a biting satire of the structure and workings of network television, Amory recounted in *TV Guide* that the show — ultimately renamed *O.K. Crackerby!* to appease its star, Burl Ives — bore no resemblance at all to his original idea. And along the way, any reference to Amory as creator of the show was virtually eliminated (his name was not even on the visitors' list of Samuel Goldwyn Studios on the day executives were to see the pilot, he noted). Credit instead went to the many vice presidents, advisers, story doctors, and others who took over the show. Ultimately, *O.K. Crackerby!* aired for seventeen episodes during the 1965–66 television season.

Amory's retelling of the adventure, subtitled "The Confessions of a Man Who Fathered a Fiasco," is good-natured and full of the detail and absurdities that characterize much of his writing. The theme of the piece is that the novice Amory was at first impressed by everything: the "suits" who were in control of selecting shows, the writer selected to write his show, the actors, and everything else in Hollywood. His experience, though, leaves him sadder but wiser.

He sets the stage by describing the board meeting in which top executives hear brief pitches for new shows, then make quick decisions on what to select: "They're thrilling, these meetings. . . . Around a huge table sit all the top network brass — Mr. Leonard Goldenson, the president in charge of all the other presidents; Mr. Thomas Moore, the president in charge of all the vice presidents; and the vice presidents themselves, men in charge of so many things it gives you a charge just thinking about them." Much to his delight, Amory's show is chosen after his pitch — he is the show's "creator" but not its writer. Instead, another writer will pen the show each week.

After the meeting, Amory has another one with Cramer's assistant, who has a question about the show's premise and the concept of the "tutor-companion." "Cleve," he asks, using the nickname that all the network executives have for Amory, "just between friends, what is a two-door companion?"

But Amory is not to be deterred: he is thrilled that the show's writer will be none other than Abe Burrows, then a well-known playwright and screenwriter who was famous for redoing and fixing the scripts of many of the era's most popular television shows. And well-known character actor Burl Ives is cast as Crackerby, much to Amory's delight.

But his pleasure is short-lived. Burrows's fame allows him to take almost complete credit for every aspect of *Crackerby*, and Amory's name appears only briefly in the credits, camouflaged by many others. By now the show was "created by Abe Burrows and Cleveland Amory," according to the credits. Further, Burrows's version of the show is far different from Amory's. The character of St. John is not a "tutor-companion" but has become an agent; Crackerby is not an outsider but the ultimate insider who controls his environment; and the portrayal of "society" in the scripts consists of a dinner at an expensive restaurant. Worst of all, all elements of the show as a satire are gone, Amory believes, and what is left is a hodgepodge of unrelated scenes and characters.

And while Ives does have name recognition, his fame is a double-edged sword. As a star, he requests the series be named after him — hence, *O.K. Crackerby!* — and he wants the show itself to revolve around the title character, not St. John.

Amory notes that he did personally make appeals to the executives at the studio, including the executive vice president in charge of television production for United Artists, who was the picture of confidence, assuring Amory the revised version of the show would work. "Cleve, boy," he says, "From now on the bullet has left the gun. It either hits the target or it doesn't."

The bullet apparently missed the target. On the day the pilot show was to be tested, Amory received several warmhearted congratulatory notes from the show's executives. ("Only you, Cleveland Darling, could have ridden through all these months with such unbridled enthusiasm and charm," wrote Cramer from New York to Amory's suite at the Beverly Hills Hotel.) While test audiences loved the pilot episode of the show, it fizzled in the middle of the first season, leaving "Cleve" Amory sadder but a lot wiser about the workings of network television.

▷ ▷ ▷ Amory did occasionally write longer pieces for *TV Guide* that were not reviews. In the fall of 1967, for instance, the magazine ran a five-part series called "Who Killed Hollywood Society?" — mainly a historical story about how Hollywood had changed from its glory days of the studio system, before competition from television. The editors at the magazine gave Amory substantial space for the stories and featured the first one in the series as its cover: "Who Killed Hollywood Society?" the magazine asked in large letters that took up most of its front cover, with Amory's name played prominently. And the tone of the articles was characteristic Amory: casual and low-key, written in first person. The second story in the series, in fact, is a long essay written in first-person plural in which he describes his daylong outing playing croquet at Samuel Goldwyn's Beverly Hills estate. As Amory, Goldwyn (who was eighty-five), and a friend of Goldwyn's play, Goldwyn reminisces about the old days at his studio, and occasionally utters one of his famous Goldwynisms.

Amory also occasionally wrote personality profiles for the magazine, including one long story in 1972 about Doris Day, an animal lover who had been friends with Amory, mostly because of their common interest in the anticruelty movement. The headline read, "The Dog Catcher of Beverly Hills" and was placed next to a large photo of a smiling Day cradling a small dog. The story opens, "Let's face it. Doris Day is a nut. Not just an ordinary nut, mind you. A real nut nut. Miss Day is a nut about animals and these days, when you say Doris's 'career has gone to the dogs,' in one way it has." Day, who was starring in a weekly television series when the article was published, spent much of her time picking up stray dogs and cats in Beverly Hills and then finding homes for them. Her own home, as Amory notes, housed many of the animals while she sought good homes for them. She also lobbied heavily against the wearing of animal fur, and went to great lengths to warn pet owners against leaving their dogs and cats alone in hot cars — a plotline that had been featured in her half-hour television show that season.

Most of the article focused on Day's extensive activities on behalf of animals, including a question about whether she was vilified by some people for her activism. Amory apparently was treading relatively lightly when it came to promoting animal causes in *TV Guide*. But he could not manage to stay out of trouble completely, as *TV Guide* editors learned.

*

Chapter 8 ▷▷▷ Hunting the Hunters

> Each week we have a curious assortment of white hunters
> in living color, about all of whose fearless exploits we
> hear ad nauseam — particularly as, armed with a full
> arsenal of weapons, they boldly advance to test wits
> and match virilities with, say, a mourning dove.
>
> ▸ AMORY's review of *The American Sportsman,*
> February 25, 1967

*A*mory's role as chief critic for *TV Guide* was in many ways the perfect
job for him: his editors gave him a wide berth to express his opinion as he
saw fit (and to employ puns as he saw fit), he could add cultural and social
references into the mix, and he could exercise his talent for writing and his
sense of humor. His opinions and expertise about television made him an
even more sought-after guest on television talk shows and on the lecture and
cocktail circuit.

But it is an understatement to call Amory a man-about-town during the
1960s and early 1970s. He was a man about the world. During the 1960s,
Amory had regular opinion columns in two respected magazines, a syndicated newspaper column, a syndicated radio show, and he was a regular guest
on daytime and evening talk and game shows. His trilogy of books about
society — *The Proper Bostonians, The Last Resorts,* and *Who Killed Society?* —
were widely read and still in print. (*The Proper Bostonians* remained in print
for several decades; Amory collected royalties on that book for many years.)
He also wrote freelance reviews and articles for several national publications.
In addition, he was widely quoted in a remarkably eclectic variety of magazine and newspaper articles, such as a mention and photo of him in *Ballroom
Dance* magazine, in which he described the movement of ballroom dancing in characteristic colorful fashion: "Like you're drying the derriere with
a towel while grinding out a cigarette with the toe." He and Martha were fixtures at celebrity events and cocktail parties in New York and Hollywood,
mingling and dining with Cary Grant, Doris Day, Katharine Hepburn, and

many other stars of the day, and he had been a guest on Aristotle Onassis's yacht. Based on photos and mentions of the couple that appeared in magazines and newspapers, one might well suppose the Amorys were the ultimate in East Coast sophistication: Cleveland with his dry wit and quick retorts, and the elegant and slim Martha, her hair in a smooth French twist. The pair even coedited a cookbook with actor Vincent Price and his wife, Mary, in 1965 that featured favorite recipes from the world's best restaurants. Martha appeared regularly in society and fashion columns, occasionally with a description of her clothes ("Mrs. Cleveland Amory in black crepe with black satin side-inserts," as one *Women's Wear Daily* item noted).

If Amory felt one could be judged by the quality of one's enemies, he may have felt also that one could be judged by the quality of one's mail: he routinely received invitations and personal notes from people like Steve Allen, Cole Porter, Oscar Hammerstein, and many others, who indicated a familiarity with him. Richard Rodgers, for instance, while thanking Amory for an article about him and his wife, noted that "Dorothy [Rodgers's wife] and I . . . will miss you at the chess board and . . . we will just miss you. . . . as ever, Dick."

The Amorys appear to have lived a charmed life in the 1960s and early 1970s. Martha and her husband were constantly in motion. As Martha's daughter, Gaea, remembered, Martha also worked hard with her husband for the cause of animal rights, and was the editor of much of his work. (Gaea remembers her stepfather walking the halls of their apartment, reading his television reviews out loud and getting comments about them from his wife, whose opinions he took very seriously.)

Even though his forte was writing about society, culture, and television, Amory could also be considered a serious writer. His monthly columns for *Saturday Review* continued into the 1970s, and *Saturday Review* editor Norman Cousins let his friend write what he wanted to write. The era during which Amory wrote this freewheeling column was an important one. The 1960s and early 1970s were a time of social upheaval and had everything: the civil rights movement, the second wave of feminism, and widespread and intense political activity in part because of the war in Vietnam, expansion of the drug culture, and the development of music as a social and cultural force. The era was perfect for someone as opinionated and articulate as Amory.

But things are rarely as they seem, and the mid- and late 1970s were the best of times and the worst of times for Amory. They certainly brought with them dramatic changes in his life.

▷ ▷ ▷ During the first few years of his tenure at *TV Guide*, Amory wrote little or nothing in that magazine about animal rights — either he was chastened by his experience at *Today* or he felt he had other public platforms for his activism. Sometimes the programs Amory reviewed dealt directly or indirectly with animals or issues related to his cause, but until the late 1960s he was uncharacteristically quiet. In early 1965, he reviewed *Flipper* on NBC and the ABC show *The American Sportsman* in one column. One would think that the writers and "actors" in *Flipper*, in particular, would have had to go a long way to please an animal lover like Amory. But, oddly, they did please him:

> Take a show with a static premise, poor actors, incredible dialog and highly improbably situations and what do you have? Not very much. But when you stir thoroughly, add water and, most important, a fish, what do you have? *Flipper*, probably the best new children's show on the air and one that is curiously engrossing week after week for adults. . . . It's all due, of course, to the fish. And make no mistake about it, Flipper, whose real name is Suzy, is no ordinary fish. In fact, she isn't even a fish at all. Like all good dolphins, she is a mammal; and as a porpoise with a purpose, she's something.

Amory liked the show, but he could not say the same about *The American Sportsman*, a hunting show. Of course, anyone who knew him would realize that the show, by virtue of its subject matter, did not have a chance with Amory. But his review of *The American Sportsman*, negative as it was, was oddly subdued. The show, as he noted in a brief review, consisted of four hour-long specials:

> Here the narration is inept, the fishing is boring, the bird shooting pathetic and the "he-man" exchanges embarrassing. . . . In one sequence actor Robert Stack "bravely" shoots, at a distance of approximately one light-year, a feeble old lion who is billed as a "killer." In another Joe Foss brings down, again a country mile away, an elderly, bewildered one-tusk elephant who is gently trotting along.

Amory saves his apparently muted sense of outrage for the last line of the review: "In one show we heard the 'Sportsman' defined as 'the certain sense of good in each of us.' Honestly, Sport, that's what the man said."

If Amory was restraining himself during those early years at *TV Guide*, that restraint gradually eroded as the 1960s progressed. By the end of the decade his activism was growing, and it expanded considerably with the founding in 1967 of what would become one of his most enduring legacies: the Fund for Animals, a fund-raising organization that Amory would describe as a "Red Cross and Ford Foundation for animals." Amory's founding, with Marian Probst, of the Fund for Animals was a pivotal event and would inform his activities for the rest of his life.

By the early 1970s, *TV Guide* had started to change its image. When editorial director Merrill Panitt hired Amory in 1963, it was as part of the revamping of the magazine and an attempt to be taken seriously by readers. As Altschuler and Grossvogel note in their history of the magazine, Panitt and publisher Walter Annenberg told members of the staff that they "aspired to be the industry's *Atlantic Monthly*, its *Life*, its *Harper's*, its *Time*." By the early 1970s, the magazine's writers were not discouraged from criticizing television or from being candid in personality profiles. Of course, part of this stemmed from the magazine's existence in an era when investigative journalism and other forms of innovative journalism came to the forefront. Altschuler and Grossvogel wrote, "*TV Guide* had two different but complementary tones. Its profiles were sharp, sassy and skeptical, up-to-date and increasingly appropriate in a journalistic climate of credibility gaps, where personal peccadilloes were fair game." Panitt took pride in the fact that writers for the magazine would not write down to its readers and, in fact, assumed that they had a high level of intelligence. That is why he commissioned articles periodically by some of the nation's most brilliant, interesting, or controversial personalities, including Betty Friedan, Chaim Potok, Benjamin Spock, Gore Vidal, J. Edgar Hoover, and Arthur Schlesinger Jr.

The cultural references by Amory, meanwhile, must have been just what the editor had ordered. Consequently, Amory's sometimes brutal candor was not censored by his editor and may even have been encouraged. The zeitgeist included the fight for women's rights, equal opportunities for blacks and minorities, and debates over issues such as abortion and the war in Vietnam; these issues were dealt with on television and consequently begged for comment by a television writer. Altschuler and Grossvogel write that Amory "could always be counted on to play the male chauvinist in his reviews," although that was not necessarily the case. Altschuler and Grossvogel offer as an example Amory's point when he discussed the new role of female secret agents in a new espionage show. "Girls and secrets — the very idea is a contradiction in terms," Amory wrote. This phrase may be simply be an example of Amory's humor — he would have just as likely made a similar stereotypical comment about men. Examples of similar chauvinism did not stand out in his reviews over the years, nor did any published letters to the editor point them out. His stepdaughter, Gaea, who went on to become a college professor, indicated that Amory expected the most of her intellectually and scholastically and certainly never indicated she need not excel professionally because of her gender.

Indeed, Amory remained critical in his reviews and public comments not about the expanding role of women in society but about the expansion of what he felt was lewd subject matter on television. On an appearance on the *Tonight* show in 1973, for example, he noted that the medium is "more and more sex-oriented. Words, phrases, and concepts which were previously forbidden are now not only commonplace but subject matter for sitcoms." Amory was asked in particular about a controversial two-part episode of the comedy *Maude* that dealt with the previously taboo subject of abortion. The audience reaction to it, Amory said, was ironic. "A remarkable thing happened: the same women who have for years delighted in the adultery, violence, and perversion of soap operas are those most opposed to the same subject matter at prime time."

If the period from 1963 to 1967 brought a brief respite from Amory's proselytizing about some of his favorite subjects outside television, he started returning to those topics with a vengeance by the late 1960s. The protection of animals was, of course, his top priority and would continue to be. But Amory was growing just as obsessive about Israel and its role in the Middle East peace process by this time. He had written several times about Israel's role in the Six-Day War for the *Saturday Review*, but now commentary about his affection for Israel and its culture was finding its way into speeches, much to the chagrin, apparently, of the lecture bureau that helped arrange his lectures.

In September of 1970, the president of a lecture bureau that arranged Amory's speaking engagements warned him, in a letter, against arranging by himself speeches to Jewish groups. The purpose of the lecture bureau, said W. Colston Leigh, president of the bureau, was for it to arrange his talks: "Dear Clip, There is a considerable amount of confusion arising out of your conversations with Jewish groups — and frankly, with all of your good will toward Israel and the people here who are helping the Israelis — I think you are doing yourself more harm than good. . . . I do think that some of your conversations with these groups are placing us in a very awkward position to try to negotiate with them in your behalf."

Leigh was probably not pleased, then, by a letter he received a year later from the program chairwoman of the Officers' Wives Club of Wright-Patterson Air Force Base in Dayton, Ohio, who said Amory was fifty minutes late for his speech — and did not extend it at the end — and did not talk solely about his assigned topic, "Your TV and You," but also about vivisection. The group wanted part of its money back.

Amory's obsession with Israel continued to intensify during the years following the 1967 Six-Day War, after he made several visits there. He was the author of a widely read and quoted article in April of 1970 in *Reader's Digest*, in which he was unabashed in his admiration for that country and its people. "I am hopelessly smitten with this land, " he wrote. Amory began the article by noting the contradictions in Israel's spirit: "Israel is a paradox — a nation in siege, yet a nation with such a thriving tourist business that the whole country might be defined as a resort," he said. "Peace is the hope but hardly the expectation." Amory was adamant in his support for Israel politically, arguing that only 4 percent of Americans were "pro-Arab" before the Six-Day War, yet after the war Americans saw Israelis as oppressors: "Television news, which before the war showed fanatical Arab crowds screaming, 'Death to the Jews,' now shows wretched refugee camps, starving women, weeping children. And Arab terrorists are glorified in their training while Israel's raids are vigorously condemned."

The Israeli culture and way of thinking fascinated Amory, and, as he liked to do, he made connections between the history of Israel and its society. He quoted Amnon Rubenstein, a professor of law at Tel Aviv University, who commented that, unlike their counterparts in the United States, Israeli college students were not political activists who demonstrated in the streets. Israel had no free colleges, few scholarships, and no reduced-tuition public universities like those in the United States, the professor said, and students took their education very seriously: "The difference between America and Israel is that in America, the fathers of the present generation, the men who went through the Depression and war, were pragmatists, so their children, who are now making the riots in the colleges, are idealists," Amory quoted Rubenstein as saying. The opposite was true for Israel: "In Israel, on the other hand, it's just the other way around. Our fathers, who founded the country, were the idealists, and we are the pragmatists."

It was clear from letters found among Amory's papers and accounts of his speeches that Israel was a topic that was much on his mind. In August of 1970, a headline in the *Washington Post*, for example, may have said it all: "Amory Charms Hadassah," it read. "Cleveland Amory had 2,500 Jewish women at his feet as he delivered a rousing pro-Israel speech to the 56th annual convention banquet of Hadassah, the Women's Zionist Organization of America," the lead read.

This was one group that did not mind that Amory's speech did not center completely on television. But the women apparently did hear some of the speaker's comments about animals. At the podium, the story noted, Amory turned to the president of the organization and remarked, "I'm glad to see you didn't wear a fur tonight," to which she replied: "And I'm glad you're not speaking to us in January."

Amory reminded the group that in *The Proper Bostonians* he quoted a woman who said she began studying Hebrew in her late eighties because "she wanted to be able to greet her Creator in his native tongue." But Amory went beyond using humor to charm the women. He had sharp words for the U.S. government and its stand on Israel. After the Six-Day War, he said, America was willing to spend lives and money in Southeast Asia but would not even sell planes to Israel. "What manner of madness is in our State Department. . . . What kind of muddleheaded, mealymouthed men are they?"

Amory's friends say that the topic of Israel often made its way into their conversations with him; ironically, as Amory's activism intensified and his comments against the wearing of fur garnered national attention, he drew criticism from furriers, some of whom were Jewish, according to Lewis Regenstein, who once ran the Fund for Animals Washington office. "They called him anti-Semitic [for his antifur activities], which made him angry," Regenstein said.

Whether it was the founding in 1967 of the Fund for Animals, the fact that his marriage was failing, or a general ambivalence about the current direction of his life, Amory by the late 1960s was becoming much more vocal in his activism and in the defense of his beliefs. In *TV Guide*, for instance, his reviews were getting increasingly candid when animals were concerned. His 1967 review of *The American Sportsman* is far harsher than the one he wrote two years earlier—it is downright brutal. He starts the review by noting that it is difficult for a reviewer at times to select the best show on television because the competition can be stiff. But there is little doubt as to what is the worst show on television: *The American Sportsman* on ABC.

Amory notes early in the review that the network could have learned how to produce high-quality shows about animals from other networks that produced shows like *Flipper, Wild Kingdom,* and *Lassie.* "If the men who run ABC themselves find enjoyment in such a 'sport' [hunting], it is sad news," he wrote. "When they inflict it on the public, however, it is the public's business, and an outrage." Amory goes on to criticize the blandness of the show's host, noting, also, that he will not identify anyone associated with the show in order to save them from embarrassment. He also ridicules the show's guest "stars," each of whom "has to be identified as a 'television personality' because otherwise you wouldn't know he had one, let alone is one."

The theme of the review is the cowardice of hunting and the bravado of the hunters: "Each week we have a curious assortment of white hunters in living color, about all of whose fearless exploits we hear ad nauseam — particularly as, armed with a full arsenal of weapons, they boldly advance to test wits and match virilities with, say, a mourning dove." At the end of the review, *TV Guide* ran an interesting disclaimer of sorts, noting that "Mr. Amory has written many articles protesting inhumane treatment of animals" and adding that he was a founder of the Fund for Animals "and a director of several other antiviolence organizations."

Amory wrote years later that animal lovers had been furious with the show, and by the time the review appeared, they had sent letters of protest to both the network and the show's "guests." Actor Cliff Robertson, who had appeared on one of the shows, later appeared in what Amory called a "pro-elephant" show to indicate he was sorry he was part of *The American Sportsman.* And Bing Crosby, who had done promotion for the show, abruptly stopped supporting it. Eventually, a mail "war" broke out over the show, with hunters supporting it and animal activists and animal lovers (including many celebrities) seeking its demise. Ultimately, Amory wrote, the show's two main sponsors, Eastman Kodak and Chevrolet, dropped the show. By 1971, four years after Amory's second review, the show announced a new policy in which the broadcasting of the hunting of big game would be replaced by segments on the rescue and relocation of animals.

While *The American Sportsman* review was one of his most negative, Amory did get other, smaller digs in at those he felt were hostile to animals. In a lukewarm review of the show *Emergency!* for example, he described some of the action, noting that the team of regulars had to rescue a hunter who found himself on a mountain ledge. Amory could not resist: "Since he was a hunter, we were cheering for the ledge," he wrote. "But no matter. It was still a spectacular sight."

Amory was, of course, complimentary about many animal shows, including *Born Free* and *The Adventures of Black Beauty*. The creators of *Black Beauty* could have had trouble pleasing Amory, whose favorite book as a child was Anna Sewell's *Black Beauty*. But he notes this humorously at the beginning of the review, explaining that it was his favorite piece of writing "except for the things we wrote ourselves." Amory notes that, sadly, the horse himself, Black Beauty, is not the focus of the show, as he is in the book, but the human actors are effective and the show, overall, is watchable.

In his *Born Free* review, Amory did something he had not done before in his *TV Guide* reviews: he publicized a book he had written. The "star" of the television show — which was based on the true-to-life film of the same name — was Elsa, a lioness who was domesticated and then retrained to go out in the wild. In the televised version of the story, when Elsa is sent back to the wild, she never strays far from her home, so she may not be quite prepared for the perils of the wilderness. Sending tamed animals back into the wild is a real problem, Amory writes. "In our new book, *Man Kind?*, we point out that no animal anywhere is safe from man's infinite capacity for cruelty." The 1974 book was a discussion of the problems and politics of wildlife management in the United States, and it pointed out how many wild animals were, intentionally and unintentionally, mistreated.

As usual, though, Amory managed to slip some humor into the review to amplify his point that it is usually people, and not animals, who misbehave. "One of the troubles [with many animal shows], at least with the African-type shows, is those fear-maddened natives facing those 'rogue' animals," he wrote. "We've never believed that it's the animals that give them all that fear. Our theory is it's those rotten parts. You know, rogue producers."

Panitt made it clear over the years that he would give Amory a free hand in what he wrote. Only two letters in Amory's cache of personal papers indicate that viewers did criticize his rare negative mentions of hunters. But hunters and others who read his column may not have used *TV Guide* as their venue to complain. In his book *The Politics of Extinction*, Regenstein noted that after they read the mention of the hunter on the ledge in Amory's *Emergency!* review, hunters reacted explosively in the pages of *Shooting Times*. The magazine carried an editorial with the headline "Cleveland Amory's Death Wish for Hunters, " and an editor called the remark "one of the most irresponsible and what we view as insane, anti-hunter remarks we've ever read," one that "demanded instant rebuttal."

It's incredible that any man would cherish lower forms—the hunter's prey—while wishing harm or even death to the highest life form of all—man. . . . Only a bigot, an unusually sick bigot, would say in print to the more than 16 million readers of *TV Guide* that he would wish harm, even death, to another human being because that man was a hunter.

As Amory and the producers of the *Today* show had learned years earlier, the hunters of the world were not a group that kept their opinions to themselves. And their sheer numbers and organization made them a force to be reckoned with. As Regenstein knew, the hunters' lobby closely monitored all forms of media to see how their ranks were portrayed. Amory wrote in *The Best Cat Ever* that the editor of *Field & Stream* called him on the phone to tell him that the line "was the most despicable thing that has ever appeared in a national magazine." Amory said he informed him that magazines had been around a long time, and that "surely somewhere, sometime, possibly in the dim past, something equally as 'despicable' must have been allowed to slip by." The editor was not amused.

▷ ▷ ▷ It is difficult to determine why Amory's activism accelerated by the late 1960s, but the formation of the Fund for Animals—and all the dedication it took to develop and maintain the organization—was no doubt a key factor. Amory had never been an extremist—he was not a vegetarian, nor did he believe in violent or intrusive methods to convey his points—but he had became increasingly frustrated by the activities of some animal advocacy groups, which he believed were timid and hesitant to take bold action. He also condemned some activist groups for what he believed were their ambivalent platforms. For instance, the Audubon Society and many other similar groups made contributions to wildlife organizations that advocated hunting, although many contributors did not know that, he believed. And he thought that many organizations paid their presidents and staffs far too much money for administrative duties. Amory liked to say that he started the Fund for Animals with only $800—and its beginnings were inauspicious. He and Marian Probst rented quarters in a cramped apartment on West Fifty-seventh Street in Manhattan, down the street from Carnegie Hall. Probst, who by this time had worked for Amory for about six years, was his typist, proofreader, sometime researcher, confidante, and general right-hand woman. (Amory did not type his magazine articles and speeches but wrote them in longhand on a yellow legal pad and gave them to Probst, who typed them for further editing and then retyped them.) By the time of Amory's death in 1998, Probst and Amory had been a team for more than thirty years and could virtually finish each other's sentences — or as Amory would joke, she could finish *his* sentences because of her phenomenal memory. In some published interviews, when Amory was about to spout a fact or figure, he'd pause and Probst would provide it off the top of her head.

Three years after its formation in 1967, the fund was able to hire Patricia Forkan as its executive director, but the group's survival still was not ensured, and it was a combination of hard work by its principals, luck, and the kindness of friends that allowed the fund to survive. For instance, pro bono advertising work by the advertising firm of Young & Rubicam — initiated by Amory's friend Edward Ney, CEO of the advertising firm — gave the fund a shot in the arm. Attorney Edward Walsh began doing pro bono legal work in 1970 for the fund. In 1977, it received its first major inheritance — $400,000, left in a will. The Fund for Animals soon moved to bigger headquarters in the same neighborhood, and its staff grew slightly. Not surprisingly Amory had rather unorthodox "hiring" practices. Few people who worked for him underwent an extensive interview process; he had gut feelings about people and made hiring decisions, such as they were, on the spot. As Probst recalled, Amory casually mentioned that he expected her to report to work shortly after they met, even though nothing official was ever said. Lawyer Walsh said, also, that he was silently "assigned" to be the fund's lawyer after he did some outside legal work for the organization. In a summary of the fund's early days, lobbying researcher Jeffrey M. Berry wrote that Amory's key goal for the fund was to be "action-oriented" in focusing solely on educational efforts. "From the stray alley cat to the endangered polar bear, there had already been too much talk and too little positive assistance," Berry wrote. Of course, because of Amory's strong views that advocacy groups should use nearly all the money they collect for their cause and not for salaries, fund workers were paid very low wages. Regenstein, who ran the fund's Washington bureau, remembered that during the first few years of the fund's existence, workers would get a few years of experience at the fund and then take higher-paying jobs with the Humane Society of the United States, prompting fund workers to joke that the fund provided a good training ground for HSUS work. Amory took no money at all for his work with the fund and lived on patched-together income from his writing — his real job — and from the royalties his books generated. Probst was paid a very small salary as his assistant and as a vice president of the fund.

Amory would comment tongue in cheek throughout his life that he came to regret the name he gave the Fund for Animals. It sounded as though the group was not seeking money but instead that it was a philanthropic foundation looking for ways to distribute it, he would say. But because its founder was a writer, the Fund for Animals frequently received free publicity. In 1967, for example, Amory made the first plug for the fund in his *Saturday Review* column. After a few items about current legislative action regarding animals (including news that laboratory dogs at Harvard University, Amory's alma mater, were being cruelly abused), he wrote about the founding of the fund, quoting from its brochure:

> The Fund is not merely one more humane society. Rather it is an organization which is specifically designed to help specific projects of existing societies or persons who are not now organized in a society. Above all, the Fund is designed to serve on a local, national and even international scale.

Amory went on to say that the fund would be available for disasters and would assist in daily humanitarian work. "Humanitarians can leave money to The Fund in the sure and certain conviction that such money will, after their death, continue to be used as wisely and as widely as possible, in the order of the most pressing need weighed against the greatest good for the largest number of animals." Further, he said, the fund would battle all the ills of the world that animals face "from the terror and torture of the hunt and trap to the misery and despair of the slaughterhouse and the laboratory." Amory was going to discover very soon that his work and the work of the fund would quickly go far beyond "the hunt and trap" and the laboratory — and into areas that he could not have predicted.

Although it is enormously difficult to create and organize an advocacy group like the Fund for Animals, its founding by Amory was probably inevitable. During the 1960s, he served on the boards of several animal advocacy groups and of course was a tireless promoter of animal rights. But, as his friends and colleagues are quick to point out, Amory was not always content simply to sit on a board and approve the work others had done; he had to take a much more active role. "He's not someone you just have on your board," Regenstein said. "Cleveland liked to be in charge. He was a very dominating personality."

Amory was a key player in several Humane Society actions of the 1960s, including an effort to ban bullfighting, a practice that had long been on the top of Amory's hit list. Always an advocate of the grand gesture, Amory once stepped into a field of one hundred bulls to prove the animals were docile unless provoked. He also worked with the Humane Society on a series of unannounced visits to laboratories in New York.

Indeed, activism overall was a key part of the 1960s, and most other successful social movements had charismatic and energetic figureheads who became symbols. Amory was perfect for that role. For starters, he was physically imposing — at six feet three and about 265 pounds by middle age, he had a deep baritone voice and could be physically overwhelming. Amory also looked perennially rumpled, with his wrinkled jackets and pants, stained neckties, and uncombed thatch of stiff, auburn gray hair, but the disheveled look just added to his persona. The former Harvard debate champion also was quick with a clever retort, and there was little he loved more than countering an illogical argument. Most important, though, were his contacts. Amory had friends and acquaintances all over the world — but mostly in Hollywood, Washington, and in the literary and media spheres. And his role as columnist and lecturer gave him access, directly or indirectly, to millions of people. With the founding of the fund, he could officially channel all his access to a cause he loved.

As many of his friends and coworkers note, Amory consistently earned the devotion of those with whom he worked. But that does not mean working with him was easy. He would call his friends and coworkers in the middle of the night and would expect them to take his calls. And woe to those who did not return his calls later if they were not available when those calls first came. He had a temper if provoked and a tendency to dominate any room he occupied. "He wasn't easy to work for — you checked your ego at the door," Regenstein said. But Regenstein, like Probst, Walsh, and many others, loved Amory and believed the extra effort was well worth it. They loved how he made them feel they were an integral part of an important cause; they loved his boldness and his quick sense of humor; and they loved watching him work — there was no telephone call or letter that was too trivial to merit a response from Amory. And, as his editor and friend Walter Anderson noted, if he did get angry, it usually was easy to defuse that anger with a joke or humorous comment.

Regenstein's experience with Amory was classic. When the fund first started, it did not have a Washington office, presumably because Amory was looking for just the right person to run it. And he found that person in 1971 when he met Regenstein. Regenstein, who held two degrees in political science and had worked for the CIA, met Amory when he worked as Washington representative for the Committee for Humane Legislation. Amory had read many magazine articles and op-ed pieces by Regenstein, who felt that writing such pieces in support of various forms of legislation was his forte. Regenstein had been pivotal in securing passage of the federal Marine Mammal Protection Act, which provided a moratorium on the killing of dolphins, porpoises, sea otters, whales, and other marine mammals.

Regenstein came from an affluent family with deep roots in Atlanta; they had once owned the Atlanta department store of the same name. Regenstein first met Amory at a hearing, although each man knew about the other. "I just went up to him and said, 'Hello,' and he said, 'Would you like to work in my Washington office?'" Regenstein recalled.

The fund's newly opened Washington office consisted of four rooms in a row house in Washington's Dupont Circle area. Two of those rooms served as Regenstein's home. As Jeffrey Berry noted, the quarters were emblematic of the fund's limited resources: "The furniture is old, and there is little in the office of comfort or luxury," he wrote in 1972. "Posters and pictures of various animals give the otherwise drab office a bit of color." Regenstein and others like him who worked for the fund and other animal-protection groups knew they did not have conventional jobs. The long hours they put in, combined with very little pay, meant that their job was their passion. But the life apparently agreed with him; he worked in the fund's Washington office for eleven years before returning to his hometown.

Despite Amory's contacts and complete devotion to the fund, he had much to learn when he founded the organization. Lobbying for legislation took some finesse, and pure force — tackling issues quickly and with brutal candor — did not always work. "You need a group that could lobby Congress and testify at hearings," Regenstein said. "Cleveland just attacked people head on — senators and congressmen. You have to do that, but he became controversial." Like the leaders of other social movements, Amory learned that special skills are required for specific activities. With his magnetic personality and unlimited energy, Amory was at his best out in the field mobilizing people: informing individuals or small groups of the goals of the organization, seeking funds from those individuals, and publicizing the fund. The subtleties of lobbying may have been best left to those who had experience with it. But Amory was a quick study, and he soon was able to match his staff's talents with the requirements of their jobs. "He ended up with the best staff and the best volunteers of any [animal advocacy] group," Regenstein said. That group included Donna Dixon, a fund field agent from Michigan; Wayne Pacelle, who would later become president and CEO of the Humane Society of the United States; Michael Markarian, who later became president of the fund and then an executive vice president of the HSUS; Patricia Forkan, who became president of the Humane Society International; and many others. And of course Marian Probst continued as Amory's assistant for his literary and activist pursuits.

Regenstein and the other top employees of the fund worked well together because of the loose structure of the organization. Amory trusted their judgment and respected their intellect and energy. He managed like this for several reasons. First, he had an inherent trust in the people he selected for top positions; second, he wanted the workers to love what they did so they would carry on long after he was gone. The fund raised $300,000 in 1972, six years after its founding, and by that time had 35,000 members. The standard membership fee was $10, with larger contributions encouraged. Anyone giving more than $50 received a personal thank-you from Amory. By the time the Fund for Animals merged with the HSUS in 2005, it had 200,000 members and constituents, a budget of $7 million, and $20 million in assets.

Amory's awareness of the power of celebrity was put to use when he organized the structure of the fund. An executive board met occasionally and had authority over the organization, but Amory made most of the final decisions. But Amory also formed a "national" advisory board that consisted mainly of celebrities — people like Dick Cavett, Jack Paar, Helen Gurley Brown — whose names were used for publicity and fund-raising purposes.

The politics within the animal-protection movement were — and remain — complex. Not everyone in the movement was on the same page when it came to methods and philosophy. Some groups preferred a softer approach regarding their opposition to hunting and trapping, the wearing of fur, and other activities, while others preferred more confrontational tactics. Groups within the movement also disagreed about the definition of "humane." In the eyes of many of his adversaries—particularly those in the hunting lobby—Amory was a radical. But that was not the case. He did not preach against eating meat or wearing leather shoes, nor did he oppose completely the use of animals in laboratories. He was a realist, and he knew he would never put an end to hunting or trapping, nor would he stop scientists from using animals in laboratories. His goal was to keep such activities at a minimum, create more humane environments for animals that were part of such activities, and try to educate the public about what was going on. Most important, Amory realized that progress develops, ultimately, from a series of small steps. "Cleveland's attitude was that a partial victory was better than no victory," said Judy Ney, who serves on the boards of several anticruelty organizations and worked with Amory on the fund board. "Cleveland always felt a little progress is OK—maybe next time a little more progress. In this movement, that's unusual." But his rhetoric could be volatile. Regenstein remembered that, in some speeches, Amory would say that some fish and game officials would shoot their own mother if she were on four legs. And Amory would say that to anyone—animal-rights audiences as well as game audiences. "He had no fear," Regenstein said.

Amory was very vocal in his beliefs that officials of groups like the Humane Society of the United States were sometimes overpaid. His disagreements with former HSUS president John Hoyt were well known to people in the movement and led to Amory's resignation from that group's board of directors in 1974. But even Amory's friends acknowledge that few if any people—particularly heads of large organizations—would work for virtually nothing, as Amory did. And few people could fall back on royalties from best-selling books, as Amory could. By the time Amory founded the fund, his work as a columnist, broadcaster, and freelance writer was earning him only about $1,000 a week, which was barely enough for him to maintain an apartment and buy food and other incidentals.

But Amory and the fund workers he gathered together were in the right place at the right time. The HSUS was founded in 1954 because of a philosophical disagreement some activists had with the American Humane Association, which was a coalition of state and local societies. The early members of HSUS wanted a group that would be aggressive in seeking federal anticruelty legislation. By the late 1960s, the animal-welfare movement was expanding dramatically, and organizers began paying far more attention to legal, political, and public relations activities. In short, the movement was getting more sophisticated than it ever had been. At this time, many animal-rights organizations were beginning to expand their efforts beyond domesticated pets and into wildlife. And it was with these latter efforts that the Fund for Animals put itself on the map.

Chapter 9 ▷ ▷ ▷ Man Kind?

A faster talker was never found outside a carnival.

▶ *Field & Stream* editor JACK SAMSON

*I*n some ways, all of Amory's "part-time" jobs — that is, his radio commentary, two regular magazine columns, and freelance writing — equaled more than one full-time job. Heading the Fund for Animals was certainly more than a forty-hour-per-week endeavor. From 1963 to 1967, he offered brief commentary on WPAT radio New York City, and from 1968 to 1970 he was a social commentator on a radio show syndicated by Westinghouse's Group W. During the late 1970s, Amory also wrote a popular syndicated newspaper column called Animail, in which he answered readers' questions about their pets and other animals. In this column, Amory was in his element; there was little he loved better that reading and responding to questions and comments from audiences. Most who contacted Amory received a personal reply of some sort.

The Fund for Animals, though, did not have an easy birth. It was trial and error at first for Amory and for Probst, even though the two were brilliant and had tireless workers — mostly volunteers — who thoroughly believed in their cause. Amory defined it as an organization that defended animals through "litigation, legislation, education and confrontation." The team of Amory and Probst was perfect in some ways: Amory was the charismatic and visionary leader of the organization, while Probst took care of the hundreds of details that needed attention. And Probst was probably one of the few people who could keep up with Amory physically and mentally. As Judy Ney noted, they were a perfect pair. It was unlikely the fund would have survived with one but not the other.

Amory traveled extensively during the first few years of the fund, making speeches, debating adversaries, and visiting local organizations. He also became the target of derision and ridicule from many hunters and sportspersons who opposed the fund's work in the area of wildlife preservation. By now, his enemies list had grown considerably to include not just hunters and some scientists but also furriers and many government agencies whose job it was to regulate wildlife. Outdoor writers in particular — in newspapers and in such publications as *Fur Age Weekly, Outdoor Life,* and *Field & Stream* — set their sights on Amory, who by the late 1960s was much more visible than ever as an anticruelty activist.

Things started cooking for the fund by 1970. The organization relied on its founder, of course, to spread the word around the nation, and it sent out a newsletter. Amory sought contributors and volunteers by developing what he called his "army of the kind" — implying that everybody who loved animals should join the club and be willing to fight for their beliefs. Amory of course had a way with words, and that came in handy for him as head of the fund. Another slogan he created was, as could be expected, a pun. Hunters, of course, had the right to bear arms. The fund offered a similar "right" — the right to arm bears.

By 1970, Amory and Probst had begun to develop a specific focus for the organization: it would concentrate on the wolf, which Amory had long believed to be one of the most misunderstood and maligned animals in the world. As he frequently explained, wolves do not attack and kill human beings, as was widely believed, and, in fact, they have a very complex and sophisticated social system within their species that closely resembles the human family. In addition to possessing great intelligence, wolves are pivotal in maintaining the balance of nature as they prey on rodents and other potentially harmful animals.

Wolves were the targets of settlers in the United States in the last half of the nineteenth century, and Amory learned that by the mid–twentieth century wolves in Alaska were routinely being shot from helicopters. He testified before Congress and helped pass in 1971 the Airborne Hunting Act, which prohibited the aerial killing of wolves and other wildlife. But in the bigger picture, the fund's efforts toward wolves were more important than just establishing some limited protection for the animal; they also helped establish the fund as the voice for wildlife, a group that had not been seriously protected by anticruelty groups. Protecting animals in the wild was naturally a tough sell for most anticruelty organizations — after all, they were not cuddly, and most people did not have firsthand experience with them. Until this time, the protection of wildlife was left to environmental groups, organizations that did little to actually protect animals. And Amory tried to stress that although people did not keep wild animals in their homes, many activities of humans — their eating habits, their clothing, their industries — affected the natural habitat of wildlife.

Amory and the Fund for Animals had a very effective ambassador for wolf rights in a timber wolf named Jethro, who made the rounds to schools, shopping centers, theaters, and even the U.S. Capitol to show that the wolf is a benign — and in the case of Jethro, entertaining — creature. Born in a California zoo, Jethro was, in the words of his owner, "tame" but not "trained," and he toured on behalf of the Fund for Animals and several other anticruelty organizations. Jethro was a gentle presence, and he occasionally pleased crowds by doing something unexpected, like gnawing on a plaque that was once presented to him naming him "Animal of the Year," or grabbing and munching the placard of an "anti-wolf" protester at one of his appearances. Jethro was later joined by another timber wolf named Clem, who made visits with him. Sadly, though, both wolves may have been victims of the politics of animal rights. After one event, Jethro and Clem were fed poison as they waited in a locked van in Brooklyn. Both died within two days.

Lewis Regenstein was pivotal not just in his efforts as head of the fund's Washington office but also because he helped introduce Amory and the fund to the plight of marine mammals: whales, seals, dolphins, and other animals in the ocean. Regenstein had been working on what was to be known as the Marine Mammal Protection Act, designed to ban the killing of marine mammals. (The law also banned the importation of products made from marine mammals.) A seasoned lobbyist, Regenstein was a shrewd marketer who knew how to get the attention of an audience. Both he and Amory were aware of the power of numbers, and both knew that there existed an army of potential supporters who were not aware of the vast numbers of mistreated or murdered animals. And Regenstein learned early that publicizing the plight of the cute and cuddly seal pups was a good way to educate the public about the mistreatment of other marine mammals. A direct-mail campaign featuring the seals had prompted more mail to Capitol Hill over a certain period of time than the war in Vietnam.

The idea that many people were oblivious of the plight of some animals was driven home to Amory at the 1964–65 World's Fair. Officials at the fair agreed to give Amory and some other animal-rights organizers space for one year to display seventy-six animals, not in a zoo or circus setting, but behind glass walls in barnyard fashion. Initially, Amory said, fair officials considered the exhibit a dead zone that would draw very few visitors. Instead, within weeks, "Animal Kingdom" had broken several fair exhibit attendance records and drew the fifth-largest crowds at the event, outdrawing exhibits by the likes of General Electric and IBM, Amory wrote.

As worldly as he was, even Amory could be naive in some ways about the politics of animal rights and the ways of Washington. As he learned quickly, the so-called wildlife and conservation groups in the United States could be enemies of wildlife, as could state and federal wildlife agencies. And because the U.S. Constitution did not protect animals, they were at the mercy of state governments (which, Amory and others believed, were greatly influenced by the hunting lobby). To Amory, nearly all literature from the federal Fish and Wildlife Service and its Bureau of Sport Fisheries and Wildlife espoused the virtues of hunting and "the nonvirtues of nonhunting," as he wrote.

What further angered Amory and his workers was the Orwellian language employed by wildlife and conservation organizations, most of which, he believed, were beholden to the hunting lobby and advocated hunting in one form or another, supposedly to regulate animal populations. Nearly all groups with the word "wildlife" in their title — and the National Audubon Society — were controlled in part by hunters, he believed. Even the seemingly benign National Geographic Society, which took supposedly pro-animal stands in magazines and on television, was afraid to support any organization it believed was at odds with hunters, he suspected.

Amory also learned that legislation passed by Congress was not always what it appeared to be. In a lengthy article in the *Christian Science Monitor* in 1966, he described how amendments and other riders horribly weakened some animal-rights legislation to the point of making it toothless. In the article, he used as an example legislation he helped pass designed to protect animals used in laboratory experiments. "The amendments literally stop at the laboratory door," he wrote.

If Amory, Probst, Regenstein, and the others felt they had formidable opponents in the government agencies, wildlife associations, and hunting lobbies, those groups had a formidable opponent in Amory, who was catching on quickly to the mechanics of running and anticruelty organization. By the early 1970s, the stakes were getting higher.

▷ ▷ ▷ Cleveland Amory had always been a champion debater, and he took great pleasure in using humor to dismantle his opponents' arguments. At no time in his life were his debating skills more indispensable than during his early years at the Fund for Animals. But his skill at debating also inflamed many of his opponents. And like those who worked for the fund and other anticruelty organizations, members of the hunting and wildlife lobbies were relentless when promoting their cause.

Of all the debates in which he participated, Amory's friends and colleagues like to describe two in particular. One dealt with the time Amory tripped up a scientist who advocated widespread use of animals in the lab, and the other involved the time Amory debated himself. In the former, Amory was involved in a heated debate with the publicist for the American Medical Association over use of animals in laboratories. Amory, who maintained that many of the experiments done on animals were unneeded, noted that he had heard of a ridiculous experiment in which scientists decided to put the eyes of a cat in a dog. "What good could that do?" he asked. His debating partner noted that such an experiment was a part of "valuable ophthalmologic" research. Then the sly Amory pounced. "I made that up," he responded. "To show that you would defend anything."

Another time, in Michigan in 1969, Amory sought a debate with an *Ann Arbor News* outdoor columnist named Doug Fulton, an outspoken critic of Amory who wrote a regular column called The Naturalist's Journal. Amory could not wait to sink his teeth into Fulton, who offered what the fund considered the same old, tired arguments advocating hunting: that it was really a form of conservation, that hunters indirectly support animal rights because of the fees they pay each year to the government, and that most animal activists were radical bleeding hearts who manipulated facts. Fulton wrote in a column in October that he had no intention of debating Amory, and he attacked him not only for the fund's stand on hunting but also for its comments about the use of animals in laboratories: "I have no intention of engaging in an emotional harangue with Mr. Amory," he wrote, adding that Amory could be "witty and charming when talking about society," but "I doubt . . . if Mr. Amory has ever seen a bow and arrow. . . . The literature they [the fund] send me is a curious brand of belief in Good causes, naivete, half-truths and misrepresentations of fact." He went on to object to "the [fund's] misleading use of isolated instances to degrade worthwhile programs, valuable research and the efforts of sincere and dedicated conservationists. [Amory] manages to create the impression that all experiments involving animals, laboratory-raised or dogs taken from pounds, are inhumanely done. . . . He doesn't say that the government gets millions of dollars from hunters in taxes and licenses. . . . A pox on Mr. Amory. Let him go back to high (or low) society and leave conservationists alone."

Amory enjoyed a good fight, and he would not take no for an answer when it came to Fulton's refusal to debate. On a Detroit radio program, he declared that he had heard the arguments of the other side so many times that he could actually present both sides of the hunting debate. He donned a safari hat and parroted all the arguments of hunters in defense of hunting. A hatless Amory then provided more "logical" arguments against hunting. Meanwhile, everyone watching in the wings howled with laughter:

> AS FULTON: Da hunter puts his money where his mouth is. The hunters put up the money. Da hunters put up all the money for all the wild-life out there. Now, I want to know what all you bleeding hearts are doing. . . .
>
> AS HIMSELF: We are not putting up any money and I'll tell you why we are not. Because my ancestors who came from Massachusetts threw lots of tea into the water because they didn't want to pay taxes or pay tribute to anything they didn't have representation on. You own the DNR, the Michigan Department of Natural Resources, you own the Fish and Game Department. You own them lock, stock and barrel. . . .
>
> AS FULTON: I am not going to take my hunting lessons from Doris Day, Amanda Blake, Mary Tyler Moore and all the rest of you bleeding hearts. . . .

By 1974, the usually prolific Amory had not published a book in fourteen years, although he was read by millions each week in *TV Guide* and other publications for which he wrote on a freelance basis. But for someone who had written or edited six books in about fifteen years, this was uncharacteristic. In 1974, Amory used his talent for writing and researching to publish *Man Kind? Our Incredible War on Wildlife*, a detailed description of — and attack on — the role of government and lobbying groups in animal protection. In particular, the book tackled the issue of protecting animals in the wild and defined the philosophy of those in the anticruelty movement and the politics within the movement. *Man Kind?* was unlike any other book Amory had written up to that time. It has a serious theme, and, with the exception of a light introduction that describes how the English language itself discriminates against animals (for instance, the use of terms like "animal" to connote a brutish person; "chicken" to connote cowardice; and negative phrases like "go ape," "dumb bunny," and the like), there is relatively little humor. Amory was unable to rely on anecdote as much as he did in previous books, but the anecdotes he did include are compelling — for example, a lengthy and funny retelling of the North Carolina bunny bop episode. As in his other books, the style of Man Kind? is quick and breezy, and easy to read. Also as in his other books, Amory uses light sarcasm to make a point. But owing to the serious nature of the book, the satire comes off as slightly hard-edged. The book packs a punch — whether the reader agrees with it or not — and it was difficult for his adversaries to ignore. The photos in it combine images of cute baby animals — small kangaroos, polar bears, and wolves — with brutal and bloody trapping and hunting scenes. One photo depicts a long line of dead coyotes strung up on poles: "Coyotes strung up, " the caption reads. "To teach other coyotes a lesson." In another, a small fox is shown dying agonizingly in a trap: "Here's what that darling fox jacket came from," the caption reads. "Only it takes about six foxes like this and it takes them so long to die." These captions, in particular, illustrate some of Amory's major points in the book: that hunters kill and maim for no real reason other than to collect trophies, and that much killing takes place in the name of fashion. Amory writes over and over again that many hunters see their actions as a courageous "man-against-the-environment" proposition when in fact nearly all wild animals are harmless and defenseless. And, he implies, there is little that is more trivial and foolish than inflicting such widespread pain for the vanity of fashion.

Amory and others in the anticruelty movement had varying opinions about how graphic they should be in depicting cruelty and violence toward animals; they wanted to illustrate the widespread brutality that existed, but they did not want to alienate people by being too graphic.

Another of the photos in Man Kind? shows a controversial and much-publicized fund advertisement: a classic full-page, fashion-page shot of five beautiful, well-known actresses wearing lovely fur coats — all made of synthetic fur, of course. The original ad, which was sponsored by the fund and E. F. Timme Co., a fake-fur manufacturer, consisted of the photo and another full page of quotations about why the stars would not wear real fur. The group of five actresses — Doris Day, Amanda Blake, Jayne Meadows, Angie Dickinson, and Mary Tyler Moore — were all friends of Amory's and were members of the fund's national board.

To launch the publishing of Man Kind? in September of 1974, Amory's brother hosted a gathering of Amory's friends as a book party. The book never achieved the best-seller status of some of Amory's other books, nor did it get reviewed in as many publications. But it did get the attention of some powerful people — and is still considered by many in the animal-protection movement as the work that launched a major antihunting effort in the United States in the latter part of the twentieth century. And the ripple effect of the book established Amory as the figurehead in the nation's antihunting movement. Overall, the book received positive reviews, and even the magazine *National Review*, which historically has advocated loose restrictions on gun ownership and other politically conservative causes, gave it a thumbs-up. The review calls Amory "eloquently angry" and one who "makes his case brilliantly, with wit and passion." It notes that he is particularly effective "in the section in which he describes the hunting of whales, especially the blue whale, which we have just about butchered to biological extinction, and in his descriptions of the aimless and brutal attempts to exterminate wolves and coyotes." The reviewer does take Amory to task, though, for failing to recognize that some people in some areas of the world must kill animals in order to survive. But the reviewer also acknowledges that if he did contemplate buying a fur for his wife, "I would not even consider . . . a coat made from an animal that was clubbed, trapped or poisoned for its fur. And I didn't feel this way before reading *Man Kind?*"

A review in *School Library Journal* notes that Amory collected "an impressive amount of data. . . . At times his strident belaboring of a point makes it hard to stay with him, but it would be difficult to wear a fur coat after reading this."

The *Christian Science Monitor*, in a glowing review, notes that the book was written at the perfect time — when environmental and animal groups were coming of age. Yet, the reviewer writes, Amory is bound to make many enemies: "He [Amory] is aware . . . that he would undoubtedly provoke the ire of many industries which use animals as a means to economic gain." The reviewer also writes that Amory's story is not a pretty one: "The reader will not like what he reads; he may shake with pity, anger, yes, even with wrath. Yet, assuredly, he will read on. . . . Yet here and there are delightful bits of humor which perhaps explain how he can continue to pursue this disturbing topic."

But one of the book's biggest boosts came from the *New York Times*, which, in an editorial against leghold traps, mentioned Amory and his book specifically. The lengthy editorial, headlined "Man Kind?" begins by saying the hunter and trapper have become "vestigial" figures in today's urban society, since few if any people in the United States hunt to get essential food to live. And few people realize the cruelty of leghold traps:

Most Americans have never hunted or seen a live animal caught in a leg trap. What the great majority of people in this country fail to realize is that they dwell in a sea of unimaginable — and totally unnecessary — suffering inflicted on wounded deer, on lead-poisoned birds, on small animals which may writhe in their death agonies for days after being caught in a neglected trap.

In an ironically titled book, *Man Kind?* Cleveland Amory presents a vivid indictment of the hunting and trapping cult. Mr. Amory is one of those rare writers who can illuminate deep moral indignation with hilarious anecdotes and sardonic wit. His book deserves to be read by every state legislator and member of Congress; for it is the ignorance or indifference of legislators across the country that permits this hideous cruelty to wild animals to continue.

The editorial goes on to give the vast numbers of animals killed and wounded in traps, and briefly quotes Amory's graphic description of animals wildly tearing at their own limbs to escape the traps.

The editorial in the *Times* — as well as one that appeared seven months later — was a tremendous boon to Amory and the fund. The *Times* was and remains one the most prestigious news outlets in the world, and is read by many influential people. The editorial page at the time was edited by John Oakes, a cousin to then-publisher A. O. Sulzberger and an outspoken environmentalist and anticruelty advocate. And Sulzberger's mother, Iphigene, was a vocal opponent of the wearing of animal skins. So Amory and the fund did have some natural allies in that newspaper. Later that year, the newspaper ran a brief editorial titled "Agony and Finery," which lauded a campaign by the international World Federation for the Protection of Animals that deplored the wearing of furs by humans and condemned the use of the leghold trap. The three-paragraph editorial, which describes how the trap clamps down on the animal's leg or paw "with bone-crushing force," quotes Amory again: "Imagine having your fingers crushed in car door for 24 to 48 hours."

While the publicity given *Man Kind?* was more than enough to introduce the cause, the firestorm resulting from a related television special certainly made millions of people aware of Amory as a serious and tireless activist.

▷ ▷ ▷ By the mid-1970s, the public had certainly heard about the use of leg-hold traps and the availability of synthetic fur. Whether people agreed with the sentiments of the fund and other anticruelty groups was one thing, but their awareness of these issues overall was very real. So, as broadcast news shows have done for decades when an issue becomes a topic of debate in the culture, CBS aired a documentary special about hunting on September 5, 1975, called *The Guns of Autumn*, which it said was prompted by *Man Kind?* The ninety-minute news special was narrated by Dan Rather and produced, directed, and written by veteran journalist Irv Drasnin. Even before it aired, Drasnin and the management of the CBS News Division were given a first-hand lesson on the size and clout of the hunting lobby in the United States.

One of the themes of the special was that the advent of modern technology, which brought hunters high-powered rifles, scopes, two-way radios, and four-wheel-drive vehicles, had eliminated the fairness of most hunting — the hunter clearly had the advantage. The special also showed, among others scenes, footage of bears being led to a garbage dump where they were first hand-fed and then blasted by hunters. It also was filled with testimonials from hunters boasting about their high-tech equipment and noting, as one hunter did, that hunting "gets in your blood — like an addiction."

Hunters had gotten wind of the show in late July when *TV Guide* published an item about it. The magazine noted that the program "would describe hunting 50 percent from the animals' point of view." (Amory was on hiatus from *TV Guide* during the summers and did not write the item.) That sentence served as a red flag for the hunting lobby, and the Washington office of the National Rifle Association launched a letter-writing campaign stressing that the show could threaten the right of Americans to own handguns. The campaign began to make advertisers nervous. Finally, the NRA managed to slip a representative into a network affiliate's screening of the show a few days before it aired and noted all the show's advertisers. By the time the show aired, nearly all the show's advertisers — Datsun, Exxon, Lennox Industries, Coca-Cola, and Aquatec — had withdrawn their advertising. Block Drugs kept its sponsorship.

Within an hour of the show's airing, hunters mobilized to protest it with calls and letters. And, within days, many outdoor columnists were condemning it — particularly those in Michigan, where much of the footage was shot. "CBS Report on Hunters Hits a New Low," proclaimed the column of *Detroit Free-Press* outdoor writer Tom Opre two days after the show aired. Ten days after the program, a statement from OETA-TV in Oklahoma City quoted the president of the Oklahoma Wildlife Federation and sent a copy to Amory: "Quite frankly, there are some people in the anti-hunting movement that are in it for the dollars. . . . That would motivate a lot of people to become involved. I'm not talking about the concerned people that send in the dollars. I'm talking about the Cleveland Amorys and people like that, that sparkplug in the anti-hunting movement." Other wildlife and hunting groups sent similar letters to media outlets across the country.

The deluge of letters prompted a CBS News official to issue a statement that said the network had received more than one thousand letters about the special, with the ratio of negative to positive at six to four. He said the New York office alone received one hundred calls. About 80 percent complained about the program.

Chicago Tribune television columnist Gary Deeb noted that the program touched off a rare and bitter ideological debate among hunters, advocates of animal protection, gun lobbyists, and gun supporters. Deeb quoted an unnamed CBS official as saying that the sponsorship withdrawal would not affect future CBS News programs: "It's clearly a campaign to intimidate."

Not everyone who spoke out was against the show. Author and historian Garry Wills, in a column titled "The Gun Nuts of Autumn," noted the special also pointed out that large numbers of people are killed in hunting accidents each year. But Wills was particularly outraged by the fact that several sponsors pulled their advertising from the show: "Big companies like Datsun ran scared, yielding to pressure," he wrote. "Guns not only kill people; they try to kill television documentaries." Wills asked, "How many other producers will risk the gunman's ire? There is something deeply emotional, sentimental and pathological about the gunmen's fear that they will be deprived of their weapons." Wills congratulated Block Drug for refusing to withdraw its advertising.

Time magazine wrote about the controversy and quoted an NRA official as saying the publicity it generated helped membership. "Hunters are not the slobs and killers that the show made us out to be," the unnamed NRA official said. "'Guns of Autumn' didn't show people going out and really enjoying the companionship of others, the wonders of being outdoors and how the hunter has restored the wildlife habitat."

But the debate over *The Guns of Autumn* was far from over. The Federal Communications Commission had initially said it would investigate the program to see if it violated the federal Fairness Doctrine, a rule requiring the broadcast media to offer equal time, on shows airing political opinions, for contrary political viewpoints. But three weeks after the airing of the program, the FCC said it would delay a decision until after the airing on September 28 of another CBS documentary about hunting called *Echoes of the Guns of Autumn*. This program centered on the controversy generated by *The Guns of Autumn* and aired brief interviews with some animal activists — including Amory — and also with Drasnin, the show's writer/producer. But it also attempted to give "equal time" to the hunters and the hunting lobby.

Eventually Michigan hunters, under the auspices of the Michigan United Conservation Clubs, brought a defamation case against CBS, saying the network conspired to slander and libel Michigan hunters. The lawsuit sought damages of $300 million on behalf of the state's licensed hunters. More than five years later, in July of 1980, a federal district court in Michigan granted summary judgment in favor of CBS News. The decision was later affirmed by the U.S. Court of Appeals for the Sixth District.

The reaction to *The Guns of Autumn* revealed the depths of the rift between the hunting lobby and animal activists — and it reminded everyone of the large numbers of people who belonged to both groups. Later that year, Drasnin received a Directors Guild of America award for *The Guns of Autumn*, for outstanding direction of a news special, but questions remained: Did the overwhelmingly negative reaction to the special and the withdrawal of advertising serve as a deterrent to CBS and other networks when it came to airing future shows that focused on animals, hunting, or the environment? And did the show and the resulting reaction to it help fire up thousands of complacent hunters who now began to fear they could, at some point, be kept from participating in that activity? Those questions can never be answered, but *The Guns of Autumn* offered a hint of how ferocious the battle was becoming. And Amory would remain on the front lines.

▷ ▷ ▷ When it decided to focus its efforts on wildlife in addition to domestic pets, the Fund for Animals naturally became a target for the hunting and gun lobbies; and the power of those groups far outweighed that of scientists and doctors, some of whom criticized Amory's comments about the treatment of animals in laboratories.

But Amory's high-profile role also served the hunting and gun lobby — he provided a face and a name for their wrath. The outspoken and very visible

Amory was to them the living embodiment of greed and arrogance — a naive "bleeding heart" who represented everything negative in the animal-protection movement. No longer did animal-rights opponents have to direct their ire at vague and impersonal organizations or unknown lobbyists. They were unified in their anger at — some might say hate of — Amory. The start of an editor's column in *Field & Stream* sums up the tone and attitude of some of these writers: "Well, we suppose it was inevitable. Cleveland Amory and his happy band of dreamers in The Fund for Animals have called upon the nation to recognize the wolf as our 'National Mammal.'" The column ridicules the fund's "defense" of wolves, its argument that wolves and humans are similar in the organization of their social strata, and its explanation that wolves eliminate excess numbers in herds by preying on weak, sick, and old animals. "Right on, Cleve!" the editor writes, disagreeing with the latter premise and noting that, in reality, wolves are not such particular or delicate predators. "But how is Cleve going to explain to all of his 'show biz' pals . . . that the wolf is really a sterling character in spite of his somewhat brutal way of obtaining breakfast lunch and dinner. Don't worry. Old Cleve will think of something. A faster talker was never found outside a carnival."

The editor goes on to say that Amory convinces his "theatrical friends" — fund supporters Mary Tyler Moore, Katharine Hepburn, and Princess Grace of Monaco — that all hunters are "rural, red-necked, bib-overall-wearing yokels who sit on stumps swilling beer while enjoying the slaughter of animals." Yet, the editor notes, Amory would not dream of stereotyping other groups of people: "Those famous names would have nothing to do with a man who preached that all blacks have rhythm and are crazy about watermelon." Indeed, the testimonials of Amory's friends in Hollywood enraged some hunters and gun owners, who realized that star power gave publicity to Amory's cause. And they believed that most of the celebrities involved with Amory were fed lies about the cause.

In 1976, *Field & Stream* published a long article called "Cleveland Amory and the Kingdom of the Kind," focusing on what the reporter felt was fraud, hypocrisy, and lavish spending in the anticruelty movement overall. The reporter begins her argument by mentioning a recent *Los Angeles Times* exposé about rampant mismanagement by the Sacramento-based animal-protection group Animal Protection Institute of America, which, the *Times* article said, spent most of the money it raised on salaries for its employees. But as the article progresses, it also slams Amory, bringing up what the reporter felt was lavish spending on travel and items peripheral to the fund's mission. Clearly, the reporter was bothered by Amory's penchant for publicity: "Cleveland Amory has moved his crusade far afield from . . . early, rather narrow confines," she writes. "Judging by his increasing number of appearances on TV, radio, flower shows, college campuses and other public meetings, he is now heavily into the business of selling doctrine and copies of his new book, *Man Kind?* Here, as well as in his syndicated column, 'Animail,' Amory has been able to give his much-touted 'sardonic wit' full play. He has been able to increase his celebrity, travel around the country, pow-wow with actresses and generally achieve McLuhanesque fame. He may not take any direct salary from his work as President of the fund, but power and celebrity can be almost as worthwhile." Accompanying the article was a line drawing of an angelic Amory, complete with halo and wings, rising above a sea of well-dressed fat cats who hold signs that carry words like "bombast," "waste," "sophistry," "travel expenses," "propaganda," and the like.

Amory and Probst were meticulous in their record keeping and their spending, and it would have been difficult for anyone to find evidence of illegal or improper spending by the fund. And besides, neither was interested in material possessions. Later in his life, Amory was still living on royalties from various books (including three best sellers he wrote late in his life), from a small amount he made for his writing, and from what he earned on his investments. It allowed him to have a modestly furnished apartment in Manhattan, a car, and the luxury of dining out on most days.

The fact that he was a thorn in the side of many scientists, hunters, and gun lobbyists drove Amory to do more. For example, in the early chapters of *Man Kind?* he revisited the Hunt-the-Hunters Hunt Club he had aired eleven years earlier when he was a commentator on *Today* (which had so enraged hunters, who called NBC en masse to complain). To Amory, the commentary was still timely, and now he had a new generation of readers. Even the reporter of the long *Field & Stream* article alluded to the Hunt-the-Hunters Hunt Club, noting that a "TV critic" invented it "right before a nationwide audience at breakfast time." (When Amory first created the Hunt Club for *Today*, he did not yet work for TV *Guide*.)

The Hunt Club was revived with *Man Kind?* but in 1973, a year before the book's publication, Amory made some revisions to the club's philosophy, based on what he had seen and heard as president of the fund. In the *Sierra Club Wildlife Subcommittee Newsletter* (San Francisco Bay chapter),

Amory writes tongue in cheek about his updated Hunt-the-Hunters Hunt Club, mimicking arguments and phrases that hunters have repeated to him: "In the years since I have founded the Hunt-the-Hunters Hunt Club, many people have put the knock on us. I have myself, if you can believe it, been subjected to a steady barrage of pot shots from *bleeding hearts* and *hunter lovers,*" Amory writes, mimicking the name-calling that animal advocates are "bleeding hearts" and "Bambi lovers." Then he moves on to the responses from hunters when they are told their actions might lead to the extinction of some species: "It has been said, for example, that the Hunt-the-Hunters Hunt Club favors the extermination of hunters. Nothing could be further from the truth. . . . Hunt-the-Hunters Hunt Club has never once in its history to our certain knowledge favored the extermination of a single species. All we have ever sought to do each fall is to trim the herd and, sure as shooting, if we did not crop the surplus each year, nature would."

Besides, as a member of the Hunt-the-Hunter Hunt Club, Amory notes, it would be absurd and impractical for him and others like him to advocate the extinction of hunters: "If we exterminated hunters, what would we have for game?" he asks. He concludes that those who hunt hunters "are sportsmen. We love the outdoors and — this is the thing that the hunter never seems to realize — we love hunters."

Amory was fearless when it came to conveying his points, and he never backed down when he was criticized or ridiculed. Nor was he ever physically intimidated, even as he grew older. Amory's friend and colleague Lewis Regenstein said Amory never feared the prospect of violence against him, even though that possibility was very real. Regenstein said he did worry that Amory might one day be in the wrong place at the wrong time — that one of his adversaries would resort to physical violence. Regenstein doubted that anyone would hurt Amory on a premeditated basis but felt that such an act was possible in the heat of the moment. "He would go and give these speeches and demonstrations right there where the hunters were," Regenstein said. "He wasn't afraid of anyone."

Chapter 10 ▷ ▷ ▷ In the Belly of the Beast

> He was someone who gave me wise advice. I did not
> always listen to it. But one bit of advice was: you must
> never be concerned what people think of you. You
> must do what you think is right. And because of that I
> have a lot of enemies today. But I did the right thing.
>
> ▶ Activist PAUL WATSON

*A*lthough Amory's book *Man Kind?* never achieved the best-seller status of his early society trilogy, the book did firmly establish Amory as a key figure in the animal-rights movement. (According to one estimate, it sold about sixty-six thousand copies.) More important to him, though, was the fact that publicity about the book introduced many people to what he and others believed were the inhumane methods of killing frequently associated with hunting and trapping. Amory and others in the movement believed that cruel practices continued in part because the public was not aware of them.

But his growing status as the leader of a social movement also placed him squarely on the radar of those who disagreed with him. While Amory did not necessarily mind this (and, in fact, often enjoyed their taunts and their accusations), many scientists, hunters, and gun owners were watching his every move. They were certainly reading what he wrote in his columns for *TV Guide* and the *Saturday Review*.

By the early 1970s, Amory had been a regular columnist for *Saturday Review* for two decades. His friend and editor Norman Cousins let him write about whatever he wanted, and did little or no editing of his column. But the readership of that magazine was not the same as the mainstream readership of *TV Guide*. *Saturday Review* readers were more upscale and more liberal in their political beliefs than their counterparts at *TV Guide*—and Cousins, a legendary editor, made no secret of the fact that he was antiwar and actively opposed what he considered lax pollution regulations, cigarette advertising, and violence in the media. In fact, Cousins once said that he edited his magazine "to please myself." The circulation of Cousins's magazine was much smaller than that of TV Guide, which had more than 10 million readers by the 1960s and nearly twice that by the late 1970s. (Under Cousins's editorship, though, circulation of Saturday Review grew from 20,000 in the 1950s to a high of 600,000 by the time he retired in 1977.) So Amory's occasional comments and complaints about animal cruelty in his Saturday Review column did not create much of a stir. In fact, he was probably preaching to the choir, for the most part.

The content of Amory's Saturday Review column changed little over the two-decade span in which he wrote it, but the column went by various names. It started under the name Trade Winds during the early and mid-1950s, was called First of the Month in the early 1960s, and, as the name indicates, was published near the beginning of the magazine once a month. By 1974, Amory's column was known as Curmudgeon-at-Large. He ended the column in 1977, the same year Cousins retired permanently as editor of the magazine. (Cousins did not edit the magazine from 1971 to 1973.) Amory was gradually changing his image once again. In his Saturday Review columns and during his guest television appearances, he had established himself as somewhat of a good-natured curmudgeon — someone who, in a light-hearted way, grumbled about contemporary society — its attitudes, its conventions, and its newfangled tools. He began driving home this image by the mid-1970s, and it may have been the right time. Born in 1917, he was entering his fifties by the late 1960s; by the 1970s, he was perhaps the proper age for a curmudgeon.

Amory's Saturday Review column in these later years still contained brief items about plays, film, television, and speeches, as it had before. But Amory began focusing more on humorous advertisements he found, slips of the tongue that were quoted in magazines and newspapers, and other items that reflected the absurdity of modern life. For instance, in 1970, he quoted a want-ad that a reader had sent him from the Ramona (Calif.) Sentinel: "WANTED: Part-time housekeeper for retired Nudist Non-Smoker. Must have valid California Operator's license." Amory's reply? "The license of the freeway, we say, is not a license for licentiousness." Amory loved double entendres, particularly unintended ones. He quoted this one from a television listing guide in the Jackson (Mich.) Citizen-Patriot: "Mon. — A Private's Affair ('59): Sal Mineo, Barbara Eden. Uncle Sam's swinging privates and how the gals went for them." Amory's observation: "We can only hope it was rated G — for, you know, the general public."

Double entendres and spoonerisms were not limited to the nation's magazines, newspapers, and signs, as Amory noted once, quoting an envelope addressed to the Fund for Animals: "Fun Fur Animals," the envelope said. Amory's response in the magazine: "At any rate, the letter didn't start 'Dear Fur.' One letter to the fund did come, though, addressed to the attention of—and we didn't make it up, either—'Miss Treatment.'"

Part of Amory's curmudgeonly demeanor depended on observations about the changing role of women in the 1970s. At times, he could not resist commenting on the current state of affairs regarding feminism. In one Curmudgeon-at-Large column in 1975, he quoted a *Houston Post* column a reader had sent: "A mercifully unnamed Houston policeman, being interviewed by a TV newsman on whether he could trust women police officers in patrol cars: 'Well, I guess we'll just have to feel them out to see how they're going to do.'" Amory's response? "Sounds like to us like a Msdemeanor." In another, he quoted at length two writers who wrote—pro and con—about the Miss America pageant, a contest that was beginning to be criticized in the era of women's liberation. On the "pro" side, *Sports Illustrated* writer Frank Deford noted that the pageant could be lucrative for its winners, that it offered women what athletics offered men, and that it provided entertainment. On the "con" side, author Mort Weisinger said that the pageant discriminated against black women and—oddly—against women with large busts. (Weisinger, who was serious, noted that small-busted women nearly always win the title of Miss America. He also called the pageant "cold," "humorless," and "uptight.")

Amory was born and raised during an era of some stifling assumptions about women's roles, and he was somewhat startled by aspects of the feminist movement of the 1960s and 1970s and the changing role of women. On talk shows, he frequently decried what he thought was the increasingly graphic content of television. But his political views were liberal on most topics, and, as his stepdaughter observed, he certainly believed that women and men were equal intellectually and should be given equal educational and vocational opportunities.

▷ ▷ ▷ Although Amory's career had undergone several dramatic changes throughout his life, there was one constant in each reincarnation: he always used humor to convey his ideas—at times, under some less than comical circumstances. It was this humor that was Amory's signature—it was what made him so readable and so colorful. And nothing pleased Amory as much as reacting to the questions and comments of others, whether it was in debates with those who opposed him about animal rights or in his Mail Bag column in *TV Guide*. So it is no surprise that he would combine his animal-rights beliefs, his quick wit, and his curmudgeonly demeanor to publish in 1976 a compilation of the best of his newspaper column, Animail.

In the column, Amory took questions about — as that name indicates — animals. Much of the column's subject matter was pets, but Amory of course also loved to talk and write about wild animals. In his book *Animail*, he was able to answer questions, pontificate against such phenomena as bullfighting, and, in general, give animals a lot of positive public relations. At times, though, people mentioned in the book do not come off as well. Amory delighted in stories like the one about the whaling captain who harpooned a pregnant whale; while the crew attempted to get the animal aboard, the fetus shot out of the whale's belly and onto the ship, decapitating the captain in the process.

Animail was the perfect forum for Amory because he loved communicating directly with this audience. And, before the age of the Internet, he may have been ahead of his time — the audience loved interacting with him. Amory could not have created the questions that some readers asked — they were often perceptive, funny, and sometimes just strange. Take, for example, one question he answered in a section in his book titled "Animals and Their Famous Friends": "Q: Is it true that Sammy Davis Jr., has a dog that is also [like Davis] blind in one eye? — T. N., Tuscaloosa, ALA." Amory, who always provided detailed and complete answers, replied yes — and the dog, a Lhasa apso, was named Thurston, because he was always thirsty. He added the background of Davis's accident that had cost him an eye and noted that the Davis family had four other dogs, all poodles. Other readers wanted to know if domesticated pets are left- or right-pawed, why some cats watch television, and whether any type of animal can be housebroken. The questions were diverse, but to Amory, however, one common theme emerged: that in temperament and demeanor, animals were usually superior to their human counterparts.

As a *Los Angeles Times* reviewer wrote, "Cleveland Amory, famous for his discriminating enjoyment of high society in books such as 'The Proper Bostonians' and 'Who Killed Society?' has an extraordinarily unprejudiced view of the animal kingdom. His sociability, which extends, paradoxically, to all kinds of animal life, falls short of including human beings who are cruel to animals and, by implication, to one another."

A thumbnail review in *Library Journal* sums up the book:

This compilation of questions and answers from Amory's newspaper column, "Animail," is fun to read or just browse through. Both amusing and sad anecdotes about wild and domestic creatures of all sorts, an astrology chart to match pets and owners, occasional poems, stories, and even a recipe for vegetarian dog biscuits are included in the six major sections. Amory wittily describes a seeing-eye cat, a dog who fought in the Civil War, the low "divorce" rate among penguins and more.

Although he had always been careful not to discriminate or show favoritism when it came to animals and species, Amory — the dog owner — indicates in the book that he has a soft spot in his heart for cats. That may have been a harbinger of things to come regarding both his personal life and his career.

▷ ▷ ▷ Heading the Fund for Animals was a learning experience for Amory. He was getting a crash course in the politics of various anticruelty organizations, and he had to navigate the internal politics of Washington, D.C. Lewis Regenstein, who ran the fund's Washington office, knew firsthand about the subtleties of Washington lobbying, but that was all new to Amory when he first founded the organization. What might have come more naturally to him, however, was public relations; Amory was a natural in getting the fund publicity, a knack that infuriated his critics and his opponents.

Amory — oblivious to criticism — may have believed the old adage that there is no such thing as bad publicity. He began writing letters to the editor to the *Washington Post* in response to stories it published about national and local issues regarding animals, and he certainly knew that a little controversy was bound to generate publicity. For instance, he was not afraid to cause a stir at an event covered by one of the *Post's* star reporters, Sally Quinn.

Amory had been invited to a Washington fund-raiser for the American Horse Protection Association, which featured an exhibition of horses painted or sculpted by famous artists. Proceeds from sales of the art were to go to save the lives of wild mustangs. A similar event on Long Island had been successful, and sponsors in Washington hoped the event at the Washington Gallery of Art would yield similar results. They did not count on the fact that Amory was always one to speak his mind, no matter what the circumstances. Under the headline "Horse Lovers Fight about Goose Hanging," Quinn's lead paragraph sums up the event: "It all started out as a high-minded fund-raising venture with Remingtons, Wyeths, and a Toulouse-Lautrec for sale. It ended up more like one of those cockfights that Cleveland Amory is so against."

Quinn went on to explain that one of the paintings, a $50,000 Remington, depicted a horse, all right—but it also showed the rider grabbing the neck of a goose, which hung by its feet from a beam. The painting, of course, caught Amory's eye: "I don't like my name being associated with a guy hanging a goose, no matter whether it's a Picasso, a Rembrandt, or what," he is quoted as saying. The comment caused a great stir among the event's planners, whose aim was to show "the nobility of the horse," as one planner said. Another of the event's planners was a bit more candid with her irritation at Amory: "Amory keeps complaining about 'you people who come down here in furs and don't care about horses,'" exclaimed a braless Mrs. Mac Vicker Snow of Oyster Bay. "'Why, I grew up in the Hunt Country of Far Hills. I could ride before I could walk. If he wants to see inhumanity, he should go to Vietnam. I'm getting so tired of the attitude.'"

As Quinn wrote, the brouhaha died down when Amory agreed to allow the painting to remain on the wall, provided he could post a signed note of his own under the price tag. "This picture illustrates a sad use of the mustang—for a despicable 'sport,'" it read.

Because of the controversy, the event—which under normal circumstances may have merited a two- or three-paragraph story, or none at all—was played prominently on the front page of the third section of the newspaper. Amory could not have been displeased by the publicity it generated.

Amory also long understood the impact of large numbers when making an argument. He never hesitated to offer them when discussing the large numbers of animals who were abused and killed inhumanely. He also knew how to deflect the influence of his opponents' numbers, and a common topic of debate between Amory and hunters in particular centered on the number of hunters in the United States and whether it was increasing or decreasing.

For example, in a radio debate between Amory and NRA president Harold Glassen, Glassen pointed out that 40 million people in the United States hunted birds and game each year—and they paid more than $145 million in taxes and licenses. That money, Glassen said, was returned to the wild in the form of animal conservation. "How much money has Amory's group put into conservation?" Glassen asked. "You get the impression from Mr. Amory that animals in the wild would die comfortably. . . . He doesn't realize that animals don't die of old age in the wild."

Amory, meanwhile, had heard these arguments many times. He noted that the hunting and gun lobbies greatly inflated the number of hunters each year, and he believed their ranks were actually declining. Further, as he said consistently, "conservation" was a term used by hunters and wildlife agencies simply to justify killing. As Amory was accustomed to saying, he would hate to see what would happen if hunters did *not* like animals, since they shot the animals they apparently did like.

He knew the impact of celebrity, thanks to his experience as a social historian and lecturer, and he consistently enlisted celebrities to help publicize the anticruelty cause: glamorous and well-known actresses Mary Tyler Moore, Doris Day, Amanda Blake, and many others donated their time and images to an extensive antifur campaign, and many other well-known actresses publicly supported other causes of the fund. Others sympathetic with the cause, such as Dick Cavett, Jack Paar, author Jacqueline Susann, and Betty White served at one time or another on the board of the fund. Katharine Hepburn, a longtime friend of Amory's, was at one time international chairwoman of the fund. (Cavett and other talk show hosts at the time, including Merv Griffin and Art Linkletter, had Amory on their shows and let him talk about his anticruelty efforts.)

But Amory also knew there were other ways to lure people to his cause — he had to appeal to whatever it was that interested *them*. As part of his "curmudgeon" image, Amory frequently conveyed his belief that children should, literally, be seen and not heard. While he was an animal lover, those positive feelings did not necessarily extend to children, who, he felt, were often spoiled by their parents and given far too many liberties. (One time he began his Curmudgeon-at-Large magazine column with an item about a national conference he attended for "non-parents." The conference, hosted by the "National Organization of Non-Parents," decried what it labeled "pro-natalism," defined as the belief that women's destiny is tied to reproduction, and that most people do not have free reproductive choice. The organization's slogan, "Communicate before you procreate — you *can* question the stork," was in earnest.)

Amory was smart enough to realize that many people had more positive attitudes toward children then he did. So he conveyed the idea that those who are cruel to animals can easily be cruel to children. In an article he wrote for the *Christian Science Monitor* in 1966 titled "From Human Society to Humane Society," Amory explains why he stopped writing about society and began writing about animal cruelty. He notes that Henry Bergh, who founded the American Society for the Prevention of Cruelty to Animals in 1883, also founded the first Society for the Prevention of Cruelty to Children. And, he adds, "Today those of us in the organized humane movement . . . believe, whatever our differences, in one basic creed — that the least cruelty to the least creature diminishes us all."

Amory was also quick to point out that federal legislation designed to protect animals creates in many people a false sense of security — that is, people support the legislation and read about its passage and naturally assume a protective law is in effect when exactly the opposite may be true, he wrote. He used as an example a bill passed in 1966 that prohibited the stealing of pets, some of which ended up being sold to laboratories. Although the bill carried amendments designed to provide for the humane treatment of laboratory animals, those amendments provided no protection during experimentation. Here, Amory appealed to readers and their own love for their cats and dogs, implying that they and their pets could be personally affected by anticruelty legislation and its loopholes.

▷ ▷ ▷ Running the Fund for Animals was more than a full-time job for Amory and Marian Probst. Amory was adamant that he could not take a salary for his work at the fund, even though his income from writing and other sources was relatively small. He was paid $350 a column by *TV Guide* instead of a regular salary, and only $15 per column for his syndicated Animail column. Probst remembered that Amory was often still writing his *TV Guide* column at 10:00 p.m., and she typed and retyped it into the night. Amory also earned some money for his lecturing — and it was relatively easy money since he was naturally a charismatic speaker who loved taking questions from audiences. But speeches were a double-edged sword for Amory. Because he traveled so frequently on the lecture circuit, he was able to give very similar versions of the same speech, although the talks had varying titles. But correspondence between Amory and officials of the speakers' bureaus representing him show that he occasionally frustrated bureau workers. They occasionally received complaints from audience members who believed Amory talked too much about animals or Israel and too little about television or society — charges that Amory always emphatically denied. Probst remembered one incident in which a big fan of Amory's once told him after a speech in Cleveland that he had heard him speak in his hometown of Pittsburgh and had enjoyed the talk so much that he had traveled to Cleveland to hear him again. But, he told Amory, the speech he gave in Cleveland was nearly identical to the one he had already heard in Pittsburgh, although the titles were different. With his verbal sleight of hand, Amory did not apologize but blamed the speakers' bureau for a mix-up: "Cleveland said, 'Sir, we have to get to the bottom of this,'" Probst remembered. "'These lecture agents have been getting away with murder for years. . . . Now you write down where you were when you heard that speech and I'll go right to the head person.'" He and the man shook hands.

Like most good speakers, Amory never lost his aptitude for improvisation, even late in his life. Walter Anderson, who was his editor at *Parade*, recalled the time Amory, in his seventies, was the guest of honor at an event where he was due to get an award. A harried Amory was running late and hurried to the podium, apparently thinking he was there to deliver some kind of speech: "I know why I'm here. You know why I'm here," Amory told the audience, launching into one of his standard speeches, but apparently *not* knowing why he was there. A gentleman next to him on the podium gently tugged at this sleeve and whispered that Amory was about to get an award. "And this award means something not just to me, but to each and everyone one of you," he continued, barely missing a beat.

Life at the Fund for Animals headquarters was chaotic. Phones were constantly ringing, new crises arose hourly, and bags of mail arrived each day. But Amory reveled in the confusion, and, with his eye for the absurd, his activities always became fodder for his writings and speeches. For instance, he frequently told the tale of how, on one of his busier days, he was in a hurry to fly out of Ohio to an engagement in another state. "To the airport!" he yelled to his limousine driver. Unfortunately, though, as both the driver and Amory learned when they arrived, he had jumped into the wrong limousine. It did not matter to Amory, who tried to reserve the man's services for future trips.

An article in *Publishers Weekly* in 1979 describes the lumbering Amory as he sat at his large wooden desk at fund headquarters, nearly hidden by mounds of papers and books: "His capacious room and the wooden desk he sits behind combine to shrink Cleveland Amory. He is further obscured by the disarray of industriousness around him. Piles of papers, files and books lie on available flat surfaces. Pictures, posters and newspaper clippings on the wall remind a visitor of Amory's passion for all creatures great and small." The usually polite Amory cannot stand up to shake hands — he is weighed down by a large black-and-white cat named Benedict who sits on his lap.

The reporter for this article was interviewing Amory because his newest book, *The Trouble with Nowadays: A Curmudgeon Strikes Back*, had just come out. It was in some ways a narrative version of Amory's short syndicated radio show, *Curmudgeon at Large*. The book allowed him to elaborate on some of his favorite rants as a curmudgeon: the changing role of women, bloated and inefficient government, children, and other favorite topics. One of the reasons for the popularity of Amory's grumpy persona was, no doubt, that he was usually funny and never bitter when enumerating his gripes. In *The Trouble with Nowadays*, however, some of that lighthearted humor had turned heavy — some of the book can be read, perhaps, as an occasionally unfunny diatribe.

The Trouble with Nowadays, published in 1979, was written during what may have been one of the most depressing times in Amory's life. The fund, founded in 1967, went through some tough times during its first five or six years of existence, and running it required nearly all of Amory's and Probst's time. Beyond that, though, Amory's professional career was undergoing yet another metamorphosis in the mid- and late 1970s. His employment with *TV Guide* ended in the summer of 1976, and his column in *Saturday Review* was discontinued a year later with the retirement of Norman Cousins as editor. Probst remembered decades later that Amory was not sorry to see the *TV Guide* column go — it required a lot of work for little compensation, although it certainly gave Amory a national platform. Amory never used the magazine to directly publicize his activism, but he did insert occasional, subtle proanimal phrases in his reviews — such as the idea that he had "rooted for the ledge" when a hunter who appeared in one show nearly fell off a precipice — and he was able to review shows that featured animals. Little or no fanfare accompanied Amory's departure as television critic after the 1976 television season, although he did write a few feature-length stories for *TV Guide* later on, indicating that he and editorial director Merrill Panitt still had a positive relationship after he left the magazine.

It is impossible to determine whether *TV Guide* received letters complaining about Amory's activism, although among Amory's papers is a copy of a letter from Panitt to Joan Silaco of New York, dated October 19, 1976. Silaco apparently wrote to Panitt and enclosed a newspaper clipping stating that TV *Guide* had received eleven thousand letters — mostly from hunters — about Amory's TV *Guide* columns. Panitt responded that the figure was wrong and that the magazine had received "more like 100." "It was mutually decided that because of his time-consuming efforts on behalf of animals and because TV Guide was interested in finding a new critic, Mr. Amory would not longer write regularly for the magazine. . . . Please don't believe everything you read in gossip columns."

By the 1970s, the biggest change in Amory's life was the end of his marriage to Martha Hodge Amory, from whom he separated in 1975. The two were divorced two years later. The Amorys had been married for twenty-two years, although they had lived apart for the last several of those years. For many years, Martha Amory had been a faithful companion to her husband, serving as his unofficial editor, sharing his interest in animal rights, and accompanying him to a variety of social and cultural events. Martha's daughter, Gaea, believes the marriage ran out of steam, in no small part because of Amory's philandering. But one might also suppose that Amory harbored some animosity toward Martha, based on a possible reference to her in one of the chapters of *The Trouble with Nowadays*. Amory writes in first person but adopts the persona of a fictional member of a gentlemen's club who is appalled by many conventions of current society. In a mock discussion of "types" of women, Amory writes, presumably tongue in cheek, "when you're talking women, right at the start you're talking nice girls, and you're also talking the other kind. . . . I don't care how far this damn liberation goes. Even your nice girl category, as a matter of fact, breaks down into at least four subcategories. At the top you've got your real ladies, and then underneath them you've got, in order, your ordinary women, your shop girls and finally, your flibbertigibbets." ["Flibbertigibbet" is defined as a silly, flighty person.] Then Amory gets personal — sort of. His persona in the book notes that he has been married twice: first to "Cornelia" and then to "Muffie." (Amory's first wife's name was Cora, and his second wife's, Martha.) The Amory character is not charitable to either wife, and Muffie bears the brunt of his resentment. Cornelia, he writes, "wasn't a flibbertigibbet. . . . She wasn't the brightest woman in the world, and God knows she wasn't the prettiest, and she would try the patience of Job . . . but the point is she was no flibbertigibbet." Muffie, on the other hand, "was a flibbertigibbet. Honestly, she didn't have the sense God gave little fishes. It wasn't so much she didn't think —

she literally couldn't think." Why did he marry her? "Because love is blind," he said, answering his own question. "But the only kind who ever should have married Muffie should have been blind and deaf. God, how that woman could talk. . . . You really can't imagine what it was like, trying to think what was going on in her mind, at the same time that awful little baby voice was going on and on."

The descriptions of the fictional wives seem uncharacteristically bitter for the usually affable Amory. Amory said in interviews, though, that he was not necessarily the book's narrator; instead, he assumed the voice of many of the curmudgeonly, conservative types he had met at men's social clubs. "All the bores I've known in clubs throughout my life were more funny to me than boring, and I wrote a book about what they think of modern times," he said.

The Trouble with Nowadays itself was interpreted differently by different reviewers. The book, overall, was not reviewed in as many publications as most of Amory's previous books, nor did it sell as well. But, for the most part, it received positive reviews. The reviewer for *Library Journal* noted that it is "hard to imagine anything more boring than having to listen to someone who thinks like Archie Bunker explain what's wrong with the modern world," but that Amory's satire "manages not only to keep torpor at arm's length, but to actively entertain." *Best Sellers* called Amory a "lovable lunatic. . . . Amory is ludicrous and lucid." In a thumbnail review of the book in 1981, when it was published as a paperback, the *New York Times*, also, reacted positively: "[Amory] is one of those rare writers who can illuminate a deep moral indignation with hilarious anecdotes and sardonic wit."

In the *Publisher's Weekly* interview, Amory told the reporter, presumably tongue in cheek, that change is never for the better. The only change for the better in his lifetime, he added, was the invention of Scrabble. (Marian Probst recalled that Amory once vainly tried to win at that game with the unlikely word "underailed." His rationale? He had recently read an account of a train accident in which several cars were forced off the track while others, a rail official explained, were "underailed.")

In 1975, Amory moved to an apartment on Central Park South overlooking the park, two blocks from the fund's offices near Carnegie Hall. Despite the prestigious address, his friends say that he lived modestly—and, as one reporter noted in a 1991 story, the apartment was hardly lavishly decorated; in fact, it was barely decorated at all. "The walls are painted a dull dark brown and are hung with countless cutesy animal pictures. But then, what did you expect?" He did insist on having a car, although he was a terrible driver late in his life, as one friend noted, and spent much time at the Harvard Club in New York. Despite his longtime use of the club, Amory was none too pleased that it was decorated with the stuffed heads of wild animals. He liked to say that those trophies on the wall bore an amazing resemblance to some of the club's older members.

▷ ▷ ▷ Most histories of the animal-rights movement in the United States note that the 1970s were a pivotal decade for it, owing to a combination of societal and cultural factors. In their history of the movement, James M. Jasper and Dorothy Nelkin note that the cultural atmosphere of the 1970s was ripe for increasing activism in anticruelty efforts. That decade brought with it a disdain for conformism and large bureaucratic organizations; a questioning of authority and the way things had always been done; and an ambivalence about science and technology. "The critiques of animal research picked up many of the same themes," they write. Other issues of the 1970s also had an impact on the growth of the animal-protection movement, including the momentum of liberation itself. The 1970s brought expansion of the civil rights, feminist, and environmental movements and increasing involvement by many in social and cultural reform. In the mid-1970s and early 1980s came the formation of more radicalized animal-rights and environmental groups, including People for the Ethical Treatment of Animals (PETA) and the Animal Liberation Front. Greenpeace, considered by many a radical environmental group, also was formed during this era. In 1977, Australian ethicist and writer Peter Singer wrote a pivotal *New York Review of Books* essay, "Animal Liberation," which had been published in his book about the ethics of the animal movement. The essay was widely read and discussed by activists and others involved in the movement. Singer has continued over the decades to write and edit books and articles about the ethics and morality of animals and animal rights and grounds his writings on basic ethical theories, basing his arguments for the humane treatment of animals on a utilitarian perspective — that the suffering of animals should be taken into account in their treatment. "Ethical decisions should be made by adding up all pleasures and pains that would result from different choices, and choosing the option yielding the greatest aggregate pleasure," as Jasper and Nelkin summarize it. Under Singer's theory, animal experimentation, for example, need not be banned completely but instead may be permitted if suffering is limited and the research is likely to yield practical results — that is, if the benefits ultimately outweigh the pain. Singer was the first to widely use and pan the concept of "speciesism," the idea that human beings are naturally superior to animals, thus justifying inhumane treatment of animals. As the name indicates, speciesism is to some people an injustice parallel to sexism or racism. Singer writes: "Speciesism is, in brief, the idea that it is justifiable to give preference to beings simply on the grounds that they are members of the species *Homo sapiens.*" In his 2006 book, *In Defense of Animals,* Singer goes into great detail about the arguments for and against speciesism. He writes, for example, that one defense of speciesism is that just as a parent has a special obligation to protect his or her own children over the children of others, we have a special obligation to protect those in our own species. Singer quotes supporters of speciesism as saying that ethics arise from an unwritten social contract stating, "If I do not harm you, you will not harm me." Because animals cannot participate in this contract, we have no special duty to them. But the most commonsense argument given against granting full rights to animals is simply that animals do not have the powers that humans have to communicate, argue, or reason, nor do they have, obviously, a sense of justice or high intelligence. The response to that, Singer writes, is that some humans, also, do not have those qualities (an argument that Amory frequently made, albeit tongue in cheek).

In his rejection of speciesism, Singer is careful not to accept ludicrous contentions. For instance, he writes, animals and humans do not have equal interests across the board; it would be absurd to give animals many of the rights of humans, including the right to vote, freedom of speech, and the like, just as it is ridiculous to give such rights to small children. He summarizes his beliefs: "The rejection of speciesism . . . requires us to make only the more limited and defensible claim that where animals and humans have similar interests — we might take the interest in avoiding physical pain as an example — those interests are to be counted equally. We must not disregard or discount the interests of another being, merely because that being is not human."

Of course, the history of the animal rights and protection movement worldwide is a complex one that consists of various definitions of terms and philosophies. On its website, the Animal Liberation Front labels itself an "animal rights" group that differs from what it calls "animal welfare" groups such as the Humane Society of the United States. The website explains the group's views of the difference: "Animal welfare theories accept that animals have interests, but allow these interests to be traded away as long as there are some human benefits that are thought to justify that sacrifice. Animal rights means that animals, like humans, have interests that cannot be sacrificed or traded away simply because they benefit others." The website also defines ALF as a group devoted to taking "direct action on behalf of animals," and one that vehemently opposes considering animals as property. (The group has acknowledged it has broken into animal laboratories to free animals and destroy records, and it has been accused of more violent acts, including arson.) In May of 2005, the FBI and Bureau of Alcohol, Tobacco, and Firearms declared ALF a terrorist group.

PETA, meanwhile, describes itself as an "animal rights" group because "animals are not ours to use for food, clothing, entertainment, experimentation or any other purpose." The most well-publicized act of PETA over the years has been the splashing of paint on women wearing furs as they walked down city streets. On its website, it states that the animal-rights movement "is nonviolent. One of the central beliefs shared by most animal rights activities is the belief that we should not harm any animal — human or otherwise."

All successful social movements have philosophical underpinnings — and leaders of those movements can have certain deep-seated beliefs without even being able to give name to those beliefs or describe them in words. When Amory was young and first became active in the movement, the environment for activists was simpler. Amory rarely spoke or wrote about the philosophical reasons for his beliefs. But because the Fund for Animals was coming of age during a time of great growth of anticruelty organizations, he could not avoid the politics or conflicting beliefs of other similar organizations. But Amory's philosophy was a curiously contradictory one. One of the reasons he formed the fund was that he believed current animal organizations were toothless and did not go far enough in their anticruelty efforts. Yet he certainly was a member of the utilitarian or pragmatist wing of activism that states humans can use animals when the benefit outweighs their suffering, or when their suffering is kept at a minimum. The Fund for Animals sought to ensure animal welfare through legislation, legal action, negotiation, and protest. Consequently, Amory was willing to compromise on certain issues. For example, like most other anticruelty activities, he did not believe in the concept of zoos and thought it cruel to keep animals penned outside their natural habitats. And he certainly did not believe in routine radical actions to convey his point or to get results; in that way, he can be considered a moderate. Judy Ney, a friend of Amory's and a member of the Fund for Animals and the HSUS boards, shares Amory's philosophy—but she also believes more radical ways of thinking and acting can ultimately help more middle-of-the-road groups like the fund: "The far edges of a movement . . . push people toward the center," she believes. Amory was not religiously devout in the conventional sense, but he did grapple with the question of whether animals had souls. He was Episcopalian, but as his friend Edward Walsh noted, that was the religion of people in his social class, and if he did attend church on holidays, it was for social reasons rather than reasons of faith. Still, Amory was perplexed over the idea that humans were actually God's chosen species. Historically, some of the leading animal-protection agencies of the twentieth century had religious roots: the HSUS — which was formed in 1954 after it split from the American Humane Association — was founded as a "ministry" for animals by Coleman Burke, who was head of the American Bible Society. John Hoyt, a president of the HSUS from 1970 to 1996, was a Presbyterian minister; his successor, Paul G. Irwin, HSUS president from 1996 until 2004, was a Methodist minister.

Amory's friends and colleagues acknowledge today that his attitude about eating meat and wearing clothes made from some animal by-products would not fly today, so to speak, in the animal movement. During the last decade or so of his life, after groups like PETA were formed and the movement grew, Amory was sometimes asked by interviewers why he ate meat, and why he wore clothing made of wool. (He was vehemently opposed to the wearing of fur.) He frequently made a joke of it, saying at times that his cat was a carnivore and so was he, but the truth is that many in the movement gave Amory a pass on his consumption of meat and animal by-products because of his age, Probst said. When Amory first became active in the anticruelty movement as a young man, vegetarianism was not considered an element of the animal-protection movement, and if vegetarians of the era avoided eating meat, they usually did so for personal health reasons rather than philosophical ones. As the movement matured into the 1970s and 1980s, few leaders of it could get away with eating or wearing any animal products. Today, in fact, many believe in veganism, which prohibits the eating of all animal products, including eggs, dairy products, honey, and others. (Probst remembers running across the street during a breakfast business meeting to seek out an omelet for breakfast. One of her colleagues who saw her vowed to keep her "shameful secret.") But the respect others had for Amory's age and for his activities during the latter part of his life allowed him to maintain his lifetime dietary habits as a meat eater.

And while Amory did not routinely pose spiritual questions to those he met, he obviously had given thought to such issues and how they related to animals. He was quoted in one interview about a disagreement he had with a Catholic priest about the church's teachings that animals had no souls: "I told the good Father that if he and I were going in the future to some wonderful Elysian Field and the animals were not going to go anywhere, that was all the more reason to give them a little better shake in the one life they did have," he said. In comments he made during Amory's memorial service, Amory's friend Ed Ney remarked that Amory, a few months before his death, was happy to receive a letter from Sister Joyce Munson, a nun in Greenville, South Carolina. She wrote that after much thought and prayer — and, apparently, after communication with Amory — she had concluded that animals do indeed have souls and will go to heaven, where we will see them after our own death. Amory responded to her as follows: "What a delight to receive your letter and read your thoughts on animals and heaven. Coming from a higher authority, as it were, I'm taking your opinion as gospel. That it matches my own is icing on the cake. In any case, I'm most appreciative of your taking the time to write me and I look forward to meeting you and your animals in the faraway future when we can crow over the fact that we were right after all."

Amory at Black Beauty Ranch with his
granddaughter, Zoe, who is riding a rescued pony.
From the personal collection of Gaea Leinhardt.

Chapter 11 ▷▷▷ Getting Their Goats

> The man [Cleveland Amory] is a not altogether
> domesticated being himself.
>
> ▸ Reporter PATT MORRISON, as she wrote
>   about Amory's attempt to rescue 3,000
>   wild goats on San Clemente Island

*A*mory's longtime regular writing jobs — his columns in both *Saturday Review* and *TV Guide* — were gone by the end of 1977, but that by no means meant he stopped writing. He wrote a regular Los Angeles Times Syndicate column about celebrities and Hollywood called Status Quotes, and he kept turning out freelance articles for national publications. Whether he liked it or not, he was still seen as a chronicler of the rich and famous; until late in his life, he would never lose the reputation as the social historian who had written the trilogy about American's blue bloods.

Amory still lectured extensively, not only around the country, but occasionally on cruise ships. In 1977, he was one of seven personalities who lectured on the luxury liner *Queen Elizabeth 2*. The job not only gave Amory the opportunity to enjoy, gratis, an eighty-one-day cruise to four continents, but it also served as fodder for his writing. Certainly Cleveland Amory could never spend nearly three months captive with thirteen hundred of the wealthiest people in the world and remain mum about it. In a twelve-hundred-word Travel essay for *New York* magazine, Amory offers a glimpse into the world of the QE2, where the highest-priced cabin, he notes in the second paragraph of the story, goes for $125,000. The ship comes complete with fully equipped gymnasium, golf driving range, a "host of masseurs," and, of course, an overabundance of caviar (1,150 pounds of it) and champagne (2,750 bottles). Despite every luxury they could possibly want, Amory implies, many of the wealthy passengers are not content — they still strive to one-up fellow passengers when it comes to spending. In Hong Kong, one passenger purchased more than $90,000 worth of imperial jade, "a fact that she worked casually into her every ensuing conversation, " he writes.

During that same year, Amory wrote an article for *Esquire* about the Italian-made Stutz, one of the most expensive cars in the world. Uncharacteristically for Amory, but in keeping with the tone of *Esquire*, then considered a "men's" magazine, it was full of off-color references and double entendres. In the lead of the story, for example, he notes that anyone who enters the Stutz showroom to look at the $100,000 car is immediately told the following by the salesman: " 'The man who drives a Stutz and can't get laid is dead.' " The car, Amory is told, "is the ultimate male phallic symbol." Amory goes on to identify some of the celebrities who own the car (Frank Sinatra, comedian Dick Martin, Evel Knievel) and the demographics of the owner: a man "forty-five or over, who probably has a young lady with him who is at least fifteen or twenty years his junior" — and a man who no doubt wears Gucci loafers and a Rolex watch.

Since he coedited *Celebrity Register* in 1963, Amory maintained that celebrities and movie stars had replaced America's well-bred blue bloods as the country's "aristocracy." So it was natural that Amory, the social critic, would write about celebrities. He did so in several magazines and in a regular column in the *Los Angeles Times*. Besides, because of his status as a writer, lecturer, and man-about-town, he knew many celebrities personally. His column Status Quotes ran about 750 to 800 words and usually opened with a five- or six-paragraph item about one star in particular, then went into brief one- or two-paragraph gossipy items. In one typical column he catches up with Ginger Rogers, who was appearing in Los Angeles in a nightclub revue. In a brief interview, he asks Rogers, then fifty-five, why she keeps dancing and wants to know her opinions about such topics as marriage and the current morality. (Rogers had been married five times.) She responds, perhaps ironically, that she is a religious person who does not take relationships lightly. "But that's just the point," she says. "I married them." Amory also writes about a recent survey by a group called Man Watchers, Inc., that compiled the names of the ten most watchable men. In another column, he conducts a brief interview with Charo, the flamboyant wife of bandleader Xavier Cugat. The reason? Amory had recently learned that, per minute, she was the highest-paid performer in the world (earning more per minute than Barbra Streisand, Elton John, and Lassie, he notes).

Although much of Amory's freelance writing in the late 1970s focused on the rich and famous, the bulk of his time was spent raising money for the Fund for Animals and identifying causes on which to spend that money.

During that time, the fund was still struggling but was about to begin coming of age, thanks in large part to Amory, the natural public relations man.

▷ ▷ ▷ It would be impossible to overestimate the effect Amory's own celebrity status and his contacts had on his anticruelty efforts. They certainly gave him access to talk about the cause on the many daytime and nighttime talk shows that aired in the mid- and late 1970s; but to have key television and movie stars lend their names and faces to a cause was priceless. Animals were almost always photogenic, and the perceived abuse of them, on the face of it, always horrendous. And people like Bob Barker, longtime host of several game shows including *The Price is Right*, allowed their beliefs in the animal-welfare movement to seep into their profession. Barker would not allow fur coats as gifts on his shows, nor would he slip a fur coat onto the winner of the Miss America pageant when he was host.

Late in his life, Amory reminisced that the first dozen years or so of existence of the fund were tough. The organization had billed itself as one that would impose change through "litigation, legislation, education and confrontation." During that first decade, "confrontation" did not exactly lead the list, although one of Amory's favorite mantras was that the fund needed to "put cleats" on the "little old ladies in tennis shoes" who supported animal welfare. In other words, he wanted to give donors and supporters some clout in accomplishing their goals and improving life for animals. As he acknowledged later, though, even he had no idea what hard work lay ahead for the fund and its supporters. "Looking back to those days, I don't think I could imagine the kinds of confrontation we would later have." The year 1979 was pivotal for the fund: it ushered in an era of aggressive activism for the organization, although others might term it radicalism. And it all began with a few rabbits.

Amory was an equal-opportunity animal lover who did not favor any one species — his efforts on behalf of wolves and other wild animals attest to that. And he often could sense intelligence and other personality characteristics in animals that others overlooked. Christopher Byrne, who ran the Black Beauty Ranch animal sanctuary for many years, said that Amory had a deep insight into many animals and often saw unique qualities in certain species. Amory insisted that prairie dogs, for instance, were particularly fascinating and had interesting personalities. A longtime dog lover and dog owner, Amory had a soft spot in his heart for two types of animals in particular:

rabbits and cats. He believed that domesticated rabbits and cats were partic-ularly defenseless and completely reliant on the kindness and care of human beings for comfort and survival. So he could not have been pleased when he got a call from a woman in New York about some abused rabbits. But the call, indirectly, led to a big step by the fund toward more aggressive activism.

As Julie Marshall explained in her book *Making Burros Fly*, a woman named Caroline Gilbert called the fund one day after she had discovered seven dead rabbits that had been abused by a man who was breeding them and selling them for two dollars apiece as possible Easter gifts. When the fund received the call, Amory was already very aware that life was cheap for rabbits—millions were abused and killed each year for meat, for drug and cosmetics testing, for their skins, and for holiday gifts. He even had a name for the fund's efforts to save rabbits: "Hope for the hopeless."

Amory suggested that Gilbert rescue the bunnies the easy way: by pay-ing the two dollars per animal that the man requested. Gilbert did that, and became so attached to the animals that she later went several steps further. With financial help from the fund, Gilbert turned a thirty-acre farm she had bought in Simpsonville, South Carolina, for raising horses into a rabbit shelter housing as many as two hundred rabbits, many of which were crip-pled, blinded, starved, and otherwise abused. Then other people who had learned of rabbit abuse staged rescues and dropped off the rabbits at what was becoming a sanctuary. Ultimately, the fund donated money so Gilbert could renovate facilities; she destroyed most of the small cages that housed the bunnies and instead gave them ten-foot-square wood-covered "rabitats" where they could run and exercise. The funding also allowed Gilbert to pur-chase fresh vegetables and fruit for the bunnies so they could live the rest of their lives in comfort.

If the fund started out small—literally—with its intervention efforts on behalf of rabbits, 1979 also brought with it an event that would put the orga-nization on the map and serve as a turning point in its overall philosophy: the rescue of more than one thousand baby harp seals off the ice floes of the Magdalen Islands in Canada.

▷ ▷ ▷ At Amory's memorial service in 1998, activist and conservationist Paul Watson, a cofounder of Greenpeace who later left that organization and bit-terly denounced it for its complacency, spoke with great reverence about his mentor and friend. Amory, he said, was "the most compassionate man that

I have ever had the privilege to know . . . a soldier of kindness. . . . a father to a movement of compassion that is changing the world." But the relationship between Amory and Watson was symbiotic. In 1977, when Amory, who was sixty, met Watson, twenty-seven, it was the perfect storm: a seasoned visionary and brilliant tactician met a brash and fearless young idealist on a crusade. The result was a dazzling spectacle that became one of the most talked-about news stories of the year, and one of the turning points in the modern history of animal welfare.

Amory had long heard about what he considered the senseless and brutal slaughtering of baby harp seals each March near Newfoundland; each year, herds of female seals struggled to the ice floes off the Magdalen Islands to give birth, and they remained there for several weeks until their babies could swim by themselves. And each year, teams of men in fishing vessels crashed through the ice and clubbed to death many of the week-old seals as their mothers watched. As Amory explained it, the Canadian government determined each year how many seals might be killed — in 1980, the limit was 180,000. The furry skins were used for linings in gloves and boots and to stuff children's toys.

As president of the Fund for Animals, Amory was used to hearing each day about horrendous acts of animal cruelty. Still, he was a realist who realized that tireless efforts often yielded only small victories. And fighting the abuse against the seals would seem to make little sense: the annual harp seal "harvest" involved the activities of another country, it was legal, and it had little effect on the daily life of most people. But then he met Paul Watson, a captain without a ship.

In the mid-1970s, Paul Watson was a full-time volunteer for the Greenpeace Foundation, an organization he had helped found in 1972. He led two Greenpeace seal campaigns to Labrador in 1976 and 1977 and served as first officer on several Pacific campaigns against Soviet whalers. Like many environmental and anticruelty activists, Watson embraced his volunteer work as an all-consuming lifestyle: his "homes" were either on Greenpeace ships or in Greenpeace offices or quarters. Eventually, Watson and Greenpeace parted ways after a bitter disagreement about the group's mission and philosophy (at one point, he called the organization the "Avon ladies of the environmental movement"). He thus became a captain without a ship, and an activist without an organization.

Watson knew of Amory through the latter's involvement with the passage of the Marine Mammal Protection Act, which prohibited Americans from participating in the seal slaughter. The two had corresponded briefly by the time Watson contacted Amory to explain his dilemma and describe his devotion to the baby seals. Amory requested a meeting with him, and the two soon hatched an unorthodox plan: they would get a ship, sail to the seals, and "paint" them with red organic vegetable dye, rendering their skins useless for commercial purposes.

Such a plan was easier said than done, though. The fund gave Watson $120,000 to purchase a retired fishing vessel in London. The 789-ton ship, called the *Westella* but renamed the *Sea Shepherd*, needed to be cleaned and renovated before it could make the trip from Hull, England, to Boston, where eighteen tons of concrete were poured into its bow to allow it to break through the ice for its journey. In March of 1979, the *Sea Shepherd* began its journey down the Gulf of St. Lawrence, west of Newfoundland and east of the Magdalen Islands, with Amory, thirty-two crew members, and a dozen reporters on board.

The fund got its money's worth with the ship. For four days and four nights, the *Sea Shepherd* rammed through the ice of the St. Lawrence, getting stuck on several occasions. Once, the crew literally went over the side and hacked at the ice with axes. As it neared its destination, the ship met with more ice that seemed insurmountable, and at the same time an ice storm hit. At their lowest point, the crew members witnessed what they viewed as a miracle: the storm subsided and actually broke the ice that was impeding the ship. Within a few hours, just after midnight, the *Sea Shepherd* reached the seal herd.

As Amory described it, the sight was breathtaking: the first things the crew saw were the bloody and mangled carcasses of dead baby seals, their mothers sitting nearby and moaning. But on the other side of the ship were baby seals frolicking on the ice. The crew immediately jumped off the ship and began playing with the seal pups, even bringing one on board to get its photo taken. Meanwhile, as planned, eight crew members donned survival suits, grabbed heavy canisters of dye, and fanned out, spraying a thousand baby seas with red dye. Everyone's morale was now soaring.

The crew's jubilation was short-lived, though. At daybreak the next day, Canadian police and government helicopters hovered over the scene. Watson and seven volunteer crew members of the *Sea Shepherd* were arrested, with Watson shackled to the deck of the Coast Guard cutter for hours in the subzero temperatures. He was later jailed. Eventually, Watson and his volunteers were fined a total of $5,000 for painting the seals, $5,000 for being within half a mile of a seal and not killing it (as Amory later wrote), and $200 for resisting arrest.

As Amory and the crew had suspected from the start, the publicity garnered by the trip made it worth all the trouble. The *Sea Shepherd* got international headlines and earned the seals the sympathy of millions who saw, read, or heard about their plight. "Save the seals" became embedded in the lexicon of popular culture. Footage of mangled baby seals was beamed into television screens all over the world, along with the angelic, furry faces of those who escaped slaughter, as Amory made the rounds on daytime talk shows. Afterward, Amory organized a postcard-writing campaign in which citizens were urged to tell the prime minister of Canada and the Canadian Tourist Industry Association that they would not visit the country unless the seal killing was stopped. More than 300,000 people wrote postcards. In London's Trafalgar Square, 70,000 demonstrators voiced their opposition to the killing. Thanks in part to the pressure resulting from the anti-seal-clubbing momentum, the Canadian government banned the clubbing in 1988 — but it was permitted again ten years year later.

As Amory knew, publicity for a cause had a way of reproducing itself and creating a domino effect. He also knew it could have a short shelf life. So a year after the event, he wrote a long article for *Good Housekeeping* in which he described the plight of the seals and replayed the fearless adventures of the *Sea Shepherd* crew. Accompanying the article was a large photo of Amory in a hooded coat, hugging a furry, white baby harp seal, whose whiskers and big eyes dominated the frame.

It is no surprise that Amory's relationship with Paul Watson did not end with the seal rescue. Amory by this time was not a young man, and while he did not actually climb off the *Sea Shepherd* to paint the seals, the trip itself was probably strenuous for him. He may have left the heavy lifting to younger men like Watson, but Amory shared Watson's enormous mental energy, drive, and dedication. And he was happy to listen to Watson's more radical views about how to accomplish the goals of rescuing animals in an increasingly technologically advanced and hostile world.

Watson was not about to stop at painting seals, and his arrest and incarceration were no deterrent to similar actions; in fact, they probably encouraged him. Flush with victory from the seal rescue — and a captain once again — Watson had another idea and hoped Amory could help: he wanted to use the

Sea Shepherd to go after a pirate whaling ship called the Sierra. The crew of that vessel had long violated international whaling laws and in a decade harpooned at least twenty-five thousand whales. Watson decided he wanted to find the Sierra and put an end to its illegal activities by ramming and sinking it.

At a meeting with Amory, however, Watson's mentor was not convinced of the wisdom of the action. First, he thought it would be dangerous for Watson and his crew; second, the illegality of the action concerned him, in part because he did not want to risk the Fund for Animals' tax-exempt status and in part because Amory was hardly a radical when it came to animal protection and did not believe in radical acts; and, finally, he doubted whether Watson and his crew would even be able to find the Sierra in the vast Atlantic Ocean. "It would be like finding a needle in a haystack," as Lewis Regenstein said decades later.

Watson understood Amory's concerns but knew he could change his mind. Amory "was not often asked to sponsor a sea battle," Watson wrote many years later. "Protecting animals was one thing; waging war on their behalf was a different matter entirely." Although Amory was reticent initially, "I could tell . . . the old bear would come around," Watson wrote. "It's his nature to be stubborn, but he hated the bloody whaler as much as I did." (It is ironic that Watson referred to Amory as a "bear"—it is the same analogy Amory used when he wrote about Watson in his autobiographical The Cat Who Came for Christmas. Amory said that his persnickety cat, Polar Bear, took an immediate liking to Watson: "Perhaps, I decided, because Paul looks rather like a bear—large in size that he is, however, Paul is strictly the 'Gentle Ben' kind of bear.")

Amory, indeed, did agree to give Watson financial support from the fund, and, in the summer of 1979, the Sea Shepherd, with an unarmed crew of sixteen, sailed off to find the Sierra, its bow packed with sixty-three tons of concrete. Miraculously, Watson and his crew found the rogue whaling ship off the coast of Portugal almost by accident—they had happened to stop to observe some frolicking sea turtles when one crew member spotted the boat. The Sea Shepherd first smashed into the Sierra's bow, taking off the harpoons and paraphernalia for killing whales. Then it rammed into its middle. The Sierra found its way to port with two huge holes in it, and later sank. But no one in either vessel was injured. "It was Moby Dick turned inside-out," proclaimed People magazine in a retelling of the event.

Predictably, Watson was arrested once again. To his and Amory's surprise, though, a judge ordered that the *Sea Shepherd* be given to the owners of the *Sierra* to help repay the damage done to the whaler. It was the latter action that saddened Watson — so much so that, at night, he sneaked over to the *Sea Shepherd* and opened its air valves, causing it to sink. He could not bear that his and Amory's ship would belong to the owners of the *Sierra*.

Once again, the glamour and boldness of the move ensured that the event would receive worldwide publicity. Amory arranged for Watson to make the rounds on morning news shows and talk shows, and he issued statements that while the fund did not condone illegal activities, he felt it must be noted that the *Sierra* had initiated the illegal behavior. He also noted that one must admire the courage of the small, unarmed *Sea Shepherd* crew, who had been willing to take on the larger — and armed — *Sierra* crew.

Watson would live to fight even more daring sea battles in the name of animals and the environment. The illegal attack on the *Sierra*, though, was a bold move for Amory, who went on to stage a few more high-profile — but legal — rescues. Many years after the attack on the *Sierra*, Watson wrote at length about his philosophy regarding environmental and animal rescues, and charges by some that he was in some ways a terrorist: "Terrorists do not take precautions to protect people from death or injury," he wrote. "Terrorists attack innocent people [and he does not]. Terrorists do not hold news conferences to announce what they have done, and finally, terrorists do not offer to turn themselves in to address the legal and moral consequences of their actions."

▷ ▷ ▷ Amory's sense of humor and his enormous charisma naturally contributed to the fund's ability to get publicity for its activities. But the bottom line for the Fund for Animals *was* the bottom line. Obviously, it needed to collect more money than it spent if it was to survive. Publicity for its causes certainly helped the fund get donations, but often the high-profile activities that garnered such publicity were very expensive themselves. So it was the role of Amory and others in the fund during its first decade of existence to help shape public opinion and gauge when they would be successful in doing so. In 1981, when the fund underwrote an effort to airlift more than five hundred burros out of the Grand Canyon, Amory and his colleagues showed that, with a bit of creativity and effort, they could manipulate public opinion to their advantage.

The saga of the wild burros in the Grand Canyon dates back to the 1920s, when park rangers first began shooting the animals, ostensibly to protect the ecosystem of the park from the burros, which, they thought, were over-grazing and causing rock slides. Between that time and the time park rangers announced in 1979 that they would resume the practice, nearly three thousand burros had been destroyed. Naturally, animal-protection activists like Amory were enraged. In addition to being defenseless, the burros, which were shot from the air, often died a slow, painful death. In 1979, the fund began a campaign on behalf of the canyon's wild burros after a ruling in Washington that they may be shot and killed. Not only was the practice brutal on the face of it; the reasons for the killings were not valid, the fund believed. Several environmental groups maintained the wildlife and landscape in the canyon were not hurt by the burros.

In their campaign, Amory and others once again learned about the futility of some federal protection laws. They also learned, again, that some of the organizations formed to protect wildlife could actually hurt it. In 1971, the U.S. Wild and Free-Roaming Horses and Burros Act was enacted to protect free-roaming horses and burros from "capture, branding, harassment, or death," based on the idea that they were "living symbols" of the spirit of the American West. The law, however, did not extend to burros on public lands that were a perceived threat to the ecosystem. Further, several wildlife federations and groups supported the park's intentions to kill the burros, believing that they did threaten the environment around them.

In 1976, a National Park Service announcement that it would shoot the burros launched a wave of protests from individuals and organized groups, prompting the U.S. secretary of the interior to temporarily halt any efforts to kill the animals. Three years later, though, the Park Service once again announced it was going kill the burros. But this time, Amory came up with a plan. The fund would arrange to airlift, by helicopter, all the burros from the canyon and then find a home for each one. The plan was widely ridiculed and derided by officials and many large wildlife organizations, including the Sierra Club and the National Audubon Society, which thought the plan unworkable, mostly because of its scope. The Grand Canyon is nearly one mile deep and covers more than one million acres. And, as Amory knew, it is hot in the summer. As he told the *New York Times*, "[Summer] is not my favorite time of year to begin such an operation. You are talking about 120 degree heat down there. I don't give a damn about the cruelty to people, but I do care about the cruelty to horses."

Amory, once again, marshaled his forces and garnered the support of the usual suspects — celebrities and movie stars, whose ranks this time included Princess Grace of Monaco, Steve Allen, Angie Dickinson, Cindy Williams, Mary Tyler Moore, and others. And his old friend Ed Ney, who happened to be head of Young & Rubicam, one of the leading advertising agencies in New York, designed a fund-raising ad for a nominal fee that was placed in *Parade* magazine. The full-page ad, hardly subtle, depicted a baby burro under the headline, "If you turn this page, this burro will be shot." Ney also helped with other public-service ads about the effort.

The fund forged ahead. The roundup began at 3:00 a.m. on a hot August day and of course provided great photo opportunities for Amory to use later in his publicity tour. It was unlikely newspaper and magazine readers or television viewers had ever seen large four-legged creatures airlifted en masse seven thousand vertical feet. Ultimately, two years later, the rescue yielded 575 burros. The effort cost $500,000, an unusually high cost per animal. But fund donors absorbed much of the bill, and Amory believed the worldwide publicity for the event — which also made people aware of the Fund for Animals and its mission — was worth it. Amory also believed the rescue would earn the approval of young people and raise their awareness of animal cruelty. "I bet if you asked young people if what we did is right, 98 percent would say 'yes,'" he said in an interview at the time. "All this hasn't been for the benefit of old fogies like me, but for generations that follow. They'll be around to enjoy the animals we've managed to save."

Of course, once the burros were rescued, they needed homes. Several of the celebrities who had promoted the airlift, including Williams and Dickinson, took some of them, but most were adopted by people who had a deep interest in their welfare and the facilities to keep them. And the fund was careful about who could adopt them; it charged $400 per animal in the hope of keeping out unscrupulous owners. It also encouraged people to take at least two burros so they could keep each other company. Still other burros traveled southeast to live out their lives in the East Texas countryside at Cleveland Amory's favorite project of all time, Black Beauty Ranch.

▷ ▷ ▷ Amory's connections went far beyond celebrities. He also had a wide circle of friends he knew from Harvard — and that group included many heavyweights in government, literature, the media, and education. And those connections, of course, led to more. Ed Ney, for instance, who helped publicize and raise money for the wild burro rescue, met Amory in the mid-1950s through their mutual friend Norman Cousins, and the two remained friends until Amory's death in 1998. Another of Amory's longtime friends would come through for him in another highly publicized animal rescue. This time it was *Harvard Crimson* colleague Caspar Weinberger, a 1938 Harvard graduate and, later, secretary of defense during the Reagan administration. It was Weinberger who helped Amory and the fund save the goats.

When it came to politics, Amory was in many ways an enigma. He was an unabashed admirer of Franklin Roosevelt and John F. Kennedy (both Harvard graduates, like Amory), and those who knew him as a young and middle-aged man considered him liberal politically. In his columns in the *Saturday Review,* he denounced the war in Vietnam, Richard Nixon, and other causes and people that could be deemed conservative. His stepdaughter, Gaea Leinhardt, said his politics and idealism paralleled those of his good friend Cousins, who actively participated in many liberal causes. But Amory was not necessarily a "liberal" in the modern sense of the word; he could be accused of being sexist (although some of his comments regarding women and his subtle criticism of "women's rights" were made for laughs), but he was pro-choice. Yet he always condemned what he felt was a growing use of obscenity in the media, and he claimed he hated change of all kinds. Later in his life, the few times he openly addressed politics came in speeches and writings in which he pressed for the rights of Native Americans and advocated U.S. support for Israel. By the time he reached his fifties, his friends said they barely knew his politics outside the sphere of policies that influenced animal welfare. His longtime friend and colleague Edward Walsh said Amory always avoided the personal aspect of politics, focusing more on individual people and their beliefs about Amory's favorite causes. "His politics were limited to events," Walsh said. "He may have been slightly left of center. But if he met Rush Limbaugh and liked him, it wouldn't matter what his politics were. He was not interested in politics outside of his animal-rights interests." Among his friends were, in fact, William F. Buckley Jr., founder of the conservative magazine *National Review,* and many of the Democratic congressmen from New York, including Daniel Patrick Moynihan. It is not surprising, then, that Amory would contact his *Harvard Crimson* colleague Weinberger, then a Reagan cabinet member and former budget director in the Nixon administration, to help save some wild goats.

In 1980, fifteen hundred Andalusian goats were in much the same unenviable position as the burros in the Grand Canyon. Descendants of goats left on San Clemente Island more than two hundred years ago, they roamed wild on the island, about eighty miles off the coast of San Diego, which was used by the U.S. Navy for target practice. The Navy had once allowed animal-rights groups to humanely trap and move the animals to other parts of the island but now said the goats were threatening several protected endangered species on the island, a contention with which many animal activists disagreed. After several prolonged court battles — including one triggered by a 1979 lawsuit by the fund — and several eleventh-hour stays of execution, the Navy had contracted with professional hunters to shoot the goats from helicopters. It was then that Amory sprang into action. ("Join the Navy and shoot the goats" became part of Amory's publicity campaign against the proposed shooting.) The shooting was about to begin when he and Bobbie Fiedler, a congresswoman from California, traveled to the Pentagon to make a final plea for clemency. (Amory's earlier comment — that "the Navy's answer to everything is to shoot it" — apparently did not work). Enter Benjamin Welles, assistant to Weinberger. The defense secretary had been reminded by his old friend, Amory, that the U.S. Naval Academy mascot was the goat. Weinberger, through Welles, gave the fund permission to rescue the goats.

The fund used an elaborate trapping-by-helicopter method in which helicopters swooped over the goats and captured them with nylon netting shot from a four-barrel gun. When the stunned goats fell, workers tied their legs and hoisted them on board. The goats later took an eighteen-hour trip by barge to San Diego and were put up for adoption. Once again, fund workers were particular about who adopted the animals — they insisted that each new owner adopt a minimum of two goats to make sure each had a companion. The initial goat rescue cost the fund about $100,000. About four thousand goats were rescued over a three-year period.

It may have been mission accomplished for the Andalusian goats, but, as usual, Amory was looking at the bigger picture. Goats, Amory was quick to point out to reporters, never got the respect they deserved. In fact, like all species of mammals, they were intelligent and engaging creatures, he said. "To hear him talk of them, you'd think they were his grandchildren," one reporter wrote, quoting him: "'They have this absolute fascination,' he croons. 'Sweet little things, amazingly intriguing — and so very bright.'"

In the 1980s, the fund participated in a few other high-profile rescues of animals, but none matched the scope of the goat rescue, the burro rescue, or the ramming of the *Sierra*. In the mid-1980s, the federal Bureau of Land Management put up for adoption about ten thousand wild horses that were rounded up in the western United States; it was learned that many ranchers who "adopted" the horses illegally sold them to slaughterhouses. Amory and other animal activists became heavily involved in saving the mustangs.

Despite the time, effort, and money put into these rescues, the day-to-day activities of the Fund for Animals were much more mundane. In addition to spending much time and money on lobbying in Washington, fund workers were troubleshooters who supported other anticruelty organizations. They went into the field all over the country when they heard of abuse against various animals and supported efforts already under way to clean up laboratories, puppy mills, carnivals, and other venues.

One of the fund's favorite ongoing causes was the promotion of the sterilization of pets, and it lobbied for laws to make such sterilization mandatory. Meanwhile, Amory routinely got publicity for sterilization efforts through special events. In one, which merited a story on CNN, the Bow Wow canine bakery in Manhattan celebrated Valentine's Day by featuring the sale of meat cakes made from liver in the shape of kissing lips and heart-shaped cakes made of graham crackers. Meanwhile, Amory, piggybacking, so to speak, on the promotion, offered a "neuter Benny for a penny" campaign, which, as the name indicates, allowed pet owners to get their cats neutered or sterilized for one cent at the nearby Have a Heart veterinary clinic, a facility underwritten by the fund that normally did the procedure for twenty-five dollars.

chapter 12 ▷▷▷ Nine Lives

> When the history books are written about the
> animal protection movement in the 20th century,
> [Amory] will stand tallest, rightly referred to as
> the grandfather of the movement, since he adopted
> the movement when approaching the age of 50.
>
> ▶ WAYNE PACELLE, president, Humane Society
>   of the United States

*W*hen Michael Markarian began volunteering for the Fund for Animals in 1993, he met a role model of his: Cleveland Amory, founder of the fund, who was well known as a writer and animal-rights activist. Markarian viewed Amory as *the* pioneer of animal rights. Unlike many others of his era, Amory stood up for animals who previously had no defenders — wild animals such as wolves and raccoons who, though long overlooked, still felt pain like their domesticated and cuddly counterparts and deserved to be treated humanely, Amory thought. After this first meeting with Amory, Markarian probably had little idea that, within ten years, he would hold Amory's title as president of the Fund for Animals.

Markarian had a particularly eye-opening experience when he attended the annual Labor Day Pigeon Shoot in Hegins, Pennsylvania. The shoot was a major event in that small city in Pennsylvania Dutch country, and it drew thousands of participants and spectators. Each year, about six thousand live pigeons — most deprived of food and water and otherwise abused on their trip — were trucked into Hegins from various locations. Some could not even fly. On the morning of the event, shooters who paid seventy-eight dollars apiece lined up on a field as the birds were released, a dozen or so at a time. The hunters all took aim at them. The result was a bloody and gruesome killing field of dead and maimed pigeons, many writhing in pain while the crowd cheered. Meanwhile, eight- and nine-year-old boys, called Trapper Boys, were encouraged to take part in this family event by grabbing the injured pigeons and finishing them off, either by throwing them, wringing their necks, or doing whatever else they believed was necessary to kill them once and for all.

Local humane groups had tried unsuccessfully for years to end this event. When Amory and the fund entered the fray, they were met with tremendous resistance — they were, after all, trying to put an end to a longtime community custom, and one that officials said raised money for the city. Fund for Animals volunteers began attending the event regularly in an attempt to save some of the wounded pigeons, or at least try to give them a humane death. Finally, after the failure of cajoling, threats, and even bribes (the fund offered to pay the city a flat fee of $15,000 to stop the shoot), the fund mobilized. On Amory's seventy-fourth birthday, one thousand protesters attended the event, picketing and carrying signs, handcuffing themselves to canisters of concrete and clogging traffic into the city. The event became an item on several major news outlets and even became a part of Jay Leno's monologue on the *Tonight* show. But the battle to save the pigeons was an uphill one: in 1999, anticruelty activists finally managed to pass legislation prohibiting it — one year after Amory died.

To Markarian, however, the Hegins Pigeon Shoot was emblematic of the type of event Amory particularly hated — and not just because it was a classic example of extreme cruelty. The planners justified their actions in the name of community spirit and, even worse, encouraged the participation of children, setting the stage for them to abuse animals throughout their life, he believed. Further, to Amory, it was abuse of an animal that did not naturally earn the affection of most people. Markarian admired Amory in particular for his efforts on behalf of *all* animals, not just domesticated ones. He remembered Amory's words about such animals when the fund was taking steps to protect koalas: "If we can't protect an animal as charming as the koala, what chance do the homely animals have?" Amory asked him.

The campaign against the pigeon shoot in Pennsylvania is a classic example of Amory's persistence and his attitudes about cruelty. Even though he was in his seventies at the time and suffering from arthritis, he made sure he traveled to the event to confront those participating — just as he was present in the grinding summer heat of Arizona during the first burro lift and on the *Sea Shepherd* as it cut through the ice floes of the St. Lawrence for the seal rescue. As many of his colleagues noted, he never became inured or numbed to the suffering of animals, no matter how many times he viewed it personally or in pictures, and he always seemed shocked by it. His feelings toward those initiating the abuse were a combination of disgust and sympathy, his friends say. "I can still see him walking with great patience at Hegins, Pennsylvania, around all those people who were so heartlessly slaughtering these pigeons," Paul Watson said at Amory's memorial service. "He looked at them with a combination of disgust and sorrow and pity."

Despite his participation in high-profile rescues and a schedule with the Fund for Animals that kept him busy from morning until night, Amory was still a writer, radio commentator, and columnist. Yet he found that many of his journalistic outlets were drying up by the early 1980s. Clearly, he had an ambivalent attitude toward writing. He turned sixty-three in September of 1980, and by that time he had been a professional writer for more than forty years. And while he found himself devoting more time to animal protection, Amory was still a versatile writer — of newspaper and magazine articles and columns, of best-selling books, and of essays. *Man Kind?* was certainly a success as a call to arms, so to speak, to those who opposed hunting — but the success of that book may have cut both ways for Amory. He was now seen, perhaps, as a writer on subjects pertaining to animals and animal protection. His journalistic skill had certainly contributed to the idea twenty-five years earlier that he was a social critic. He gladly abandoned that image to become a television critic and commentator about that medium. When his *TV Guide* column was taken away — not necessarily to his displeasure — he focused on writing about animal-protection issues. By the early 1980s, Cleveland Amory was about to reinvent himself again. And, once again, his new image came about almost by accident — through a combination of factors including his long-standing personal connections and his ability to connect with a new friend who understood him and shared his passion and energy.

▷ ▷ ▷ Amory was one of those longtime New Yorkers who seem to know everyone. By the time he was sixty years old, he had a diverse group of friends, many of whom he had known for decades. His close circle in New York included Marian Probst, who held the title of vice president of the fund, with whom he worked and often traveled; Edward Walsh, general counsel for fund; and Ed and Judy Ney, animal-rights activists and longtime New Yorkers. (Ed Ney had run the advertising firm of Young & Rubicam for many years.) Amory's relationship with his own family was an interesting one; he and his brother and sister had been reared for the most part by nannies in the conventional upper-class, New England style of the era in which they were born, so he was not very close to his parents when he was growing up. His mother, Leonore Amory, died in 1968, and his father, Robert Amory, passed away four years later. Amory's mother was quite ill with cancer during the last few years of her life, and his parents moved back to the Boston area from New York during this time, with Leonore living in a nursing home. Robert Amory lived in the Somerset Club in Boston for the last six years of his life, and although Cleveland lived in New York, he did meet with his father frequently for Sunday lunch.

But Amory had for the most part established a surrogate family during the last few decades of his life. He had never been close to his sister, Leonore, who had moved to California with her husband when she was in her twenties; Amory visited his sister and her family occasionally when he traveled to the West Coast, but their relationship was limited by geography. Amory and his brother Robert had a more complex relationship. Both were brilliant overachievers who had been very successful professionally. And while they were hardly inseparable, they certainly had an amiable and friendly relationship, although it was characterized by an undercurrent of competitiveness, according to Robert's son, Rob. In his autobiographical cat books, Cleveland joked that, at Harvard, he chose to go into journalism and join the staff of the *Harvard Crimson* because he could never live up to the high academic standards set there by his older brother (who was not in journalism). Robert Amory graduated magna cum laude in three years. Robert Amory makes a few appearances in his brother's cat trilogy; in one episode in *The Cat Who Came for Christmas*, Amory notes humorously that his brother, a former colonel during World War II and a member of the amphibious engineers division, was the perfect person to disassemble his dishwashing machine in search of a missing cat. Amory's half-joking description of why he joined the *Crimson* — to avoid competition with his brilliant brother — may have had an undercurrent of truth. Robert Amory did not share the national fame of his brother, but he was very well known and respected. As deputy director of the CIA during the Cold War years, Robert Amory was a force to be reckoned with in the international arena. As his son noted years after his death, Robert Amory and his brother made great contributions to society in vastly different arenas. (In one arena, though, both Cleveland Amory and his brother shared a similar passion: baseball. Both were intense Red Sox fans their entire lives, and both were serious students of the game and meticulous researchers who knew every statistic possible about their team and its players.)

Robert's son, Rob, who saw his uncle Cleveland periodically as an adult, noted also that he and Cleveland became closer after the 1989 death of Robert Jr. "There was this sense of 'we're the survivors,' 'we have this bond,'" he said. "It was something I welcomed very much."

All in all, however, Amory was probably closer to his friends and to his stepfamily than he was to most members of his own family. He had developed a loving relationship with his stepdaughter, Gaea, soon after he married her mother, and the two maintained that relationship throughout the rest of Amory's life, even though Gaea never lived in New York again after she left home for college. And after Gaea married and had a daughter, Zoe, Amory also grew close to his granddaughter. Gaea, who now is a professor of education at the University of Pittsburgh, said she usually saw Amory two or three times a year, but they would talk on the telephone several times a week. "He'd have this habit of watching two sporting events [at the same time] and then he'd call a friend or relative and say, 'Are you watching this game? You have to.'" Amory also liked to "watch" television with his friends — even though they may have been in different cities at the time. "He'd sit [and stay] on the phone with you while you watched. That was fun," Gaea Leinhardt said.

Walsh, also a sports fan, was on the receiving end of hundreds of such calls. "He was one of the brightest baseball fans I ever met," Walsh said. Amory, for instance, did not just consider win-loss records when determining the quality of pitchers, which was then a conventional method of assessing pitchers. He also took into account the number of innings pitched per year — a measure used commonly years after Amory employed it. And he may have been one of the few fans who could actually call a manager and have him take his calls. "He'd call [Red Sox manager] John McNamara in the morning to tell him how to pitch to the Yankees," Walsh said.

Amory's calls were not limited to mere chatter, though. If he knew one of his friends had plans to travel during bad weather, that person would inevitably get a call. "If I were going to a Giants game, he'd call and tell me not to go because of bad roads," Walsh said.

Amory was a loyal, trusting, and open friend — indeed, if a person agreed with his stance on animal rights, had a sense of humor, and was friendly, Amory was easily won over. By the last decade or so of his life, it was not difficult to identify some of the true members of his inner circle; they were mentioned frequently as "characters" in his best-selling trilogy of cat books, *The Cat Who Came for Christmas*, *The Cat and the Curmudgeon*, and *The Best*

Cat Ever. In those autobiographical books, his beloved cat, Polar Bear, naturally adopts some of the characteristics of his curmudgeonly owner. But Polar Bear on his own is highly intelligent and a shrewd judge of people — so shrewd, in fact, that he takes kindly to only a small group of people. And, not coincidentally, those Polar Bear likes are also Amory's closest friends.

Through the years, Amory wrote frequently about his opinion of children — he thought they were overindulged and almost always spoiled. But this did not extend to Gaea's daughter, Zoe, who, he was quick to note in *The Best Cat Ever*, became an immediate favorite of Polar Bear's — even when she was only four years old. Like her mother, Zoe was very bright and a good student, qualities in which Amory took pride. It is perhaps uncharacteristic that Amory did in some ways become a proud and doting grandfather late in his life. (In the third book of his cat trilogy, Amory writes that Polar Bear loved the song "Bless the Beasts and the Children." But Polar Bear's version of the song stresses the "beasts" and virtually ignores the "children.")

Of course, a prominent "character" in the books is Marian Probst, who appears throughout the trilogy as a temporary caretaker of Polar Bear, as well as editor, assistant, bookkeeper, and periodic traveling companion of Amory. Amory in the cat trilogy pays homage to her in a joking and affectionate way. She is mentioned at the beginning of the acknowledgments in the second and third books of the trilogy, and a theme throughout most of Amory's books is his indebtedness to her and his affection for her. "The author wishes to thank first of all Marian Probst, his longtime assistant, under whose incredible memory for irritating facts he has, with the patience of Job, long suffered," he writes in *The Cat and the Curmudgeon*. In *The Best Cat Ever*, he acknowledges her again, thanking her for her "critical judgment. . . . A judgment which, hard as it is for him to bear, was amply and often demonstrated in these pages to be infuriatingly superior to his own." (Amory, who usually dedicated his books to groups of people, such as cat lovers or other animal lovers, dedicated *Man Kind?* to Marian: "To Marian, Assistant-in-Chief for Judgment under Pressure.") But most of all, he makes it clear that she was indispensable to him as an editor. Amory usually wrote his books and articles longhand on yellow legal paper and then gave them to Probst to type. Then he would edit the typed version, give it to her, and the process would repeat itself. "Ms. Probst came to me during the Spanish War and, as far as I'm concerned, is still on trial. And make no mistake about it, a trying woman she is," he wrote in *The Cat and the Curmudgeon*. Amory wrote that he eventually discovered that after Marian typed his submissions to her, she had three policies if she did not like a sentence: she either changed it, deleted it, or left out the entire paragraph. But Amory never knew exactly what she did because she never returned the original to him, nor did she tell him.

A decade after its founding in 1967, the fund was still struggling—even though Amory and a handful of others worked long hours each day at its Manhattan headquarters and earned little or nothing. Amory's own life was not exactly at its peak during those few years, either. In addition to the dissolution of his marriage to Martha Hodge, his writing career was suffering. As he wrote a decade later in *The Cat Who Came for Christmas*, by 1978, "[The fund] was suffering growing pains [that were] close to terminal. . . . The society itself was barely subsisting. It had achieved some successes, but its major accomplishments were still in the future. . . . My own writing career, by which I had supported myself since before you were born, was far from booming. . . . I was four years behind on a book deadline and so many months behind on two magazine articles that . . . one of the things I had meant to do . . . was to borrow a line from the late Dorothy Parker and tell the editor that I had really tried to finish but someone had taken the pencil."

It was unlike Amory to feel sorry for himself, and, with his hectic schedule, he barely had time to seek sympathy. Once again, though, his life was about to change, thanks in part to the entrance of a new friend and a dirty, stray cat.

▷ ▷ ▷ It did not take *Parade* magazine editor Walter Anderson long to determine that Cleveland Amory would be the perfect contributor to his magazine. Anderson met Amory in 1981 at a party when the two were introduced by writer Dotson Rader, whom Anderson had recently hired as a contributing editor. Anderson and Amory talked and arranged to meet the following day in Anderson's office. "He had an idea that I immediately agreed to, which was an interview with Katharine Hepburn," Anderson remembered. Amory, of course, had known the Hepburn family since he was a boy, but apparently he persuaded Anderson that his would not be the conventional, sugary celebrity interview. "He and Katharine Hepburn were a perfect match," Anderson said. "I don't think any writer could have written a more evocative piece with Katharine Hepburn than Cleveland. It was beautiful work."

In some ways, Anderson and Amory also were a perfect match. A writer himself, Anderson began at *Parade* in 1977 and became editor in 1980. Under his direction, *Parade* began to publish increasingly newsworthy stories, including the first interview in the United States with Pope John Paul II, the first interview with Hillary Rodham Clinton, and others. Anderson also attracted such award-winning writers as Norman Mailer, David Halberstam, and Willie Morris. Walter Anderson was well aware of the fact that he did not edit a conventional magazine. A Sunday newspaper supplement, *Parade* had a mainstream audience — it was delivered to newspaper readers — yet it also had to serve a diverse audience of small- and large-town readers in varying geographical areas. It also served readers of all ages. So while Hollywood news was certainly of interest to its readers, Anderson did not view the publication as a celebrity rag. Instead, he began to develop a clear vision of what he wanted to do with *Parade*, and Amory, personally and professionally, fit into that vision. "I felt if someone or something exists, that's not a story," he said. "What makes it a story? What can we learn from their lives? Everyone survives or endures to the last heartbeat. But a few more do more than just survive. We get to learn something more about ourselves from their lives." The contributing editors of his magazine all had one thing in common, Anderson said. They all believed they could make a better world, all were devoted to what they did, and none was cynical. Amory's passion for animal rights was indicative of his passion for life, Anderson believed, and emblematic of his desire to make a difference in the world. But despite his tireless efforts for animal rights, "he was always a writer" who had a deep interest in people, Anderson believed.

Shortly after he met Anderson, Amory began writing periodic personality profiles for *Parade*, most of which were cover stories. With the *Parade* job — for which he was paid per story — Amory may have found the perfect situation: it allowed him to use his celebrity contacts, allude to his animal rights activities, and, most of all, exercise his talent as a writer. He frequently interviewed people he had known for years — Jack Lemmon, James Stewart, James Cagney, Rose Kennedy, Doris Day, George C. Scott, Gregory Peck, and others. Not coincidentally, most of his subjects had a deep interest in animals, and some were members of the fund board. But most rarely gave interviews or sought publicity, so they were "gets" for the magazine. Because most of Amory's subjects knew him, they apparently felt comfortable talking to him. But the profiles were far from fluffy; Amory usually spent days with his subjects, and he was not afraid to ask personal questions. And frequently tidbits in those interviews were picked up by the wire services and made national news. Amory was the first to hear from Cary Grant — another longtime friend — that Grant had used LSD. And Gregory Peck candidly discussed his son's suicide.

Amory walked a fine line in the profiles; they were far from the conventional, soft celebrity interviews that focused on the subjects' latest project or their philosophy of their craft, yet they were not insulting or too personal. Frequently, he alluded to the subject's family life, which, in the case of many of his subjects (including Cagney, Lemmon, Rose Kennedy, and some others), comprised marriages that lasted for decades. And when he did mention sensitive subjects, he often treaded lightly. For instance, in the Rose Kennedy profile, he alluded to rumors of the extramarital affairs of her late husband in a roundabout way: "She has . . . always maintained her marriage was a happy one," he wrote, implying that those who thought otherwise were wrong. All his profiles were rich in anecdote and direct quotations. Amory was a seasoned interviewer who knew how to get his subjects to open up. When he talked to Jean Kennedy Smith about her mother's fortitude and courage, she related an anecdote about how she and her mother, who was in her eighties at the time, took a walk in Central Park one evening and saw two men lurking behind a tree. One of the men approached the five-foot-tall Rose Kennedy: "Gotta match, lady?" he asked her. Kennedy glared at him. "No, I do not!" she told him. "I have never smoked, and neither should you." The men retreated immediately.

When Amory interviewed Hepburn in 1983, she was surprisingly candid, particularly for someone who did not often give interviews. In an especially colorful quote, she offers that she has lived her life "like a man." "Like a selfish man. Like a pig." But women should not try to *be* men. "Women are simply not men," she says. "And if we are, we're making a mistake — we're so different emotionally." Amory notes in the story that he has known Hepburn for many years, and that may be why she acted so casual around him. That behavior included her answering a ringing phone, pausing, saying "She's out," and hanging up the phone. If such a caller recognizes her voice, she then explains, "I tell them I'm my sister." In the story, Amory is honest with his readers. Hepburn, he confides, is the first celebrity he ever met, so he naively assumed that all stars were as wonderful as she: "I have since learned how greatly I erred," he writes. "Kate, at 75, is still my best star."

A common theme in Amory's profile pieces is the lack of pretense in those he interviews. This quality in celebrities must have appealed to Amory. Back in 1945, when he was doing freelance writing, he wrote an extensive profile for the *Saturday Evening Post* on young actor Fred MacMurray, who was content to accept minor character roles and who, according to Amory, shunned publicity, much to the chagrin of his handlers at Twentieth Century–Fox Studios. Amory writes that when MacMurray first came to Hollywood, on a trip to visit his grandfather, he gladly played an "extra" and had no designs for bigger roles. He initially turned down a proposal to have a speaking role in his first film, but then reconsidered. The MacMurray interview was in some ways the model for the type of profile Amory wrote thirty-five years later for *Parade.*

The picture Amory paints of the eighty-five-year-old James Cagney is a poignant one. Never one to seek the limelight, Amory writes, Cagney and his wife of sixty-two years live quietly with their horses, cows, dogs, and ducks in upstate New York. Cagney, who recently had a stroke and a heart attack and was confined to a wheelchair when the interview was conducted, notes that in reality, he is as far as can be imagined from the tough guy he portrayed in films. His mother, who left school at age twelve to work in a pencil factory, was his role model throughout his life, and tears came to his eyes when he discussed her with Amory, decades after her death.

Actor Jack Lemmon was also very candid with Amory when it came to what he admitted was a childhood that was far from perfect. Lemmon, like Amory, was a Boston native and a Harvard graduate. He said he was very sickly as a child, and very much a loner. Further, he felt he was in part responsible for his parents' unhappy marriage and felt that they stayed together only because of him. Like most of Amory's other interview subjects, Lemmon had been married a long time — twenty-two years at the time to actress Felicia Farr.

Cary Grant, a longtime friend of Amory's, kept a low profile, so Amory's 1985 interview with him was a coup — and one of the last interviews the actor granted. He died a year later. Amory writes that Grant initially turned him down because he "hates interviews," but when he found out Amory would write a story anyway, he agreed. That story may be apocryphal — Grant probably did the interview with Amory because he knew him, and it was not Amory's style to write a piece about a person without that person's cooperation. In the profile, Grant talks about some of his costars over the years and confirms Howard Hughes's image of eccentricity, but notes that he admired the man as a friend and colleague. "He was the most restful man I've ever been with," Grant says. "Sometimes we'd sit for two hours and never say a word to each other." He adds that he would occasionally travel with Hughes. "I'd arrive with all my matched and monogrammed luggage, and he'd arrive with a cardboard box with a couple of shirts thrown in."

Described in Amory's notes of the interview is an exchange that never made it into the story: Amory asked Grant, whose sophisticated voice and manner made him ripe for mimicking, who did the best impression of him. His answer was Tony Curtis, who first gave his famous rendition of Grant in the film *Some Like It Hot*. Grant said that Curtis once revealed to him the roots of that imitation — when Curtis was in the army, the only film in the troop ship's library was *Gunga Din*, which starred Grant. "Tony once told me that, after seeing it over and over and over again, the crew got to the point where they could turn off the soundtrack and speak the dialogue themselves," Grant said. "Tony did me." Unlike the subjects of many of Amory's profiles, Cary Grant was not in a long-term marriage. Indeed, he was married to his fifth wife at the time of the interview and said the other wives "all left me. With good reason."

Many of Amory's interview subjects had at least one thing in common other than their celebrity status: nearly all took an active role in animal protection or, at the very least, loved animals and had several pets. Walter Cronkite, who at the time of his interview had retired from the CBS News anchor desk, is shown on the cover of *Parade* holding his beloved tiger cat. And when he discussed his long career, James Stewart talked at length about one of his favorite costars: a horse named Pie, with whom he worked for twenty years. "I'll never forget anything about him," Stewart said. "I remember the day I met him. It was love at first sight from my point of view."

For a long profile of George C. Scott, the crusty actor is pictured on the cover of the magazine with his wife, actress Trish Van Devere, and his large pet mastiff. Amory was a friend and longtime chess partner of Scott's, but when he first arrived at his Greenwich, Connecticut, home, he was given a less than cordial reception. Amory found Scott and the mastiff "both growling." When he tried to placate the animal by extending his hand, he was nearly bitten by the dog and admonished by the actor. "Don't give him that 'nice doggie' bull," Scott told him. "He's not ready for it. Max is shy with strangers." On Amory's second visit to the actor's home, the reaction was even less cordial: "This was supposed to be an interview," Scott complained upon seeing Amory again. "Not a way of life." If Amory considered himself a curmudgeon, he was no match for Scott, who had a long list of complaints about everyday life, including MTV and rock music (MTV is "shabby and phony and bizarre . . . aggressive and anti-human") and even the Beatles: "I thought they were jerks then [when they first came to America] and I think they're jerks now."

In the Scott interview, Amory related a conversation between the actress Maureen Stapleton and director Mike Nichols. Scott, Stapleton said, made her nervous. "I'm afraid of him," she said. "Don't worry," Nichols told her. "The whole world's afraid of George C. Scott."

Amory asked Scott why he had turned down an Oscar in 1970 for his famous portrayal of General Patton. "I just can't stand our people — I mean actors — being put in a position of sweating in front of those television cameras and hoping . . . with all that contrived suspense focused on them. It's offensive, it's barbarous, it's innately corrupt," he said.

Amory's interview with Gregory Peck must have been special to him — notes left behind among his papers indicate that he did extensive research into Peck's life and that the story was more heavily edited than most of Amory's profiles. The story was extensive and touched on some sensitive topics, including Peck's politics, his home life in Beverly Hills, and the sudden death of his oldest son, Jonathan.

When Amory arrived at Peck's home, he noticed the actor's three-legged dog, who had lost his leg after being hit by a truck but was "OK now," according to Peck.

Amory apparently felt it fair game to ask Peck about his political beliefs — the actor had a reputation at the time for having liberal political views, but he denied the "liberal" label. "I never think of myself as that," he said. "But I don't get my politics from my movies." Peck, however, did call himself a "Franklin Roosevelt man from way back. I still am. . . . I never worry much about the fat cats. They can take care of themselves. I empathize with the people who are deprived and don't have a decent chance to get anywhere because of the social injustices."

Although Peck had been married three times, he had been married to his current wife, Veronique, for thirty-three years when Amory talked to him. Peck was still recovering from the suicide of his oldest son, who had shot himself. Jonathan Peck had been a television news reporter in San Francisco. "You look for reasons," he told Amory. "Jon had lost a girl with whom he had been in love." Peck implied that the loss, along with a breakup with another girlfriend and job pressure, may have led to the tragedy.

If Amory had trouble writing the Peck profile, as the editing indicates, Peck, at least, was happy with the result. He wrote Amory a warm note about it: "I got so many positive reactions to your story in Parade, that I had to share it with you, the responsible party. People keep mentioning it, in a very good way, and the mail keeps coming in. So much so that I got the story out and read it again this afternoon. With a couple of months of hindsight, it looks better and better. I think it is the best story anyone has ever done about yours truly. Thank you once more, and with warm regards, Greg."

Amory's work for *Parade* was not limited to personality profiles. He also wrote feature stories and occasional "list" stories — for instance, "The Difference between Bad and Good Sportsmanship: A Select List," in which Amory compiled short essays about sports figures he considered "good" and "bad" examples. (Examples to "admire" included Pennsylvania State University football coach Joe Paterno, baseball player Jackie Robinson, tennis player Chris Evert Lloyd, and others. Examples to "avoid" included basketball player Wilt Chamberlain, Ohio State University football coach Woody Hayes, New York Yankees manager Billy Martin, and others.) He also wrote a long piece, "The Best and the Worst of Everything," which comprised two- or three-paragraph explanations and examples under each category ("best divorce news, worst divorce news"; "best graffiti, worst graffiti"; "best bumper sticker, worst bumper sticker," etc.) Like *Saturday Review* editor Norman Cousins, Walter Anderson allowed Amory to get in a few plugs about his favorite cause. Under the "best bumper sticker," for example, was the Fund for Animals' slogan, "Support your right to arm bears." *Parade* also published a thought piece about animal experimentation and the rights of animals, titled "Do They Have Rights?" Amory did not write that story.

Like all good writers, Amory gathered far more material than he actually used. But for someone who claimed to hate editors, he was not hard to edit, Anderson maintained, and he almost always turned in stories that were the length requested. "Cleveland responded well to editing," Anderson said. "He welcomed it. I would raise questions occasionally, but there were a couple of pieces where I virtually had no questions." But that is not the way Amory told it, tongue in cheek, in *The Cat and the Curmudgeon*, when he wrote about Anderson's "phobia": "His particular phobia is length," he wrote. "I do not know whether this was because, as a child, he was not allowed to wear long pants until other boys in the class wore them, or whether, in growing up, he aspired to the basketball team, but I do know that whatever you give him to read, he would like it better if there was less of it."

Over the years, Anderson experienced Amory's sometimes volatile temper, but he also noted it could be defused easily with a joke. And if Anderson's behavior did annoy Amory, he got back at him with a practical joke. Anderson remembered the time he was sitting at an important meeting when a newly hired secretary (i.e., one who was not familiar with Amory's sense of humor) burst into the meeting to tell Anderson he had an emergency telephone call from S. I. "Si" Newhouse, the media executive whose company owned *Parade*. Anderson of course left the meeting to take the important call. "It's Si Newhouse," said a voice on other end that sounded suspiciously like Amory's. "You must give Cleveland Amory a raise." When Amory came into the *Parade* offices and saw a new receptionist, he always identified himself to the oblivious new hire as "Si Newhouse."

In Amory, Walter Anderson found a talented writer whose readable and engaging style was perfect for the audience of *Parade*; he also had in Amory a professional who was easy to work with, and whose enormous network of personal connections gave him exceptional access to famous people. In Anderson, Amory found what he had had in Norman Cousins years before: an experienced and accommodating editor, and a good friend. As it turned out, Anderson's influence went even deeper than that. He was pivotal in returning Cleveland Amory to the best-seller list and putting him on the map once again as an author.

Chapter 13 ▷▷▷ Ranch of Dreams

> [About Polar Bear, Amory's cat]:
> He's very Republican. He doesn't like anything
> to happen which hasn't happened before.
> ▸ CLEVELAND AMORY, on a book tour for
>   *The Cat Who Came for Christmas*

*B*y the late 1980s, Amory was spending most of his time working for the Fund for Animals and serving as a contributing editor of *Parade*. His most recent book, *The Trouble with Nowadays*, had been published in 1979, but his most recent "big" book — that is, one that received widespread attention — was *Man Kind? Our Incredible War on Wildlife*, which came out in 1974. His life at this point may have been calmer than it had ever been. There were no high-profile animal rescues like the burro or goat rescues, and the venues for his writing were more limited than they had ever been, although *Parade's* circulation of millions of readers gave Amory a wide audience.

In 1986, Amory was finishing a semiautobiographical manuscript when his friend and editor, Walter Anderson, asked to read some of it. Amory was reluctant — the book outlined his relationship with a beloved cat he had found nearly ten years earlier on the streets of Manhattan, and Amory feared it was a bit too sentimental and personal for Anderson, a former marine and a realist. The publisher Little, Brown had given him a small advance for this nonfiction account of how, on Christmas Eve in 1978, Amory had rescued a dirty, injured white cat who had been roaming the alleys of Manhattan. As he describes in the book, Amory and a friend quickly made phone calls and found the cat a home, although his new owner would not claim him until the day after Christmas. Amory and other fund workers frequently kept strays in their homes for a few nights until they could be placed in permanent homes, so this was nothing unusual. But what followed was not ordinary, Amory writes. Within a day, after Amory gave the screeching, snarling cat a bath, the two formed an almost mystical bond: the cat seemed to sense that Amory had probably saved his life, and Amory felt an intense attachment to the cat unlike any he had felt toward any animal. But Amory was hardly sentimental, either as a man or as a writer, so the manuscript he showed to Anderson was no conventional, sappy Christmas story. The main "character" in *The Cat Who Came for Christmas* is Polar Bear, the stray, hungry cat. But its secondary character, Cleveland Amory, uses the cat as a foil and confidant to talk about himself and to describe his views abut life in general. *The Cat Who Came for Christmas* is at its best when it illustrates the strong and mysterious bond that can exist between people and their pets. Perhaps that is because Amory is less sentimental than many writers, and he chooses to show this rather than try to define it. A predominant theme in the book is the unspoken, reciprocal arrangement we have with our animals: we provide them shelter, food, and companionship, and their loyalty and patient disregard of our idiosyncrasies and weaknesses give us great comfort in our daily lives.

Amory wrote the manuscript about nine years after the event — when he was still living happily with Polar Bear — and considered it a minor work with which pet owners could identify. The publisher planned initially to print fifty thousand copies, a relatively small run. Amory reluctantly gave the manuscript to Anderson, who insisted on reading it. "I read it and called him up. I said, 'Cleveland, this is a major work. This is important. . . . The American people are going to respond. It is a crackling good story, really well told.'" Amory, Anderson recalled, was stunned. To Anderson, *The Cat Who Came for Christmas* had all the markings of a best-selling book. It was written well and with a sense of humor, it had passion, and it was all true. He told Amory that he wanted to run an excerpt of it in *Parade* and use it as a cover story. Both Amory and Anderson knew that exposure like that could tremendously boost sales.

Amory received some suggestions about the book from Anderson and from Fredrica Friedman, his editor at Little, Brown. Her notes on one of the drafts of the manuscripts urge Amory to elaborate on the differences as well as the similarities between the cat and the man, and to focus on the fact that his life was about to change that Christmas. "[When bathing the cat] would it help the humor to describe the fact that you are a very tall man, bending over to wash this very small cat?" Friedman writes on a Post-It note stuck to the early pages of the manuscript. "It's always nice for the reader to be able to picture the principals — and you are one."

The result, ultimately, was the phenomenal best-selling holiday book *The Cat Who Came for Christmas*, which quickly climbed to number three on the

New York Times best-seller list, where it remained for five months. About fifty thousand copies were printed when the book first came out on October 29; those copies were sold within a week. By February, readers had requested paperback and audiotape versions. All this spawned a book tour for both author and subject, and, ultimately, two more books about Polar Bear, both of them best sellers: *The Cat and the Curmudgeon* (1990) and *The Best Cat Ever* (1993).

The tremendous commercial success of the book caused some tension between Amory and Little, Brown, which he claimed had underestimated the potential of the book and, consequently, mishandled its marketing. (As Anderson had predicted, the *Parade* excerpt gave the book a tremendous shot in the arm, which quickly translated into sales. The publisher apparently was not prepared for that boost when it decided on the initial press run for it. Consequently, orders for it came that could not be filled.) The unexpected success of the book — and the fact that the publisher ran out of copies shortly after it was published — prompted two stories in the *New York Times*. In one, Amory, with characteristic candor, called the publishing experience with Little, Brown the worst in his career. But Amory and his publishers apparently came to terms with each other. He picked Little, Brown to publish the sequel to *The Cat Who Came for Christmas*, to be called *The Cat and the Curmudgeon*. As the second *Times* story noted, by the summer, rights to the book had been sold to publishers in eight countries, and paperback rights were sold to Penguin. As Amory implied in the *Times*, money can be a great mediator — the publisher apparently offered him a large advance, and all was forgiven.

The Polar Bear trilogy is in some ways Amory at his best. Written in his very readable, humorous, conversational style, these books allowed him to pontificate about subjects dear to his heart: his beloved cat, his activities on behalf of animals, and, perhaps most important, the subtle absurdities of life in general. It was his fine sense of the absurd that made Amory's mocking of the upper-crust New Englanders so readable in *The Proper Bostonians*, and that allowed him to stay on as chief critic at *TV Guide* for thirteen years. Amory was a self-described "curmudgeon," but as most of his friends say, he was far from cynical, and was usually the first to observe and to laugh at the ironies of everyday life and human behavior. The Polar Bear trilogy also illustrates what his friend Edward Walsh said: that, while Amory understood animals, he understood humans more. The books convey universal themes about human as well as animal behavior.

In *The Cat Who Came for Christmas*, Amory focuses on his introduction to Polar Bear and how, serendipitously, the two met at lonely and desperate times in their lives. He notes that he and the cat are—not surprisingly—alike in many ways: both are stubborn, skeptical of anything new or different, and devoted only to a select few. Interspersed with the tale of Polar Bear are the author's take on the history of the cat, Polar Bear's likes and dislikes, and recollections of the author's early animal-rights activities. The second book, *The Cat and the Curmudgeon*, is more of a picaresque story that outlines the travels of Polar Bear with Amory and Marian Probst to Amory's old haunts, including his childhood home in Nahant, and to Hollywood and Murchison, Texas, the home of the fund's animal sanctuary, Black Beauty Ranch. Now a celebrity because of Amory's best-selling book about him, Polar Bear's publisher launches a book tour, much to the chagrin of the shy cat, who is clearly not as gregarious as the author who writes about him. Included in this volume also are retellings of a few of the romantic escapades of Amory, and the key role Polar Bear plays in assessing and approving of prospective paramours.

The third book of the trilogy, *The Best Cat Ever*, written after Polar Bear's death, is the most poignant. It is still hilarious, continuing with Amory's nostalgic recollections of key events in his life, including his years at Harvard, his years as *TV Guide* critic, and his short tenure as the Duchess of Windsor's ghostwriter (and Polar Bear's reaction to these events). Both author and feline are growing old at this point. Both have arthritis, which limits their mobility and affects their moods, and both suffer from other ailments: author Amory has been hit by a car, and Polar Bear has kidney problems. Amory is at his best when he describes the heartbreak of watching someone he loves decline physically, along with the denial that inevitably accompanies that observation. After Polar Bear is euthanized, Amory is fine, temporarily. Minutes later, though, in the waiting room of the veterinarian's office, he meets a friend who inquires about the cat: " 'Is he all right?' " He writes: "I could not even shake my head. Instead I did something so unknowingly, so un-Bostonian, and so un-Me—something I could not help . . . with all those other patients there, too. I burst into tears. It was embarrassing, and I was ashamed, but the worst part was, for the first time in my life that I can remember, I could not stop crying."

Overall, the Polar Bear trilogy received positive reviews from critics, many of whom noted that the books were not written only for pet owners. "This is the latest installment in the continuing saga of how a mature curmudgeon copes with the tribulations of, as the author would say, being owned by a cat who, truth be told, is a curmudgeon himself," the *New York Times Book Review* said of *The Cat and the Curmudgeon*. "This is a witty, wonderful book with universal appeal for anyone who has been owned by a pet — and even those who haven't." *Library Journal* said the author's "meandering philosophy and observations are wordy, lacking the crispness of most contemporary writing, although . . . many readers are charmed by this old-fashioned style." Of *The Best Cat Ever*, a reviewer for *Library Journal* wrote that while Amory's reflections on life and his views on humane issues outnumber his recollections of Polar Bear's antics, "[he] is a very readable writer and he is able to present his sideline comments and musings without appearing to stand on a soapbox. . . . [The book] will have animal lovers everywhere lapping it up like a bowl of warm milk."

But the best-selling and enduring Polar Bear trilogy was virtually critic-proof. The second and third volumes sold well in part because of the positive word-of-mouth advertising of their predecessors. And, more than ten years after the final book was published, dozens of reader reviews on the Amazon.com website indicate that the books — which have been reissued in paperback form — remain enormously popular. Several reader-reviewers write that they read the book as children and now, as adults, have reread them and still appreciate them, perhaps in a different way. Young adults and older teenagers indicate that they, also, enjoy the books. One reader, in his review of *The Best Cat Ever*, is particularly impressed by the trilogy's comments about life and people overall:

> Amory has been privileged to lead an interesting life that connects to many other interesting people. He does not recount the stories as standard history, or as mere gossip-columnist fare, but rather looks for overall meanings and directions in what is often a difficult pattern of discernment in life. Regardless of social status, political motivation, or intellectual stature, people are people, and will do the most remarkable, selfish, selfless, silly, wonderful things. Amory's observations of this [are] a delight to read.

To Amory, the best-selling status of the books meant substantial royalties — and, for the first time in his adult life, he had some discretionary income. Shortly after the publication of *The Cat Who Came for Christmas*, he told one interviewer that he had received about fifteen thousand letters in response to the book. He tried to read and answer most of them, he said, and was particularly touched by one writer who said that he hoped the book would encourage its readers to adopt cats from animal shelters. "If there are going to be a million books in print by 1988, if I were responsible for a lot of cats coming out of shelters. . . . I would feel that that was the best thing I had done," he said.

The Polar Bear trilogy has had an extraordinary long shelf life, perhaps in part because of Amory's easy style of writing and the timelessness of the topic, and it continues to sell. Certainly Polar Bear's legacy will live on in another way. He is buried next to the man he owned — as Amory consistently reminded the reader, cats "own" their human caretakers — with a marker that notes:

> Beneath This Stone
> Lie the Mortal Remains of
> The Cat Who Came for Christmas
> Beloved Polar Bear
> 1977–1992
> 'Til We Meet Again

Amory wrote the last line, he said, in the sincere belief that he would indeed meet Polar Bear again.

▷ ▷ ▷ Much earlier in his life, Cleveland Amory might have been one of the last people in the world to sing the praises of Murchison, Texas, a small town about ninety miles east of Dallas. First, it was a small Texas town — not that Amory necessarily had anything against small towns. He was born in one, in fact (Nahant, Massachusetts). A tiny town in the South, though, was another matter. Amory assumed (wrongly, he would learn) that tiny Texas towns had more than their share of meat eaters whose beliefs about animals in general were not exactly in line with his own. Further, he just was not accustomed to the culture, geography, climate, and general belief system of those in the South. (Amory had visited Murchison much earlier in his life when he did an exhaustive — and pointed — piece for *Holiday* about the unusual number of Texas millionaires who lived in or near Murchison, and their feelings of entitlement.)

By the late 1970s, however, Amory and the Fund for Animals needed a safe haven for many of the 577 burros they had airlifted from the Grand Canyon.

They found homes for some of them, but even the fund workers, with their great contacts with animal lovers, could not find homes for that many burros. And they were not willing to place the animals just anywhere. They wanted to make sure the new owners were humane and that the burros would live the rest of their lives comfortably.

When Amory first heard about land being available in east Texas, he was skeptical of the location, he writes in his last book, *Ranch of Dreams*. But when he saw the overgrown farm and land that would become the Black Beauty Ranch, he fell in love with it. East Texas, he concluded, was not like his view of the rest of Texas, with its green, rolling hills, small lakes, and its residents' overall benevolent attitude toward animals. The fund bought land there gradually until it ended up with thirteen hundred acres, four lakes, and a dozen ponds and brooks. The lush greenery, hills, and water reminded him of New England, Amory often said. (Still, Amory, a student of language and its quirks, could not resist noticing and being amused by the peculiar accents of Texans: "[The East Texas accent] just has to be heard to be believed," he wrote, apparently going through the alphabet. "I am not just talking here of 'all' for oil, 'are' for hair, or 'arn' for iron, or 'ass' for ice. . . . I am also talking 'bard' for buried, 'kain't' for can't, 'dayum' for damn, 'fur' for far, 'griyuts' for grits, 'hard' for hired, 'hep' for help, 'lags' for legs, 'own and oaf' for on and off, 'pap' for pipe, 'poly' for poorly, 'rass' for rice, 'stars' for stairs, 'tahm' for time and 'tarred' for tired. . . . And if this wasn't enough, all the time they are convinced they are talking the 'Kang's Ainglish.'")

And so was born Black Beauty Ranch, the animal sanctuary that would, ultimately, become a living symbol of the Fund for Animals rescue efforts and the type of animal utopia about which Amory dreamed. Although it was founded as a home for the rescued Grand Canyon burros, the ranch during Amory's era eventually housed nearly six hundred abused and mistreated animals of all types — including bobcats, buffalo, Siberian foxes, ostriches, and kinkajous. Although Amory wrote about the founding of the ranch and Polar Bear's visit to it in *The Cat and the Curmudgeon*, his last book, *Ranch of Dreams*, published a year before his death, goes into elaborate detail about the founding of the ranch and its many remarkable residents, all of whom were terribly abused before their arrival, and many of them permanently wounded.

And the ranch is indeed something to see. Because of Amory's and the fund's objections to zoos and other institutions that house animals but use them for entertainment or exhibition purposes, Black Beauty Ranch is not open to the public, although it does sometimes sponsor open houses. Many of the animals run free, and those who cannot run free for practical purposes are housed in enormous and open structures with plenty of toys and material to keep them occupied and happy. Food is plentiful, and most is fresh. Most of the animals are neutered, and mating is not permitted. The purpose of the ranch is not for the animals to be looked at, Amory would say. Instead, they are to be "looked after."

The sanctuary concept was not new for the fund; Amory himself firmly believed in the idea of a paradise for animals, where they would not be forced to be the subjects of experimentation or used as entertainment for humans. By the time Black Beauty Ranch was founded, the fund had the rabbit shelter in South Carolina and a wildlife rehabilitation sanctuary in Ramona, California, which has room for three hundred animals. The Ramona center, opened in 1985, cares for injured animals, and when they are healthy again, they are released back to the wild.

In *Ranch of Dreams*, Amory describes some of the success stories of the ranch, and goes into the often sad histories of some of its residents. He also notes that most of the abused animals — some of whom feared humans and often shunned them, while others hated humans and wanted to hurt them — grew docile and affectionate after spending time at the ranch. After being treated humanely, he said, they mingled well with humans and other animals. But if the animals could talk — and one actually could — they would have some horrific tales to tell. As one writer profiling the ranch noted, "The animals' stories begin to sound like the life histories of war veterans." Babe the elephant was a baby and living in Africa when her mother was killed by hunters — as Babe stood by and watched. She was then shipped by crate to the United States. Two of her legs and her head became misshapen after she spent long hours in the tiny space; a third leg was seriously injured later when she became a circus performer and another elephant crashed into it.

Other animals had been burned (including Conga, an elephant whose skin was badly sunburned as she performed in a Florida roadside zoo, twirling an umbrella); abused during medical experiments, where teeth and limbs were pulled from them; shot in anger by their owners; and shackled in tiny quarters for months or longer.

Even Amory, who knew much about the personalities of most animals owing to his years of experience working with them, was continually surprised by their intellect and awareness. He was particularly fond of elephants because of their sharp minds and innate cleverness. In *Ranch of Dreams*, he tells the story of the injured elephant Conga, who, when she first arrived at Black Beauty, could be moody. Occasionally she would move suddenly, bumping into caretaker Christopher Byrne but not hurting him. Amory soon grew to adore the ten-thousand-pound elephant, but he worried that she would come running toward him excitedly if she saw him from across the barn. With his arthritic hips and Conga's size, even a mild bump from the elephant could hurt him. He mentioned this to Byrne, who scoffed. The animal had affection for Amory, he said, and was smart enough to know better. "She'll stop," Byrne replied. "She's knows you can't move fast. She's not stupid — she's an elephant."

Byrne, who managed Black Beauty from 1990 until his death from a car accident in 2003, oversaw much of the growth of the ranch. He had a history almost as interesting as the animals', and Amory was immediately drawn to him. Born in Wimbledon, England, he worked as a stuntman and animal trainer in the United States and in Australia, and at one time cared for the DuPont family's horses in Pennsylvania. Byrne also worked with animals in films in Hollywood, and started Hawaii's first ecotourism business on Kauai. Byrne, like most of the workers at the ranch, knew virtually every individual animal by its human-given name. He had tremendous knowledge of animals and how to handle them — strange, considering that during his childhood he was "almost entirely animal deprived," he once said.

Like his childhood role model, his Aunt Lu, Amory believed in treating all animals fairly, and he felt all the animals at Black Beauty Ranch deserved equal treatment. But he knew that certain ones had particularly compelling stories to tell, and he did have his favorites. Amory knew that the unusual and compelling story of Nim Chimpsky, the "talking" chimpanzee, would get publicity for the ranch, and he could not help but develop a special kinship with Friendly, one of the Grand Canyon burros who was transported to Black Beauty.

Interestingly, the first animal to find a home at Black Beauty was not a burro, a goat, an elephant, or a horse. It was a small orange kitten who dragged herself down the driveway of the ranch with her front paw attached to a leghold trap. The animal, dubbed Peg, was in great pain, and the ranch workers did not think she would live. Peg was taken to a veterinarian, who was forced to remove the front leg to the shoulder. And the severely injured kitten had to stay at the veterinarian's office for a long time before she returned to the ranch. But, like nearly all the animals at Black Beauty, Peg's story has a happy ending: she devised for herself a new way to walk, Amory writes, using her three legs, and by the time Amory published *Ranch of Dreams* in 1997, the eighteen-year-old cat was still roaming around the ranch.

Then there was Friendly, one of the burros rescued from the Grand Canyon, who became of Amory's favorites when he visited Black Beauty Ranch. Amory and Friendly — who would bound toward Amory as soon as she saw him — would often stroll together through the grounds of the ranch, and she would accompany him as he sat on the steps of the ranch's main office. Amory wrote that he knew the burro was special when he first met her. Friendly had been one of the first burros to "land" at Black Beauty after the animals' high-profile rescue from the Grand Canyon. Despite the tremendous upheaval in her life, she remained serene, he writes:

> Friendly had come up in a sling under the helicopter in the very first batch of burros we rescued in the Grand Canyon. I was in the corral when she was lifted up over the rim and delicately dropped to the ground. I was also one of the crew who untied her. Friendly did not, as all the other burros had done, trot immediately and rapidly away from us — instead she just looked at us in that contemplative and philosophical way I learned was her trademark. Whatever had happened to her — the roundup, being tied in a sling, being picked up and fastened to a roaring helicopter overhead, being carried seven thousand feet up in the air, and finally being let down among all of us — it had all been sudden and uncomfortable and ridiculous and even crazy, and she surely thought that's what we all must be. But she also realized . . . that no one had really hurt her, and therefore we were not all bad.

By 2007, Friendly was still roaming the pastures of Black Beauty Ranch — the last surviving burro there of the rescue.

But certainly the most famous resident of Black Beauty Ranch was the chimp Nim Chimpsky (named after the writer and linguist Noam Chomsky), who knew more than one hundred signs of American Sign Language. Nim, as he was known, came to Black Beauty in the mid-1980s when he was about ten years old. He initially had been used by a New York psychologist and researcher who was doing behavioral science research, and eventually the chimp lived on and off in the homes of various families and researchers in the New York area. Members of one family had taught him sign language. Nim had been a celebrity in his own right before he arrived at Black Beauty (he was the subject of two books), but Amory and others at the fund were distressed to learn that he was often put in isolation and, as he grew older, certainly treated in a manner not fitting the celebrity he was — he was put in pens with many other laboratory chimpanzees and used in experiments investigating hepatitis. Amory persuaded the organization that then housed Nim — the Institute for Primate Studies at the University of Oklahoma — to move him to Black Beauty. Amory writes at length in *Ranch of Dreams* about the chimpanzee and his plight, and about the efforts by the fund to relocate him. Fund workers realized that his knowledge of sign language was Nim's claim to fame, but they were determined that he would live the rest of his life without having to learn another word of it. (But that did not stop Nim from talking; Byrne recalled an incident when a deaf woman who knew sign language visited the ranch and "talked" to Nim. "Nim told her that he must have been very bad [before he came to the ranch] because he had been locked up for a very long time," Byrne said.)

The fund built a special house for Nim and even persuaded the primate lab to give the ranch another chimp, Sally, a former circus animal, for his companion. The two lived happily until Sally's death in 1997.

Ranch of Dreams, published in 1997, was Amory's last book. It summarizes some of the autobiographical material he covered in the cat trilogy but also goes into great detail about how he came to found the ranch. Amory elaborates on how the ranch fulfilled a lifelong dream for him: "It was not long after reading *Black Beauty* for the first of many times that I had a dream that one day I would have a place which would embody everything Black Beauty loved about his final home," he writes on the book's back cover. "I dreamed that I would go even a step further — at my place none of the horses would ever wear a bit or blinkers or check reins, or in fact have any reins at all, because they would never pull a cart, a carriage, a cab or anything else. Indeed they would never even be ridden — they would just run free."

Black Beauty Ranch still exists, and is now known as the Cleveland Amory Black Beauty Ranch, a name change that took effect when the Humane Society of the United States and the Fund for Animals merged in 2004. As visitors enter the gate to the huge ranch, Anna Sewell's words greet them on an arch overhead: "I have nothing to fear / and here my story ends. / My troubles are all over and I am home."

▷ ▷ ▷ *Ranch of Dreams* would be Amory's eleventh book, not including two volumes of which he was editor. He was nearly eighty years old when it was published in 1997, and his arthritic hips had severely impaired his mobility by this time. Amory, though, had been amazingly mobile and energetic even in his seventies. In the mid-1980s, he had a small part in a film, and was also a real-life character in a made-for-television movie. In 1987, he played a small part in *Mr. North*, which was based on the Thornton Wilder book *Theophilus North* and directed by John Huston's son, Danny. The film originally was slated to star Amory's friend John Huston, who ultimately became too ill to do the filming. Amory describes in *The Cat and the Curmudgeon* how excited Probst was when she told him he was selected for the role of an "elderly" butler in the film. "'A *mature* butler,' I automatically corrected," he wrote. Amory's role in the film came at a time when some producers in Hollywood were considering making a movie of *The Cat Who Came for Christmas*, a film that, ultimately, was never made. Amory had a whopping six speaking lines in *Mr. North*, but, characteristically, the event became fodder for a funny anecdote in *The Cat and the Curmudgeon*. After the film was released, he received two fan letters (including one from his sister-in-law), he wrote. "I waited faithfully for William Morris and ICM and all the other big agencies to call me for other pictures. But not single one of them did," he wrote. "No one even wanted me to play myself in the movie about Polar Bear." *Mr. North* was filmed in Providence, Rhode Island, and starred Anthony Edwards and Robert Mitchum. Amory's acquaintances Lauren Bacall and Angelica Huston had roles in the film, as did Katharine Houghton, the niece of his longtime friend Katharine Hepburn.

Amory may never have had a chance to play himself in a film version of *The Cat Who Came for Christmas*, but an actor did portray him in a 1984 made-for-television film about his old friend and editor Norman Cousins. In an adaptation of Cousins's popular book *Anatomy of an Illness*, actor David Ogden Stiers played Amory. Stiers, a veteran actor who is best know for his role as Charles Emerson Winchester III in the television show M*A*S*H, starred along with Ed Asner, who played Cousins. Cousins — who once faced a life-threatening illness but recovered — wrote the best-selling book based on his theory that a patient's state of mind can have a dramatic effect on his or her recovery.

▷ ▷ ▷ By the time he was in his late seventies, Amory still went to work each day despite severe arthritis and other health problems. (Medication he took for an aneurism clashed with his arthritis medication, so his pain from the arthritis often went untreated.) His weakened physical state may have simply made it more difficult to write. Amory was not one to complain about his health, but as he noted in an interview when he was seventy-two, growing older was no treat for him. "You can't walk properly, you can't get all the beautiful girls, because all these stupid little kids get them," he told the reporter. Old age did have at least one advantage, though: "Decisions come easier," he said. "Suddenly, it's a question of what you want to have done, not what you want to do."

Walter Anderson, Amory's editor at *Parade*, said most of Amory's writing for that magazine required little editing. But one of the first drafts of *Ranch of Dreams* indicates that the original manuscript of the book was the target of some extensive criticism by Fredrica Friedman, Amory's editor at Little, Brown, who had edited the Polar Bear trilogy and was by this time editorial director and vice president of the publishing company. (In all three cat books, Amory thanks Friedman in the acknowledgments.) Amory clearly respected Friedman as an editor, and she was adept at pointing out problems in his writing without insulting him. In a draft of *Ranch of Dreams* — which, when Friedman saw it, was titled "Meanwhile, Back at the Ranch" — Friedman seems unusually frank about problems in the manuscript. Friedman tells Amory that his firsthand knowledge of animals and his "charm, humor and unique stylistic voice" made best sellers out of the three Polar Bear books. "But that is exactly what is missing now. . . . Chapters often have too many encyclopedic-like biographies of peripheral folk, or animal history and episodes covered before," she writes. "That material distracts the reader from the narrative thrust of the book and reads as filler. It should be replaced with relevant and new animal and human stories on or of the ranch." Friedman's notes are extensive, as she suggests that he reduce the information he includes about *Black Beauty* author Anna Sewell and elaborate instead on his lifelong dream for the ranch. ("You can tell us in your inimitable tongue-in-cheek manner how your brother, your aunt, your father reacted to your 'dream.'") Friedman tells Amory that the manuscript he submitted is not the one they discussed, and that she wants a new focus and new title: "Thus, Cleveland, I am concerned that the chapters you have shown me, these 185 pages . . . do not now succeed in telling a story of the Ranch or of the animals — the book for which you are under contract at Little, Brown and for which your audience awaits. I know your talent; I believe you can write a memorable story of the animals and the Ranch. I will be happy, as always, and as we have done before, to meet with you to work on revising the book chapter by chapter. I hope you will decide to do that." Ultimately, *Ranch of Dreams* was not published by Little, Brown but by Viking Penguin, and edited by Carolyn Carlson, whom Amory thanks in his acknowledgments. Apparently Amory and Friedman did not agree on what the book, ultimately, should say, so Amory found another publisher.

While *Ranch of Dreams* never achieved the best-seller status of the Polar Bear books, it has attained a respectable longevity. Once again, as with each volume in the Polar Bear series, readers on the Amazon.com website continued to write about *Ranch of Dreams* more than seven years after it was published. (And an audio version of it also ensured more "readers.") The book inspired superlatives from some of the reader-reviewers: "This is the best piece of non-fiction ever written," one wrote. Another reader wrote in 2003, "Someone recently asked me what I'd do if I didn't need to work for a living. I think I'd want to go to Murchison, Texas, and help care for the ranch's residents." Like the Polar Bear trilogy, *Ranch of Dreams* appealed to a wide age range and type of reader, including young adults. Part of its appeal to young readers may have been its structure — it consisted of only five chapters — and its cover, a brightly colored drawing of Amory in a chair, surrounded by a half dozen of the ranch's residents. The book received positive reviews from the leading book-review journals. "Amory tells the heart-wrenching stories of individual residents [of the ranch] in the larger context of humanity's cruelty to animals in general," according to *Library Journal. Kirkus* wrote, "Amory is a wry companion whose aristocratic humor sparkles with a biting contempt for all those who would do harm to animals. . . . Amory's simple point — that our treatment of animals should be governed by the rules of common decency and respect — is stated convincingly, with brio and great dignity." "A very moving but important work," wrote *Booklist*, whose reviewer also noted that the book would appeal to young adults.

Amory's activities for the last decade or so of his life were a function of his physical health. His Fund for Animals work required him to travel extensively, and this naturally became more difficult as he aged. His biggest problem was the arthritis, which grew progressively worse. One indication of the gravity of the condition was the fact that he wrote about it — Amory, of course, wrote about most aspects of his life but was normally silent about his physical ailments, including the severe skin disease that led to his honorable discharge from the army when he was a young man. The arthritis, though, became such a part of his daily life that he wrote at length about it in *The Best Cat Ever*, talking in particular about the lengths he and other arthritis sufferers would go to find relief from their pain. He may have considered it ironic that Polar Bear, too, suffered from the same illness. Throughout his life, Amory had always conducted intense research on any topic that interested or affected him, including, in his later years, the stock market. (He was an intelligent and informed investor who made much money on his investments.) Amory informs us of the roots of the term "arthritis," and he writes about the various forms of what is an incurable disease. He offers statistics on the number of animals and humans who have the disease: "By the time [humans] are in their sixties, 80 percent of them have it, and by the time they get to my age I have no intention of telling you what percent have it any more than I have any intention of repeating to you how old I am. But I will tell you that, by my figuring, it is well over 100 percent."

But his arthritis was nothing compared to an event that nearly killed him — he was hit by a truck while crossing the street one morning on his way to work. Amory talks about the incident at length in *The Best Cat Ever*, and it seems unbelievable that he survived it at all. As he describes it, he was crossing the intersection of Central Park South and Seventh Avenue with his cane. He nearly made it to the other side of the street when the light changed. A truck careened around the corner at him. Amory writes that the next thing he remembered was being in the ambulance, unaware of where he was and with only an inkling of what had happened. The ambulance transported him three blocks to Roosevelt Hospital. He suffered several broken ribs, a concussion, an injury to his eye, and numerous bruises and cuts to his face and neck. Ever the writer, he was intrigued by the description of the accident that the emergency-room doctor had written:

Traumatic injury to the body resulting in: fracture of the left lateral fifth, sixth and seventh ribs, resulting in loculated pleural hematoma with contusions and hematomas to chest wall; closed head trauma, cerebral concussion with unconsciousness and post concussion syndrome; facial trauma resulting in contusions and large hematoma of the left forehead and left frontal region with swelling and large periorbital ecchymosis and hematoma of left eye extending to medial right eye, resulting in complete closure of the left eye with purulent conjunctival discharge; unsightly facial scarring and/or discoloration; contusion to the left hand; contusion above and lateral to the left eye with hematoma extending down left cheek to chin and neck.

Amory joked in the book that he had to practice repeating that paragraph when friends asked him how he was. ("'Once I get that loculated pleural hematoma under control,' I said, 'and then lick that darned large periorbital ecchymosis, I will be fit as a fiddle.'")

Amory eventually recovered, and he and his friends were able to find humor even in such a serious — and potentially tragic — event. Walter Anderson remembered that after Probst told him about the accident, Amory called him from his hospital bed. But Amory was unaware that Anderson already knew about it, and he went into great detail about what had happened to him. Anderson, as it turned out, had rehearsed what he was going to say. He waited until Amory was through explaining: "'Cleveland, I have one question,' I said. 'What's that?' he asked. 'How's the truck?'" Even in his pain, Amory roared with laughter, Anderson recalled. "He loved that," Anderson said. "It was the only time I Cleveland Amoried Cleveland Amory."

In *The Best Cat Ever*, Amory tells the story of how he overheard a conversation Probst was having with an attorney when they thought Amory was out of earshot. The two were discussing a possible lawsuit against the company that owned the truck that had hit him, and the attorney told Probst that any settlement Amory would receive would be tax-free. "Don't tell Cleveland," Probst told the attorney. "He'll do it again."

After Amory recovered from the accident, his daily schedule was full as usual — he routinely traveled out of town to regional animal shelters and humane groups for fund-raisers and educational purposes; when he was in the fund offices, he was constantly on the phone. Amory famously returned as many phone calls as he could — from fellow animal lovers all over the world — and would even go to lunch with complete strangers who believed in the cause. Once the Polar Bear books hit the best-seller list, Amory had an entirely new, and much younger, audience. Obviously, some of his first readers — those who were familiar with his trilogy of social histories (*The Proper Bostonians, The Last Resorts,* and *Who Killed Society?*) — were aging, and some were not around anymore by the 1990s; and only an ever-shrinking group of readers could remember his 1960s and 1970s column in TV *Guide*.

During the last few years of his life, the Internet began to come of age. It is unfortunate that Amory saw that new medium only in its infancy, because he was a natural to take advantage of it. First, it would have been handy for him to use it for the exhaustive research he conducted on any subject that interested him; second, he could easily have spread information about animal-rights activities through it; and, third, as a great communicator who tried to return calls and letters from most who contacted him, he would have enjoyed the ease and instant gratification of e-mail. As it happened, the Internet perhaps served him best after his death. Many fans posted online tributes to him, and a continuing theme was that they appreciated his personal answers to their fan letters. One fan, Mary Beth Skeuse, described how she wrote Amory a fan letter after reading his account of Polar Bear's death in *The Best Cat Ever*: "I was absolutely stunned when he called me and suggested we meet for lunch at Trattoria Del Arte [his favorite restaurant] the following Sunday," she recalled in a posting on www.animalnews.com. "Meeting him was a thrill I'll never forget, and we corresponded from that day until his death."

Amory's life went on as normally as possible during those last years. A few years before the death of Polar Bear, he adopted another white cat, Polar Star, who made his home in the fund offices. Near the end of his life, Amory lived primarily on royalties from the Polar Bear books, plus some money he made from stock investments. But as always, and particularly during the last twenty years of his life, he lived relatively modestly. In addition to his apartment off Central Park and memberships in the New York Athletic and Harvard clubs, his only other luxury was a Cadillac that he insisted on keeping, much to the chagrin of some of his friends, who said he was not a good driver. In 1992, he was able to purchase a small beach house in Water Mill, New York, that had a view of the ocean. Because of his failing health, he had little chance to visit there and had trouble negotiating its stairs when he did go there.

By the last six months of his life, his arthritis was so severe that he had trouble walking even with two canes, and he could barely bend over. Like many of the animals he rescued, though, Amory was a creature of habit. He dined nearly each day at the same booth at Trattoria Del Arte, around the corner from the fund offices, routinely greeting many of the New York celebrities who passed by his table. (Some, like baseball player Paul Molitor, received his hearty greeting but may not have necessarily known him, Edward Walsh remembered. But that did not stop Amory from engaging him in conversation.)

Although the last few years were not easy for Amory, there was a bit of justice in the manner in which the end finally came. He had fought for many of his eighty-one years for the rights of animals — for their freedom and for their chance to live unmolested by humans. Barring that, he had advocated a peaceful and painless death if it had to be. On October 14, 1998, he returned home after working until 8:00 p.m. at the fund's offices. That night, he died at home, in his sleep, of an abdominal aneurism.

▷ ▷ ▷ Epilogue

You can tell a lot about a person by his enemies.

▶ CLEVELAND AMORY

𝒜 memorial marker for Amory stands in the most likely *and* unlikely of places — not in the Boston area, where he was born and raised, not near Harvard, where he spent some of the most enjoyable years of his life, and not in or near Manhattan, where he lived most of his adult life. Instead, he is memorialized in a location that probably would have surprised even Amory ten years before his death: in northeast Texas (out in the middle of nowhere, some New Englanders would probably say).

Amory had known near the end of his life that he would be buried next to his beloved cat, Polar Bear, just inside the entrance to Black Beauty Ranch. His memorial's tone is a simple one and asks a question: "Cleveland Amory, 1917–1998 — Why can't we all be kind?"

A day after his death, Carolyn B. Maloney, a congresswoman from New York, introduced a resolution in the U.S. House of Representatives commending Amory and his actions in behalf of animals. "Mr. Amory devoted the last 31 years of his life to speaking for those who can't as unpaid President of the Fund for Animals," the resolution says. "In his years at the helm of this national animal protection group, he has imprinted millions in our society with the notion that we should treat animals with both decency and dignity." The resolution continues:

During three decades of advocacy for animals, Mr. Amory and his group led the way in dramatic rescues of animals all over the country. He airlifted hundreds of wild burros from the Grand Canyon who were destined to be shot by the National Park Service. They joined thousands of other animals, all snatched out of harm's way by Mr. Amory, at his Black Beauty Ranch animal sanctuary in Texas.

Black Beauty Ranch now stretches over 1,000 acres and will serve as the final resting place for a man who was known as the grandfather of the animal protection community. The world needs more people like Cleveland Amory and I hope his legacy of compassion will continue to live on.

About a month after Amory died, on November 12, 1998, his friends and relatives held a memorial service for him at Cathedral of St. John the Divine Episcopal Church on Amsterdam Avenue in New York City. Nine of his closest friends, colleagues, and relatives spoke. His granddaughter, Zoe Leinhardt, read two poems: "Cat in an Empty Apartment," by Wislawa Szymborska, which deals with an owner's death from the cat's perspective, and "On the Grasshopper and the Cricket," which reflects on the simple beauty of nature. Written by Amory's favorite poet, John Keats, it expresses the importance in nature of even the tiniest creatures:

> ... The poetry of earth is ceasing never:
> On a lone winter evening, when the frost
> Has wrought a silence, from the stove there shrills
> The Cricket's song, in warmth increasing ever,
> And seems to one in drowsiness half lost,
> The Grasshopper's among some grassy hills.

"Cat in an Empty Apartment" begins:

> Die? One does not do that to a cat.
> Because what's a cat to do
> in an empty apartment?
> Climb the walls.
> Caress the furniture.
> It seems that nothing has changed here,
> yet things are different.
> Nothing appears to have been relocated,
> yet everything has been shuffled about.
> The lamp no longer burns in the evenings.

The comments of other speakers were overwhelmingly funny, engaging, and poignant, but a few serious themes emerged: first, that Amory had been a loyal and supportive friend who contacted them in one way or another nearly daily, and who worried about their well-being; second, that his instincts and first impressions of people had been so strong that most of his best friends became close within days of his meeting them; and third, that their most vivid recollection of Amory involved him with a rescued animal, or on some animal-rescue mission — even when he was in his sixties and seventies, and even when the physical requirements of being an activist were almost overwhelming to him.

Even a month after he had passed away, the speakers at his memorial service indicated surprise that he was gone. To many of them, the lively, engaging, energetic — and sometimes manipulative — Amory had seemed immortal. At the service, some of the speakers indicated that they had, in unguarded moments over the last month, half expected to pick up a ringing telephone and hear Amory. "Cleveland Amory was my friend for almost thirty years. I spoke to him during the last ten or fifteen years of his life almost every day, sometimes two or three times a day," said Edward Walsh. When he heard he had died, "who, I thought, will call me at halftime of the Giants game on Sunday to tell me how badly they're playing? Who will call me in December to tell me not to go to the Giants game because it's too cold — a man who when he was almost my age walked the ice floes to save seals would be concerned about whether I was dressed warmly enough to watch those dopes play on Sunday. Who will call the manager of the Boston Red Sox on a day when they're playing the Yankees to tell him how to pitch to Bernie Williams or to Tito Martinez? Who will call me to tell me abut this wonderful article that was in this morning's paper, to give me the page and column and section and then read it to me word for word no matter how long it took?"

Christopher Byrne, who managed Black Beauty Ranch at the time of Amory's death, remembered his first conversation with Amory. It centered on the plight of wild animals and the widespread cruelty inflicted on them. "We had a really good talk and I got his concept of his dream of how he envisioned a place where animals just do their thing and just live their lives as animals and never get harassed or manipulated or pushed around or bullied," he said. "That was in 1990, and I think Cleveland and I talked every day since then."

Like many others who held top jobs with the Fund for Animals, Byrne was hired on the spot by Amory after their first conversation, and soon became one of his closest friends. The same happened to Marian Probst, who began working as his assistant after their first meeting; to Walsh, who did some preliminary legal work for the fund and soon found himself as its chief legal counsel; to Lewis Regenstein, who ran the fund's Washington office; and to environmentalist and activist Paul Watson, whom Amory enlisted to command the *Sea Shepherd*, the boat that broke through the ice floes of the St. Lawrence to save the harp seals.

After nearly two decades, Watson said he still had vivid memories of Amory on that rescue mission: "I can still picture him, standing on the ice floes, in the Gulf of St. Lawrence, cradling a baby seal in his arms to protect it from the sealers who were moving in toward us."

Byrne's memory of Amory was as vivid, but much more tranquil. During Amory's frequent visits to Black Beauty Ranch, Amory gradually grew to know knew the names and stories of all the animals there. But one of his favorites was a burro named Friendly, who had been rescued from the Grand Canyon. Often, man and burro would amble slowly around the ranch together, checking on the other animals. So it was not hard for Byrne and others who worked with Amory to come up with a creative way to spread his ashes. Distributing them by air over Black Beauty Ranch would not work, Byrne said, because Amory hated small planes. So the workers at the ranch attached Amory's ashes to a small container placed upside down around Friendly's neck. It acted as a shaker to distribute his ashes as Friendly made her way around the ranch. Those who knew Amory knew he would approve — it was, after all, his trademark to find creative solutions to difficult challenges.

▷ ▷ ▷ It was a source of pride for Amory that he never took a salary of any kind from the Fund for Animals. After the phenomenal success of the Polar Bear trilogy, money was no object to him; still, he donated most of this royalties from the books to the fund. Most of the money in his will went to the fund, although he did leave some cash to Probst and to his stepdaughter Gaea.

Amory was born into a family of privilege, and during his life he wrote about others who had great wealth. But money and the material goods it could buy were of little concern to him. As long as he was able to live where he wanted to live and maintain the few luxuries he enjoyed (a car and membership in a few key social Manhattan clubs), money was something he could use to help prevent animal cruelty.

In 2005, about seven years after he died, the Fund for Animals and the Humane Society of the United States merged. It was a merger, top fund officials like Michael Markarian and Probst maintained, that would have pleased Amory because it ultimately maintained the fund and gave it power. And as Probst noted, Amory would have been pleased that the merger took the fund full circle — the invitation by the HSUS in 1956 that Amory join the HSUS board triggered a further level of Amory's activism and eventually led to the founding of the Fund for Animals. All fifty staff members of the fund and its entire board were invited to serve similar positions at the HSUS. Amory, Probst said, would have been pleased about the merger. "It completes the circle," she said. The fund and HSUS had worked together on a few projects during the mid- and late 1990s, including several ballot initiatives, some litigation, and several publications. Probst, who was chairwoman of the fund's board of directors at the time of the merger and who now serves on the Humane Society board, manages and maintains the fund's Manhattan office where she and Amory worked for decades. And key fund projects like Black Beauty Ranch — renamed the Cleveland Amory Black Beauty Ranch — are still operating under the auspices of the fund. Michael Markarian, who was president of the fund at the time of the merger, became executive vice president of the HSUS. One of Amory's main goals as head of the Fund for Animals was to find smart and energetic activists who would continue to work in animal protection after he was gone — and that will be his enduring legacy, according to Lewis Regenstein and others. It was Amory who created the environment for the HSUS and the fund "to implement a powerful and effective movement dedicated to the protection of animals," Regenstein said. In the early twenty-first century, the fund and HSUS rescued more than ten thousand pets that were displaced during Hurricane Katrina, helped cripple the dog-fighting industry in the United States, and helped implement legislation "that would have been unthinkable," Regenstein said.

Markarian was in Brazil at an animal-protection gathering when he heard the news of Amory's death. People there — halfway around the world from Amory's home — expressed their condolences to Markarian when they heard the news. "I was with hundreds of animal people from Brazil, Peru, Chile and other countries, most of whom had never met Cleveland, but all of whom were touched by him in some way," Markarian said. "A woman who only spoke Portuguese managed to muster up a few words of English to tell me the reason she started working to protect animals was because she read *The Cat Who Came for Christmas*, which had been translated to her native tongue, as it had into dozens of languages."

Shortly before the merger with the Fund for Animals in 2005, Wayne Pacelle was named president of the HSUS at age thirty-eight. Pacelle was one of those people to whom Amory had taken an immediate liking. Amory named him national director of the fund when he was twenty-three and only a few years out of Yale. Pacelle left the fund five years later to take a job with HSUS.

A *Washington Post* feature story about Pacelle's appointment as president of the HSUS sounds suspiciously as though it were written about Amory. The story opens with several HSUS adversaries commenting on the handsome and charismatic Pacelle. "He's enemy number one," said the head of the U.S. Sportsmen's Alliance, which advocates hunting. "A wolf in sheep's clothing," said the president of the National Animal Interest Alliance, which opposes the goal of some animal-protection groups to stop using animal products.

Pacelle was unfazed and even amused by the criticism, even though he acknowledged he had received death threats. "They all go wild on me," he said in the story. If that sounds familiar, his next comment indicates that he had not forgotten his years under Amory's tutelage: "My ex-boss . . . said you could tell a lot about a person by his friends and also his enemies," Pacelle said. "I'm happy to have some of these people as my enemies."

The quote, no doubt, would have made Cleveland Amory proud.

ACKNOWLEDGMENTS

It is impossible to truly understand someone as complex and iconoclastic as Cleveland Amory, and it is very difficult to tell the story of his varied and complicated life. I relied as much as possible on the memories and opinions of his friends, relatives, and former coworkers, and on the primary documents — such as letters, memos, drafts of manuscripts, and published interviews — that he left behind. It is a testament to him that most of the people I interviewed for this book knew him for a minimum of ten years, and many for much longer than that. And most of them agreed that he was in many ways an enigma to them despite their longtime association with him.

I am particularly grateful to Marian Probst, who was his friend, editor, assistant, and fellow activist for more than thirty years. This book would not have been possible without her encouragement, hospitality, generosity, and — as Amory noted many times in his books — her sense of humor and astounding memory. She put no restrictions on any material and was always candid and open with me. I am extremely appreciative.

I also thank Gaea Leinhardt, for her generosity in providing remembrances of her childhood growing up with Amory and for photos of their family; and Edward Walsh, for his recollections about the beginnings of the Fund for Animals and the challenges he and other workers and volunteers faced. I am also grateful to Rob Amory, who was an invaluable source of information about the background and history of the Amory family and the relationship between the Amory brothers.

Thank you, too, to Walter Anderson, Lewis Regenstein, Edward and Judy Ney, and William Zinsser. All granted me long interviews that helped immensely in my understanding of Amory and his life and career.

Much of my research was conducted by accessing the Cleveland Amory Collection in the Rare Books and Manuscripts division of the Boston Public Library. The staff was very kind and understanding during my many hours — and weeks — there, and they made it extremely easy to access and gather material. I am particularly grateful to Mary Beth Dunhouse and Sean Casey.

I am very fortunate to have many loyal friends and coworkers who gave me great encouragement and advice while I worked on this project. They include Joe Bernt, Doug Daniel, Fred Heintz, Tom Hodson, Nancy Lewis, Pat Washburn, and many others. And thank you, too, to Corinne Colbert for your skills as a copy editor.

Finally, I am appreciative to the staff of the University Press of New England and especially to Ellen Wicklum, my editor. Ellen's enthusiasm, knowledge, and confidence in this project helped me immensely. Her suggestions and ideas were invaluable, and she made the publication process relatively pain-free.

As always, with gratitude and love to Tim Doulin for his patience and loyalty.

NOTES

All letters, manuscripts, and transcripts and other primary documents mentioned here are part of the Cleveland Amory Collection located in the Rare Books and Manuscripts Division of the Boston Public Library (unless otherwise noted). The author wishes to thank librarians there for their assistance and for access to that archive.

Introduction (pages 1–5)

1 Amory's life on videotape and film: Margaret Pantridge, "The Improper Bostonian," *Boston Magazine*, June 1991, p. 71.

1 Vision of Amory with goat: Patt Morrison, as reported on National Public Radio, Bob Edwards, narrator, November 12, 1998.

1 Amory yelling at carriage driver: Dan Rottenberg, "He Fights for the Animals," *Reader's Digest*, December 1981, p. 63.

1 "Sophie's choice" by Amory: Michael Blumenthal, *Texas Monthly*, January 1999, p. 54.

2 In speeches and interviews, Amory frequently referred to the vast number of his enemies and his pride in having them. See, for example, an interview with him in *Contemporary Authors, New Revised Series*, vol. 29, p. 12. Amory was interviewed on September 15, 1988.

2 Amory as fearless: Interview by author with Lewis Regenstein, by telephone, July 20, 2005.

2 Amory giving up his writing career: Interview by author with William Zinsser, by telephone, August 18, 2005.

3 Amory spoke and wrote at length about his upbringing and how he became interested in animal protection. See, for instance, *Ranch of Dreams* (New York: Viking), 1997; *The Cat Who Came for Christmas* (Boston, Toronto, London: Little, Brown and Co.), 1987; *The Cat and the Curmudgeon* (Boston, Toronto, London: Little, Brown and Co.), 1990; *The Best Cat Ever* (Boston, Toronto, London, New York: Little, Brown and Co.), 1993.

4 Comment about furs making women look fat: Carol Flake, *Boston Globe Sunday Magazine*, "Action and Words," February 11, 1990, p. 23.

Chapter 1. The Ultimate Outsider (pages 6–11)

7 Amory's many connections: Interview by author with Edward Walsh, June 18, 2003, New York City.

8   Meeting Amory and immediately working for him: Interview by author with Marian Probst, June 17, 2003, New York City.

8   Watching television on the telephone: Interview by author with Gaea Leinhardt, by telephone, March 15, 2006.

8   Amory compared to a Newfoundland: *Palm Beach Post Illustrated*, January 8, 1960. *Boston Globe* reporter Jack Thomas described Amory as a hefty man with a rumpled jacket in his story "A Very Proper Animal Lover," December 4, 1989, p. 39. Over the years, as Amory reached his fifties and sixties, other reporters noted his appearance was a bit rumpled. As a young man, however, he was very handsome and often impeccably dressed.

9   Description of the bunny bop: Interview by author with Marian Probst. The event is described in detail by Amory in his book *Man Kind?* (New York: Harper & Row), 1974, pp. 7–14.

10   Letter by Amory about popularity: Letter, Cleveland Amory to James L. Harmon, December 5, 1988.

11   Amory often praised John F. Kennedy after Kennedy's death. He was quoted in the *Philadelphia Evening-Bulletin* to this effect in a story by Eileen Foley, "Celebrity Book Pokes Fun at People in the News," December 24, 1963.

11   The note from Rose Kennedy to Amory is dated February 21, 1961.

11   The *New York Times* story about Mrs. Kennedy's comments about the bullfight, "Mrs. Kennedy Rides on Bullfighter's Horse in Seville," appeared on April 23, 1966, on p. 9.

11   Snub of Amory by Jackie Kennedy: Interview by author with Marian Probst.

Chapter 2. The First Resorts (pages 12–26)

12   Anecdote about the Forty Steps: Amory often told this story. See, for example, Carol Flake's "Action and Words," *Boston Globe Sunday Magazine*, p. 35.

12   Robert Amory's biographical material: "Robert Amory Dies, a Textile Leader," *New York Times*, July 21, 1974, p. 34.

13   Information about Robert and Leonore Cobb was taken from an interview by the author with Robert Amory III, by telephone, August 17, 2005, and from Leonore Cobb's wedding announcement, "Miss Leonore Cobb a Bride," *New York Times*, September 21, 1910, p. 11.

14   Amory family as members of high social strata: Interview by author with Robert Amory III.

14   "Old money" versus "new money" in Amory's eyes: Cleveland Amory, "My Life with What's Left of Society," *Saturday Evening Post*, December 9, 1961, pp. 89, 91.

15   Amory's recollections of his childhood and governesses: *Cat and the Curmudgeon*, pp. 97–100.

15   Amory's comments to Murrow: Transcript of the Amorys' appearance on *Person to Person*, April 17, 1959.

15   Pronunciation of "Nahant" and "Amory": Flake, "Action and Words."

15   Pronunciation of "Harvard": *The Proper Bostonians*, p. 12.

15   Amorys and social responsibility: Interview by author with Robert Amory III.

16   Zinsser on WASPs and his summer with Amory: Interview by author with William Zinsser, by telephone, August 18, 2005, and "A Reluctant WASP," *Town and Country*, August 2004, pp. 110–111.

16   Comment about Amory's closet by *Person to Person* technician: Amory, "My Life with What's Left of Society."

17   Zinsser on being an outsider: "A Reluctant WASP."

17   Amory's first literary effort: This was described in information Amory wrote about himself for various publishers, including Harper & Row, found among his papers.

18   Amory on discussion of sex in prep schools: *Best Cat Ever*, p. 33.

18   Amory's prep school grades: The grade card is among his personal papers.

19   Amory's parents setting high intellectual standards: Interview by author with Robert Amory III.

19   Professional path of Robert Amory Jr.: Interview by author with Robert Amory III. Details of his career are outlined in his obituary in the *New York Times*: "Robert Amory Jr., 74, Ex-official of CIA and U.S. Budget Bureau," April 21, 1989, p. 19.

20   The Amorys' financial situation as Cleveland entered college: *Cat and the Curmudgeon*, p. 185.

20   Amory on his Aunt Lu: Amory wrote at length about his role model Aunt Lu. For a detailed description, see *Ranch of Dreams*.

20   Amory on Brookie: *Ranch of Dreams*, pp. 13–19.

21   Amory on learning that a horse did not write *Black Beauty*: His column in *TV Guide*, December 23, 1972, p. 18.

21   Biography of Anna Sewell: *Cat and the Curmudgeon*, pp. 186–187.

22   Amory's years at Harvard: Amory wrote and talked at length about his college days throughout his life. See, for instance, *Best Cat Ever*, pp. 43–70.

22   Amory on selection of courses at Harvard: *Best Cat Ever*, pp. 48–49.

23   Amory's sadness on hearing about Foster's death: Interviews by author with Marian Probst and Gaea Leinhardt.

24   Amory's college grades: His grade card is among his personal papers.

24   Amory's public affairs essay: A transcript of this is among his papers.

25 Paul Watson's comments on enemies: These were made during Amory's memorial service, November 12, 1998, New York City.

Chapter 3. A Pen as Sharp as a Stiletto (pages 27–44)

27 Quote from Edward Quincy: *The Proper Bostonians*, p. 292.

28 Amory's recollections of his early days at the *Saturday Evening Post* and his relationship with the Hepburns: *Best Cat Ever*, pp. 100–104.

28 Letter to Roger Scaife: This is an unsigned and undated letter on *Saturday Evening Post* stationery, found among Amory's personal papers. It was presumably written to Scaife by a top editor at the *Post*.

28 Description by Amory of Mrs. Hepburn: *Best Cat Ever*, p. 100.

29 Early history of the *Saturday Evening Post* and other "slick" magazines of the early twentieth century: See Theodore Peterson, *Magazines of the 20th Century* (Urbana: University of Illinois Press, 1975), pp. 7, 12. See also Ronald Weber's *Hired Pens: Professional Writers in America's Golden Age of Print* (Athens: Ohio University Press, 1997), pp. 217–218.

29 Amory's correction of pronunciation and his remembrances of the Endicott Peabody story: *Best Cat Ever*, pp. 109–110.

30 The Peabody story appeared in the *Saturday Evening Post* on September 14, 1940, pp. 16–17, 68.

31 Accomplishments of Robert Amory Jr.: These are discussed in his *New York Times* obituary, April 21, 1989.

31 Amory's skin problems: Interview by author with Marian Probst, New York City, March 12, 2004.

32 Description of wedding of Amory and Cora Craddock: "Cora Craddock and Lt. Amory are Wed Here," *Washington Post*, September 14, 1941, p. SA 1.

32 Amory's story about Arizona and its sunshine: *Saturday Evening Post*, January 22, 1944, pp. 18, 76.

33 Amory's remembrances of Arizona officials' opinions of his stories: These appeared in biographical material about Amory put out by Dutton, which published *The Proper Bostonians*.

33 Amory's Doc Holliday story, "The Fighting Dentist of Tombstone," appeared in *Coronet*, August 1944.

33 The juvenile night-court story, "Delinquency Can Be Licked: The Judge Cracks Down on the Parents," appeared in the *Saturday Evening Post* on April 29, 1944, pp. 29, 70.

34 Amory's comment about his "life-altering" experiences in Arizona and his illness: Interview by author with Marian Probst, March 12, 2004.

35 Amory's story about shooting a bird as a child: Amory told this story and

wrote about it many times in his life; see, for example, Jack Thomas, "A Very Proper Animal Lover," *Boston Globe*, December 4, 1989, p. 39.

35 Amory as relative of George Thorndike Angell: Amory repeatedly wrote and spoke about this. See, for example, Pantridge, "The Improper Bostonian," p. 71.

35 Amory writing *The Proper Bostonians* as a result of publisher's request: See Pantridge, "The Improper Bostonian," p. 69.

36 Plethora of John Homanses: *The Proper Bostonians*, pp. 19–20.

36 The magic of the Family Name: *The Proper Bostonians*, pp. 31–32.

37 Bostonians as mum to reporters: *The Proper Bostonians*, p. 29.

37 Life for Bostonian women begins at sixty: *The Proper Bostonians*, p. 98.

37 The *New York Times Book Review* review of *The Proper Bostonians*, "Boston, Seen through a State of Mind," was written by Howard Mumford Jones and appeared on October 19, 1947, p. 7; the *Atlantic* review was written by Edward Weeks and appeared in November 1947, p. 180; the *Commonweal* review, written by Mason Wade, appeared in October 31, 1947, p. 47; the *Nation* review, written by Perry Miller, appeared on December 6, 1947, p. 165; the *New York Herald Tribune Book Review* review, written by Ellery Sedgwick, appeared on October 12, 1947, p. 4.

38 Pronunciation of Amory as "Emery" and description of the Somerset Club: See Flake, "Action and Words," p. 29.

39 Amory writing a book about a man writing a book: See John Crosby's "A Book about an Author Who Had Written a Book," *Washington Post*, August 6, 1954, p. 45.

39 Reviews of *Home Town*: J. H. Jackson, *New Yorker* in Briefly Noted, January 21, 1950, p. 97; *Booklist*, January 15, 1950; *Chicago Sun-Times*, January 29, 1950, p. 7; Fanny Butcher, *Chicago Tribune*, January 15, 1950, p. 3; Richard Mealand, *New York Herald Tribune Book Review*, January 15, 1950, p. 4.; Richard Maney, *New York Times*, January 8, 1950, p. 26.

40 Amory's story about Nancy Davis: *Cat and the Curmudgeon*, p. 114.

41 Gould's review of the *Today* show: "Commentary on Today: NBC's Early Morning Show Needs Some Work," *New York Times*, January 20, 1952.

41 Gould remembering his most oft-quoted review: This is discussed in the book of Gould's son, Lewis L. Gould, *Watching Television Come of Age: The New York Times Reviews of Jack Gould* (Austin: University of Texas Press, 2001), p. 115.

42 Amory's story about the Bar Harbor teenager: He wrote about this in his *Saturday Evening Post* article, "My Life with What's Left of Society," December 9, 1961, p. 91.

42   Mansions as "cottages": See the book jacket of *The Last Resorts*.

42   Reviews of *The Last Resorts*: See *New Yorker*, November 22, 1952, p. 200; Lloyd Morris, *New York Herald Tribune Book Review*, November 9, 1952, p. 5; Fanny Butcher, *Chicago Tribune*, November 30, 1952, p. 4; John McNulty, *New York Times*, November 9, 1952, p. 7.

43   Amory's books converted into television shows and plays: See *Cat and the Curmudgeon*, pp. 142–144.

43   Amory's letter to his mother "reviewing" the play: Letter, Cleveland Amory to Leonore Amory, February 5, 1953.

44   Item about Amory's marriage: *Time*, "Marriage Revealed," in Milestones column, February 28, 1954, p. 90.

44   Amory's letter to his mother indicating that he might move to California: Letter, Cleveland Amory to Leonore Amory, November 12, 1954.

44   Amory's life with Martha Hodge: Interview by author with Gaea Leinhardt, March 15, 2006.

Chapter 4. His Last Duchess (pages 45–59)

45   Amory's suggestion to the Duchess of Windsor, quoted in the chapter-opening epigraph: See his story in the *Saturday Evening Post*, "My Life with What's Left of Society," December 9, 1961, p. 91.

45   Amory's comments to Edward R. Murrow: These were made during his and Martha's appearance on Murrow's show, April 17, 1959.

46   Details about Murphy's firing: Mary Van Renssalaer Thayer, "World May Get Wally's Full Life Story: Duchess vs. Ghostwriters," *Washington Post*, October 7, 1955, p. 27.

46   Amory's full remembrances of the duke and duchess: See *Best Cat Ever*, pp. 115–143.

47   Leinhardt's views on Amory and the Windsors: Interview by author with Gaea Leinhardt.

48   Amory's view that the duchess had never read a book: "My Life with What's Left of Society," p. 91.

48   Martha Hodge Amory's letter from France to Amory's parents: Letter, Martha Amory to Mr. and Mrs. Robert Amory, June 8, 1955.

49   Initial story about the rift between Amory and the Windsors: Associated Press, "Author Quits as Writer for Duchess of Windsor," *Los Angeles Times*, October 5, 1955, p. 6.

49   Walter Winchell column: See *Washington Post*, October 13, 1955, p. 53.

49   *Newsweek*'s summary of the rift between Amory and the Windsors: "Press: The Ghost Vanishes," *Newsweek*, October 17, 1955, p. 6.

49   Martha's thoughts about the Windsor debacle: Letter, Martha Hodge Amory to Mr. and Mrs. Robert Amory, September 24, 1955.

50   Amory "abdicating": See Anthony Sammarco's article about Amory in the *Milton* (Mass.) *Times*, June 13, 2002.

50   Amory's remarks about the "untitled" duchess: *Best Cat Ever*, pp. 125–127.

51   Amory's comments about the duchess and the tape recorder: *Best Cat Ever*, p. 122.

51   The duke's comments about Hitler: *Best Cat Ever*, p. 141.

51   The duchess's comments about suing Amory: Cholly Knickerbocker [pseud.] wrote this in his column in the *New York Journal-American*, June 13, 1956.

51   Amory's comments about the networks: Jack O'Brian, "Amory Tied in Windsor Knot," *New York Journal-American*, October 1955, exact date unknown.

52   Amory having "no stomach" for the Windsors: *Best Cat Ever*, p. 143.

52   Windsor episode seen as a mistake by Amory: *Best Cat Ever*, p. 144.

54   Amory, Hodge separation notice: *New York Times*, "Notes on People," May 17, 1975, p. 25.

55   Amory as skeptical of the term "society": *Best Cat Ever*, p. 145.

56   Elsa Maxwell about the Duchess of Windsor: "What the Duchess of Windsor Won't Tell in Her Memoirs," *Washington Post*, December 18, 1955, p. AW7.

57   Maxwell about Amory's book: Helen Wells, " 'I Don't Care What They Say,' " *Miami Herald*, January 30, 1961.

57   Amory on being seated next to Maxwell: "My Life with What's Left of Society," p. 91.

57   Maxwell obituary: "Elsa Maxwell, Party Giver, Dies, International Society Figure, 81," *New York Times*, November 11, 1963, p. 25.

58   Reviews of *Who Killed Society?*: Cornelia Otis Skinner, "The Rise of 'Publi-ciety,' " *Saturday Review*, January 7, 1961, p. 24; Charles Rolo, "Readers' Choice," *Atlantic*, February 1961, p. 108; Rob Nordell, *Christian Science Monitor*, December 22, 1960, p. 5; Fanny Butcher, *Chicago Tribune*, December 18, 1960, p. 1.

58   Amory's research into society terms: *Best Cat Ever*, pp. 45–46.

59   Amory's view of the United States and heredity systems: Mary Every, "Proper Bostonian Entertains with Legends about Society," *Santa Barbara News-Press*, January 18, 1962.

59   Amory looking like Newfoundland hound: Tanya Brooks, *Palm Beach Post*, January 8, 1960.

59   Reporter's comments about Amory's pronunciation: Flo Barton Smith, *Sacramento Bee*, January 19, 1962.

59　Amory claiming he is finished writing about society: "My Life with What's Left of Society," p. 91.

Chapter 5. From Mrs. Astor to Her Horse (pages 60–72)

60　Ney's comments, quoted in the chapter-opening epigraph: These were made at the memorial service for Amory on November 12, 1998.

60　Amory's column: This was reported by Ray Erwin's story in *Editor & Publisher*, "Cleveland Becomes Columnist," November 26, 1960.

60　Amory's definition of "celebrity": See Charlotte Curtis's story in the *New York Times*, "Celebrities, from Chubby Checker to Kennedys, in Register," November 22, 1963, p. 43.

61　Reviews of *Celebrity Register*: *Saturday Review*, Books, March 21, 1964, p. 55; *Vogue*, People Are Talking, December 1963; Marya Mannes, *Book Week*, January 5, 1964, p. 2.

62　Amory talked about his call from Winchell in *Best Cat Ever*, p. 161.

63　Brief history of the humane movement in the United States: James M. Jasper and Dorothy Nelkin, *The Animal Rights Crusade: A Growth of a Moral Protest* (New York: The Free Press, 1992), pp. 60–65.

63　Animal rights activities linked with "bourgeois domesticity": Jasper and Nelkin, *The Animal Rights Crusade*, p. 60.

64　Amory understanding people: Interview by author with Edward Walsh.

64　Letter critical of Amory's column as "another column of chit-chat": Letter, Fendell Yerxa to Sun Times/Daily News Syndicate, November 18, 1960.

64　Amory's response to critical letter from member of Tuckahoe Women's Club: Letter, Cleveland Amory to Mrs. Royal Cabell Jr., March 7, 1973.

65　Biographical information about Norman Cousins: See his obituary by Eric Pace in the *New York Times*, "Norman Cousins Is Dead at 75; Led Saturday Review for Decades," December 2, 1990, p. 52.

65　Gaea's remembrances of Cousins and Amory: Interview by author with Gaea Leinhardt.

67　Probst's remembrances of first meeting Amory: Interview by author with Marian Probst, June 17, 2003.

67　Amory's description of the Hunt-the-Hunters Hunt Club: Amory talked and wrote about this throughout his life. For a detailed description, see his *Man Kind?* pp. 7–14.

68　Amory getting reprimanded: Interview by author with Marian Probst, June 17, 2003.

68　Request by Morgan for transcript of Amory's talk: Memo, Al Morgan to Cleveland Amory, June 3, 1963.

77 Amory's comments on cutbacks to wildlife refuges: This appeared on September 4, 1965, in First of the Month, his *Saturday Review* column, p. 5.

77 Amory's call to boycott the wearing of seal fur: This appeared on May 4, 1968, in "First of the Month," his *Saturday Review* column, p. 5.

77 Amory on the Sinai battles and Israel: This appeared on April 12, 1969, in First of the Month, his *Saturday Review* column, p. 4.

77 Amory on the demise of the *Saturday Evening Post*: This appeared on February 1, 1969, in First of the Month, his *Saturday Review* column, p. 4.

78 Amory on the launching of *New York* magazine: This appeared on May 4, 1968, in First of the Month, his *Saturday Review* column, p. 4.

78 Amory quoting study on monogamy: This appeared on March 7, 1964, in First of the Month, his *Saturday Review* column, pp. 8–9.

78 Amory's story about the Texas oilmen: The story, "The Oil Folks at Home," appeared in *Holiday*, February 1957, pp. 2, 56, 133.

80 Anderson on Amory's reaction to being edited: Interview by author with Walter Anderson, by telephone, March 30, 2004.

81 Anderson's recollections of Amory not following an editor's request and his comments about Amory as a natural writer: These comments were made at the memorial service for Amory.

82 Amory's article about the nation's slipping morals: "Our Morals Are Slipping," *Washington Post*, January 3, 1960, p. AW6.

83 Amory's article about the lecture circuit: This appeared in the *New York Times Magazine*, January 31, 1960, pp. 22, 25, 27, 28.

83 Circulation of *TV Guide*: See Glenn C. Altschuler and David I Grossvogel, *Changing Channels: America in TV Guide* (Urbana: University of Illinois Press, 1992), p. xi.

83 Brief history of *TV Guide*: Altschuler and Grossvogel, *Changing Channels*, pp. xii–xiv.

84 Amory's financial arrangement with *TV Guide*: Interview by author with Marian Probst, June 7, 2003.

84 Amory's comments about television scriptwriters: Amory said this frequently in speeches. He is quoted as saying it in the *Des Moines Register*, October 29, 1965.

84 Amory on "copycat" television writers: He is quoted as saying this in a story about one of his speeches that appeared in the *Milwaukee Journal*, November 12, 1965.

85 Amory on the "stacking" of the FCC: Amory said this frequently in speeches. He was quoted as saying it in a story in the Plattsburgh (N.Y.) *Press-Republican*, January 15, 1966.

85   Amory's first *TV Guide* column: This appeared in the magazine on September 21, 1963, p. 15.

85   Amory recalling "the critic judges himself." *Best Cat Ever*, p. 166.

85   Panitt on the magazine's relationship with Amory: This appeared in the same issue of *TV Guide* as Amory's first column — September 21, 1963, p. 1.

85   Amory remembering why he was hired at *TV Guide*: *Best Cat Ever*, p. 181.

86   Brief history of the growth of television in the mid–twentieth century: See Mitchell Stephens's "History of Television," *Grolier's Encyclopedia*, at www.grolier.com. This is also available on the New York University website, www.nyu.edu/class/stephens.

86   The role of Berle, Benny, Burns, and game shows on the growth of television: See David Bianculli's *Teleliteracy: Taking Television Seriously* (New York: Continuum Publishing Co., 1992), pp. 56–57.

86   The "golden age" of television and popularity of dramatic anthology shows: Stephens discusses this in "History of Television."

86   Directors Lumet, Frankenheimer, Penn, and others in early television: Bianculli, *Teleliteracy*, p. 107.

86   Expansion of news programs in 1963: Bianculli, *Teleliteracy*, p. 92.

87   Rise of television critics: Horace Newcomb, editor, *Encyclopedia of Television* (Chicago: Museum of Broadcast Communication). See the entry "Television Criticism (Journalistic)," by James A. Brown. This is also available at the website www.museum.tv/archive.

87   Lewis Gould about his father: Gould edited a volume of columns by his father, Jack Gould, who was a television critic at the *New York Times*, called *Watching Television Come of Age: The* New York Times *Columns by Jack Gould* (Austin: University of Texas Press, 2000), pp. 15–16.

87   Jack Gould wrote at length about a critic's influence, the bond between critics and viewers, and the "narcotic" effect of television in two columns in May of 1957. See his *New York Times* columns on May 19, 1957, and May 26, 1957; these are reprinted in Lewis Gould, editor, *Watching Television Come of Age*, pp. 230–237.

88   Minow on television as a "vast wasteland": This is quoted in Bianculli's *Teleliteracy*, p. 72. More of Minow's speech is quoted here, also.

88   Seldes's comments on television as a "mass medium": This information was taken from a review of the Seldes biography *The Lively Arts: Gilbert Seldes and the Transformation of Cultural Criticism*, by Michael Kammen (New York: Oxford University Press, 1996). The review was written by Gill Goetz in the Cornell University *Chronicle*, July 25, 1996: "Exploring the Life and Legacy of America's Premier 'Cultural Democrat'" (www.news.cornell/96/7.25.96/kammen.html).

89   Amory's encounter with Harold Robbins: Interview by author with Marian
     Probst, June 7, 2003.

Chapter 7. Critiquing the Vast Wasteland (pages 90–106)

90   Letter from reader about the editorial "we," quoted in the chapter-opening
     epigraph: This appeared in a letter in Amory's Mail Bag column in *TV Guide*
     on June 9, 1973, p. 50.

90   Amory's book about *Vanity Fair* magazine: *Vanity Fair, a Cavalcade of the
     1920s and 1930s* (New York: Viking Press), 1960.

91   Amory's comments about Crowninshield: *Vanity Fair*, pp. 7–8.

92   Panitt's comments about Amory's reviews: See Altschuler and Grossvogel,
     Changing Channels, p. 57. Panitt made the comment in his *TV Guide* column
     on April 2, 1968, according to the authors.

92   Anecdote about Amory meeting Alan Alda: Interview by author with Marian
     Probst, March 12, 2004.

93   Amory's comments about Monty Hall and Robert Stack: Amory, Mail Bag,
     TV Guide, June 28, 1969, p. 26.

93   Quinn Martin's thank-you note: Quinn Martin to Cleveland Amory,
     January 29, 1964.

93   Note from Patty Duke: Patty Duke to Cleveland Amory, February 20, 1964.

93   Note from Bing Crosby: Bing Crosby to Cleveland Amory, February 12, 1964.

94   Reader's suggestion to move Amory past the back pages of the magazine: This
     is quoted by Amory in *Best Cat Ever*, p. 82.

94   Shakespearean quote about Tony Curtis/Roger Moore show: Amory, Mail
     Bag, *TV Guide*, June 10, 1972, p. 58.

94   Description of Buddy Ebsen: Amory, *TV Guide*, April 14, 1973.

95   Review of *My Mother the Car* appeared on June 11, 1966, p. 12; review of
     Green Acres appeared on October 27, 1965, p. 19; and review of *Hogan's Heroes*
     appeared on November 27, 1965, p. 7.

95   Review of the *Dick Van Dyke Show* appeared on February 15, 1964, p. 2.

96   Review of *Let's Make a Deal* appeared on April 5, 1969, p. 44; review of *What's
     My Line?* appeared on January 25, 1964, p. 2.

96   Review of *Hollywood Squares* appeared on June 7, 1969, p. 6.

97   Amory mellowing: Amory, Mail Bag, *TV Guide*, April 13, 1973, p. 30.

97   Amory and Queen Victoria: Amory, Mail Bag, *TV Guide*, June 28, 1969, p. 26.

97   Amory's "editorial we": This letter was written by A. Peter Hollis of Wilson,
     North Carolina, and appeared in Amory, Mail Bag, *TV Guide*, June 9, 1993,
     p. 50.

98   Review of *Jericho*, October 22, 1966; review of *Julia*, October 12, 1968, p. 52;
     review of *Sanford and Son*, February 26, 1972, p. 47.

98 Amory's comments about *Music Country USA* appeared in Mail Bag, *TV Guide*, April 13, 1974, p. 36.

98 Review of *Harry O*, December 14, 1974, p. 44.

99 Review of *The Monkees*, November 19, 1966, p. 44.

99 Amory's Second Thoughts column appeared on June 2, 1973, p. 48. His comments about *An American Family* were made in this column, also.

100 The first review of *CBS Morning News* appeared on November 22, 1973, p. 36; the second appeared on February 8, 1975, p. 34.

100 Review of *Movin' On*, January 18, 1975, p. 26; review of *Kung Fu*, March 3, 1973, p. 42; review of *Mary Hartman, Mary Hartman*, May 1, 1976, p. 36.

101 Review of *CBS Reports*, May 19, 1964, p. 25.

101 Review of *The Dean Martin Show*, April 15, 1966, p. 26; review of *The Jerry Lewis Show*, November 9, 1963, p. 47.

101 Review of *Ironsides*, June 28, 1969; review of *Get Smart!* October 20, 1965; review of *The Banana Splits*, May 31, 1969, p. 25.

102 Television's influence on American culture: Altschuler and Grossvogel, *Changing Channels*, p. xi.

102 Need by readers to respect *TV Guide*: Altschuler and Grossvogel, *Changing Channels*, p. xiii.

103 Amory's story about his experience with *OK Crackerby!*: Titled "What the Heck Is a Two-Door Companion?" this appeared in *TV Guide* on December 18, 1965, pp. 8–14.

103 Enthusiastic comment from Cramer: This was made in a letter from Douglas Cramer to Cleveland Amory, January 7, 1965.

105 The first part of Amory's *TV Guide* series "Who Killed Hollywood Society?" was published on October 28, 1967, and the following four parts ran for four consecutive weeks. The story about Samuel Goldwyn was published on November 4, 1967, pp. 29–32.

105 Profile of Doris Day: *TV Guide*, June 10, 1972, pp. 34–36, 40.

Chapter 8. Hunting the Hunters (pages 107–123)

107 Amory's description of ballroom dancing: This appeared in *Ballroom Dance* magazine, December 1961, p. 5.

108 Cookbook coedited with Vincent and Mary Price: *A Treasury of Great Recipes: Famous Specialties of the World's Foremost Restaurants Adapted for the American Kitchen* (New York: Ampersand Press, 1965).

108 Martha in "black crepe": This appeared in *Women's Wear Daily*, April 25, 1962.

108 Some examples of Amory's celebrity mail: Cole Porter sent a note to Amory on March 27, 1963, thanking him for a short profile Amory wrote that appeared in *McCall's* magazine. Television personality Steve Allen also

thanked Amory for a short article about him in *McCall's* in a note dated May 9, 1963. Richard Rodgers wrote Amory in a letter dated January 19, 1959.

109 The reviews of *Flipper* and of *An American Sportsman* appeared in *TV Guide* on March 27, 1965, p. 1.

110 Amory's description of the newly formed Fund for Animals: This appeared in his *Saturday Review* column on February 2, 1967.

110 Panitt's comments about the revamping of *TV Guide*: These were quoted by Altschuler and Grossvogel, *Changing Channels*, p. 31.

110 *TV Guide* taking on two different tones: See Altschuler and Grossvogel, *Changing Channels*, p. 59.

111 Amory as chauvinistic and his comments about female secret agents: See Altschuler and Grossvogel, *Changing Channels*, p. 143.

111 Leinhardt about Amory believing women should excel professionally: Interview by author with Gaea Leinhardt.

111 Television as too sex oriented: Amory made these comments on the *Tonight* show on October 10, 1973, but they are quoted in a transcript to Craig Tennis, an employee of the show, prior to the taping.

111 Lecture bureau concerned about Amory's speeches: See letter, W. Colston Leigh to Amory, September 11, 1970.

112 Lecture bureau telling Amory about letter it received: See letter, W. Colston Leigh to Amory, January 26, 1971.

112 Amory's article about Israel: "Israel under Siege" appeared in *Reader's Digest*, April 1970, pp. 148–152.

113 Amory's talk to Hadassah: Sally Quinn, "Amory Charms Hadassah," *Washington Post*, August 19, 1970, p. C2.

113 Amory and Jewish furriers: Lewis Regenstein noted this in his interview with the author.

113 Second review of *American Sportsman*: This appeared in *TV Guide* on February 25, 1967, p. 28.

114 Viewers angry with *American Sportsman*: Amory spoke about this in his books *Man Kind?* p. 119, and in *Best Cat Ever*, pp. 194–195.

114 Review of *Emergency!*: This appeared in *TV Guide* on April 1, 1972, p. 5.

115 Amory's review of *Black Beauty*: This appeared in *TV Guide* on December 23, 1973, p. 18.

115 Amory's review of *Born Free*: This appeared in *TV Guide* on December 19, 1974, p. 42.

116 Regenstein's comments about the reaction of some hunters to Amory's review: Regenstein discusses this in his book *The Politics of Extinction* (New York: Macmillan Publishing Co., and London: Collier Macmillan Publishers, 1975), p. 45.

116　Amory getting call from *Field & Stream* editor: See *Best Cat Ever*, p. 192.

117　Early days of the Fund for Animals: Probst talked about this in her interview with the author, June 17, 2003. It was also written about by Jeffrey M. Berry in his book *Lobbying for the People: The Political Behavior of Public Interest Groups* (Princeton, N.J.: Princeton University Press, 1977), pp. 110–111.

117　Fund for Animals as "training ground" for HSUS: Interview by author with Lewis Regenstein.

118　Amory's "plug" for the Fund for Animals: This appeared in his *Saturday Review* column, February 2, 1967, pp. 5–6.

119　Amory not content to simply sit on boards and do no more: Interview by author with Lewis Regenstein.

119　Amory entering bullring: This was mentioned in a news release put out by the HSUS in 2004, "HSUS and the Fund: A Shared Visionary and a Shared Future," by Bernard Unti, announcing the merger of the fund and the HSUS.

119　Amory's personality: This was discussed by Walter Anderson, Lewis Regenstein, Edward Walsh, and Marian Probst (June 17, 2003) during interviews with the author.

120　Description of fund offices in Washington: See Berry, *Lobbying for the People*, p. 121.

121　Amory learning about lobbying: Interview by author with Lewis Regenstein.

121　Fund's finances during the first few years of its existence: See Berry, *Lobbying for the People*, p. 112.

121　Fund's finances and membership at time of merger with HSUS: This was spelled out in a news release by the HSUS announcing the merger, November 22, 2004.

121　Structure of the Fund for Animals and its boards: Berry, *Lobbying for the People*, p. 115.

122　Amory on compromise: Interview by author with Judy Ney, by telephone, August 14, 2005.

122　Amory having "no fear": Interview by author with Lewis Regenstein.

122　Amory's income by the early 1980s: See Rottenberg, "He Fights for the Animals," p. 64.

Chapter 9. Man Kind? (pages 124–138)

124　Amory as fast talker, quoted in the chapter-opening epigraph: From an editorial in *Field & Stream*, October 1978.

124　Amory and Probst working well together: Several of Amory's friends said this. Judy Ney elaborated on it in her interview with the author.

125　Explanation of social habits of wolves: See Regenstein, *The Politics of Extinction*, pp. 168–169.

125   Fund as pioneering voice in helping to protect wildlife: See Julie Hoffman Marshall's *Making Burros Fly: Cleveland Amory, Animal Rescue Pioneer* (Boulder, Colo.: Johnson Books, 2006), p. 24.

126   Story of Jethro the wolf: Amory elaborates on this in *Man Kind?* p. 333.

126   Details of the Marine Mammal Protection Act: See Marshall, *Making Burros Fly*, pp. 24–25.

126   Fund's success in using direct mail: Marshall, *Making Burros Fly*, pp. 24–25.

126   Amory's World's Fair exhibit: Amory writes at length about the success of this in "From Human Society to Humane Society," *Christian Science Monitor*, November 28, 1966, p. 2.

127   Amory on the federal government's tacit encouragement of hunting: *Man Kind?* p. 48.

127   Amory's contention that wildlife organizations are controlled by hunters: *Man Kind?* p. 64.

127   Amory's contention that National Geographic Society is controlled by hunters: *Man Kind?* p. 72.

127   Lengthy article in *Christian Science Monitor*: "From Human Society to Humane Society," p. 2.

127   Amory on "toothless" laws: He wrote about this in "From Human Society to Humane Society," p. 2.

128   Amory making up fake experiment to trip up his opponent: Several of Amory's friends talked about this during interviews with the author, including Marian Probst and Walter Anderson.

128   Amory seeking to debate Ann Arbor newspaper columnist: See *Ann Arbor News*, October 12, 1969, p. 10.

129   One-sided "debate" between Amory and Fulton: A transcript of this debate, which aired on radio, can be found among Amory's personal papers.

131   Reviews of *Man Kind?*: John R. Coyne, "Boobs and Bunny Boppers," *National Review*, March 28, 1975, p. 355; Delores King, *School Library Journal*, May 1975, p. 75; John Wanamaker, *Christian Science Monitor*, October 10, 1975.

131   Editorials about *Man Kind?* in the *New York Times*: These appeared on March 3, 1975, p. 24, and on October 4, 1975, p. 26.

133   Sponsors of *The Guns of Autumn* withdrawing: This was discussed in "Gunfight," *Time*, September 22, 1975, pp. 73–74.

133   Condemnation of *The Guns of Autumn*: See *Detroit Free Press*, September 7, 1975, p. 8E.

134   Statement quoting the Oklahoma Wildlife Federation to OETA-TV in Oklahoma City: This was sent to Amory on September 15, 1975, and is located among Amory's personal papers.

134   Volume of letters and calls to CBS about *The Guns of Autumn*: This was

discussed in "Hunters Zeroing in on TV," *Detroit News*, September 21, 1975. The article quotes George Hoover, director of information for CBS News.

134 Gary Deeb's *Chicago Tribune* column on *The Guns of Autumn*: This appeared on September 7, 1975, under the headline "Guns TV Program Touches off a Barrage."

134 Garry Wills's column in support of *The Guns of Autumn*: This appeared in his syndicated column dated September 18, 1975.

134 Controversy over *Guns of Autumn* helping NRA membership: *Time*, September 22, 1975, pp. 73–74.

136 *Field & Stream* editorial condemning Amory: This appeared in the October 1978 issue on page 4 and was written by Jack Samson.

136 Extensive story about improprieties at the nation's animal-rights organizations: "Cleveland Amory and the Kingdom of the Kind," *Field & Stream*, May 1976, pp. 124–137.

137 Update of the Hunt-the-Hunters Hunt Club: This appeared in the *Sierra Club Wildlife Subcommittee Newsletter*, San Francisco Bay chapter, June 1973.

138 Amory as fearless: Interview by author with Lewis Regenstein.

Chapter 10. In the Belly of the Beast (pages 139–155)

139 Paul Watson made the comments quoted in the chapter-opening epigraph when he spoke at Amory's memorial service, November 12, 1998.

139 Number of *Man Kind?* copies sold: Rottenberg, "He Fights for the Animals," p. 62.

139 Cousins doing little editing to Amory's column: Interview by author with Marian Probst, June 12, 2003.

139 Cousins's life: Details of his life were taken from Pace, "Norman Cousins Is Dead at 75," p. 52.

140 Amory quoting strange want ad: This appeared in his *Saturday Review* column on November 7, 1970, p. 18.

141 Amory's column of double entendres: See his *Saturday Review* column on March 6, 1971, p. 6.

141 "Dear Fur" mention: This appeared in Amory's *Saturday Review* column on December 5, 1970, p. 12.

141 "Msdemeanor" in column: This appeared on April 19, 1975, p. 11.

141 "Pros" and "cons" of Miss America pageant: This appeared in Amory's *Saturday Review* column on October 2, 1971, p. 8.

142 Reviews of *Animail*: See Martin Lebowitz, *Los Angeles Times*, January 9, 1977, p. Q4; and *Library Journal*, February 15, 1977, p. 503.

143 Detail about American Horse Protection Association: This appeared in the

Washington Post in Sally Quinn's story, "Horse Lovers Fight about Goose Hanging," March 18, 1971, p. C1.

145 Debate between Amory and Glasser: This was taken from a transcript of the debate found among Amory's personal papers.

145 Amory's mention of the National Organization of Non-Parents: This commentary appeared in his *Saturday Review* column on September 21, 1974, p. 37.

146 Amory's commentary in the *Christian Science Monitor*, "From Human Society to Humane Society," appeared on November 28, 1966, p. A2.

147 Amory speaking to member of audience about his redundant speech: Interview by author with Marian Probst, March 12, 2003.

147 Amory forgetting he was given an award at a speech: Interview by author with Walter Anderson.

147 Amory getting into the wrong limousine: See Marshall's *Making Burros Fly*, p. 20.

147 Description of Amory in *Publishers Weekly*: This appeared in that magazine on August 9, 1970, pp. 8–9.

148 Letter by *TV Guide* editor Panitt to reader: Letter, Panitt to Joan Silaco, October 19, 1976.

149 Description of fictional wives in *The Trouble with Nowadays*: This appeared on pp. 104–105.

150 Amory on the "bores" in social clubs: He made this comment in a September 15, 1988, interview published in *Contemporary Authors, New Revised Edition*, vol. 29, p. 13.

150 Reviews of *The Trouble with Nowadays*: A. J. Anderson, *Library Journal*, October 15, 1979; Tim Murray, *Best Seller*, October 1979; and *New York Times Book Review*, July 12, 1981, p. 35.

150 Amory's apartment: This was described in Pantridge, "The Improper Bostonian," p. 71.

151 Amory's insistence on membership in Harvard Club: Interview by author with Edward Walsh.

151 Amory as bad driver: Interview by author with Edward Walsh.

151 Increasing animal-rights activism in the 1970s: See Jasper and Nelkin, *The Animal Rights Crusade*, pp. 80, 87, 168–169.

151 Singer's essay widely read by animal activists: Jasper and Nelkin write this in *The Animal Rights Crusade*, pp. 90–93. Singer wrote about his views in his 1975 book, *Animal Liberation* (New York: Avon). A second edition was published in 1990. His pivotal essay was reprinted in 1977 in the *New York Review of Books*.

152 Singer on speciesism: See his book, *In Defense of Animals: The Second Wave*

(Malden, Mass.; Oxford, England; Victoria, Australia: Blackwell Publishing, 2006) pp. 3–4, 7.

152   Philosophy of the Animal Liberation Front: See its website, www.animalliberationfront.com.

152   ALF as a terrorist group: See Justin Rood, "Animal Rights Groups and Ecology Militants Make DHS Terrorist List, Right-Wing Vigilantes Omitted," *Congressional Quarterly*, March 25, 2005.

152   Philosophy of PETA: See its website, www.peta.org.

152   Amory as a moderate: Interview by author with Judy Ney. Marian Probst also talked about this in an interview with the author, New York City, April 24, 2008.

155   Amory's disagreement with Catholic priest: This was mentioned in his *New York Times* obituary on October 16, 1998, as well as in his own book, *Best Cat Ever*, p. 258.

155   Reaction to Amory as a meat eater: Interview by author with Marian Probst, April 24, 2008.

155   Amory's note to the nun: Edward Ney spoke about this during Amory's memorial service.

Chapter 11. Getting Their Goats (pages 157–170)

157   Chapter-opening epigraph: Patt Morrison, "You Can't Get Cleveland Amory's Goat(s)," *Los Angeles Times*, July 1, 1980, p. A4.

157   Amory's story about the QE2: See "Around the World in 81 Days," *New York*, April 11, 1977, p. 68.

158   Amory's story about the Stutz: See "The Stutz Massage Parlor," *Esquire*, July 7, 1977, p.141–143.

158   Amory's celebrity columns: Amory wrote "Stepping Out with Ginger," about Ginger Rogers, in the *Los Angeles Times*, February 21, 1976, p. B8; he wrote about Charo in "All This and Charo, Too," *Los Angeles Times*, February 3, 1976, p. E7.

159   Amory's recollections about the early years of the Fund for Animals: These were found among his papers in a transcript of a questionnaire he filled out for *Contemporary Authors*.

159   Amory's understanding of animals: Christopher Byrne made these statements at Amory's memorial service.

160   History of Fund for Animals rabbit sanctuary: See Marshall, *Making Burros Fly*, pp. 36–37.

160   Paul Watson's comments on Amory's compassion: Watson said this at Amory's memorial service.

160 Number of seals killed in 1980: Amory offered this number in an article he wrote for *Good Housekeeping*, "Let's Save the Seals," March 1980, pp. 60, 64.

161 Watson's history with Greenpeace: He discusses this in his book *Ocean Warrior* (Toronto: Key Porter Books, 1994), pp. xiii–xiv.

162 Amory's description of the seal rescue: He talks about this in "Let's Save the Seals," pp. 60, 64.

163 The banning and reinstating of clubbing in Canada in 1988: See Marshall, *Making Burros Fly*, p. 50.

164 A needle in a haystack: Interview by author with Lewis Regenstein.

164 Amory's initial reticence to attack the *Sierra*: Watson talks about this in his book *Ocean Warrior*, p. 12.

164 Amory on Watson's resemblance to a bear: See *Cat Who Came for Christmas*, p. 137.

164 *People* article about the *Sierra* incident: This article by Michael Ryan, "Duel at Sea," appeared in the August 20, 1979, edition, pp. 30–31.

165 Watson on "terrorists": See Watson, *Ocean Warrior*, p. 152.

166 History of the Grand Canyon burros and efforts to save them, and the fund's rescue plan: See Marshall, *Making Burros Fly*, pp. 57–58, 60.

166 Amory on the heat of the Grand Canyon: See "Doomed Burros," *New York Times*, July 30, 1980, p. 25.

167 Description of Young & Rubicam ad: See Michael Blumenthal, "Wild Kingdom," *Texas Monthly*, January 1999, p. 52.

167 Amory on young people advocating the burro rescue: He was quoted in David Gritten's article in *People*, April 6, 1981, pp. 42–43.

168 Amory's support of Israel: Several of his friends were aware of this and discussed it with the author, including Lewis Regenstein and Edward Walsh.

168 Amory's mercurial political views: Interview by author with Edward Walsh.

168 Amory's friendship with people of both political parties: Interview by author with Gaea Leinhardt, March 15, 2006.

169 Amory's view that the Navy will shoot anything: See Morrison, "You Can't Get Cleveland Amory's Goat(s)," p. A4.

169 Role of Weinberger aide Benjamin Welles in goat rescue: See Marshall, *Making Burros Fly*, p. 88.

169 Description of goat capture: Interview with Amory in *Contemporary Authors, New Revised Series*, vol. 29, p. 12.

169 Goats as intelligent and endearing creatures: Morrison, "You Can't Get Cleveland Amory's Goat(s)."

170 Details of mustang rescue: ABC News, *World News Tonight*, March 19, 1989, Dan Noyes reporting.

170   CNN segment on neuter/spay clinic: This aired on February 13, 1997, Jeanne Moos reporting.

Chapter 12. Nine Lives (pages 171–184)

171   Chapter-opening epigraph describing Amory as the "grandfather" of the animal-protection movement: Wayne Pacelle made these comments in the obituary of Amory that appeared in the publication *Animal Agenda*, November–December 1998, p. 12.

171   Details of pigeon shoot: See Marshall, *Making Burros Fly*, pp. 103–105.

172   Amory's comments about "homely" animals: Amory frequently made comments similar to this — that cute, cuddly animals had an advantage — but this was quoted from the *Animal Agenda*, November–December 1998.

173   Amory looking at the pigeon shooters with disgust and pity: Paul Watson said this at Amory's memorial service.

174   Amory's relationship with his brother, Robert Amory Jr., late in his brother's life: interview by author with Robert Amory III.

174   Robert Amory's search for the cat in the dishwasher: See *Cat Who Came for Christmas*, p. 16.

175   Robert Amory III on his relationship with his uncle Cleveland: Interview by author with Robert Amory III.

175   Amory's relationship with Leinhardt and their telephone calls: Interview by the author with Gaea Leinhardt, March 15, 2006.

175   Amory's knowledge of sports: Interview by author with Edward Walsh.

176   Amory's comments about Probst: See *Cat and the Curmudgeon*, p. 72.

177   Amory's comments about his tough times: See *Cat Who Came for Christmas*, pp. 4–5.

177   Walter Anderson on Amory's Hepburn interview: Interview by author with Walter Anderson.

178   Background of *Parade* magazine: This information was taken from the magazine's website, www.Parade.com.

178   Anderson's view of a good story for *Parade*: Interview by author with Walter Anderson.

178   Amory's profiles in *Parade*: The Hepburn profile appeared on November 11, 1983; the Rose Kennedy profile on July 3, 1983; the James Cagney profile on August 5, 1984; the Jack Lemmon story on March 17, 1985; the Cary Grant profile on September 22, 1985 (Grant's comments about Tony Curtis's imitation of him were found among Amory's papers, in the original manuscript of the Grant interview, but were not in the published story); the profile of Walter Cronkite on October 18, 1984; the profile of Gregory Peck on December 4, 1988; and the profile of George C. Scott on October 27, 1985.

180 Amory's profile of Fred MacMurray: "Hollywood's Ho-Hum Boy" appeared in the *Saturday Evening Post*, March 3, 1945, pp. 17, 97–98.

182 Peck's note to Amory: This was from Peck to Amory, dated February 16, 1989.

183 Story on good and bad sportsmanship: This appeared in *Parade* on March 20, 1983, pp. 6–8.

183 Story listing best bumper stickers: This appeared in *Parade* on January 29, 1984, pp. 4, 6, 8, 19, 22.

183 *Parade* animal-rights story: Written by Michael Satchell, "Do They Have Rights?" It appeared on January 13, 1985, pp. 4–6.

183 Anderson's phobia: See *Cat and the Curmudgeon*, p. 71.

184 S. I. Newhouse "call": Interview by author with Walter Anderson.

Chapter 13. Ranch of Dreams (pages 185–202)

185 Chapter-opening epigraph describing Polar Bear as a Republican: Amory notes this in *Cat Who Came for Christmas*, and he also repeated it often in speeches.

186 Anderson's opinion after reading manuscript of *Cat Who Came for Christmas*: Interview by author with Walter Anderson.

186 Editor Friedman's comments about *Cat Who Came for Christmas*: These were found among Amory's papers on yellow Post-It notes on a draft of the manuscript.

187 Fans' requests for paperback and audiotape versions of *Cat Who Came for Christmas*: See Ed McDowell's Book Notes column in the *New York Times*, July 20, 1988, p. C24.

187 Amory's dispute with Little, Brown: This is described in Ed McDowell's *New York Times* story "The Misadventures of 2 Best-Selling Books," January 18, 1988, p. C20.

187 Amory's large advance: McDowell, Book Notes, July 20, 1988.

187 Amory's ability to understand people: Interview by author with Edward Walsh.

188 Amory's recollection of Polar Bear's death: See *Best Cat Ever*, p. 241.

189 Reviews of the Polar Bear trilogy: *Cat and the Curmudgeon*: James E. Butler, *New York Times Book Review*, December 9, 1990, p. 25; *Cat and the Curmudgeon*: Carolyn I. Alexander, *Library Journal*, August 1, 1990, p. 130. *Best Cat Ever*: Edell Marie Schaefer, *Library Journal*, October 1, 1993, p. 118.

190 Amory on hopes his books encouraged adoption of cats: *Contemporary Authors, New Revised Series*, vol. 29, pp. 9–13.

190 Reader review of *Best Cat Ever*: Posted on www.amazon.com, June 7, 2003, by FrKurt Messick.

190 Amory on meeting Polar Bear after his death: *Best Cat Ever*, p. 258.

190 *Holiday* story on Texas millionaires: "The Oil Folks at Home," February 1957, pp. 2–56, 133.

191 Amory's initial skepticism about Texas: See *Ranch of Dreams*, p. 46.

191 Amory's mimicking of Texas accent: *Cat and the Curmudgeon*, p. 192.

191 Mission and purpose of Black Beauty Ranch: See the ranch's website, www.fundforanimals.org/ranch/about.asp.

192 Black Beauty residents as war veterans: Blumenthal, "Wild Kingdom," p. 54.

193 Christopher Byrne's opinion on intelligence of elephants: See *Ranch of Dreams*, p. 240.

193 Byrne on Amory's knowledge of animals: Blumenthal, "Wild Kingdom."

194 Amory's recollections of meeting Friendly: *Cat and the Curmudgeon*, p. 195.

194 History of Nim Chimpsky: *Ranch of Dreams*, pp. 163–203.

195 Nim "talking" to deaf woman: This was discussed on *ABC News with Charles Gibson*, November 4, 1997, Chantal Westerman reporting.

196 Amory on his *Mr. North* experience: *Cat and the Curmudgeon*, pp. 176–181.

197 Amory on getting older: These comments were made to *Boston Globe* reporter Jack Thomas, who quoted them in his story "A Very Proper Animal Lover," December 4, 1989, p. 39.

197 Friedman's comments on draft of *Ranch of Dreams*: Located among Amory's papers.

197 Friedman's overall criticism of what was then "Meanwhile, Back at the Ranch": Memo, Fredrica Friedman to Cleveland Amory, November 20, 1996.

198 Amazon.com postings about *Ranch of Dreams*: "Best piece of non-fiction ever written": posted December 23, 1998, author unknown; reader wanting to visit Murchison: posted August 4, 2003, by William C. Stevens.

199 Amory as investor: Interview by author with Edward Walsh.

199 Amory on his arthritis: *Best Cat Ever*, pp. 107–108.

199 Amory's remembrances about being hit by a truck: *Best Cat Ever*, pp. 228–233.

200 Anderson's joke about Amory and the truck: Interview by author with Walter Anderson.

200 Conversation about Amory suing the trucking company: *Best Cat Ever*, p. 233.

201 Fan's posting about meeting Amory: Mary Beth Skeuse, posted June 29, 2001, on www.animalnews.com.

201 Amory as bad driver: Interview by author with Edward Walsh.

201 Amory's purchase of beach house: Interview by author with Judy Ney.

Epilogue (pages 203–208)

203 Maloney's congressional tribute to Amory: Maloney presented this to the House of Representatives on October 15, 1998. It is reprinted in *Congressional*

Books by CLEVELAND AMORY

The Proper Bostonians
  (E. P. Dutton Co., 1947)
Newport: There She Sits
  (Harper, 1948)
Home Town
  (Harper & Brothers, 1950)
The Last Resorts
  (Harper & Brothers, 1952)
Who Killed Society?
  (Harper & Brothers, 1960)
Vanity Fair, a Cavalcade of the 1920s and 1930s
  Cleveland Amory and Frederic Bradlee, editors
  (The Viking Press, 1960)
Celebrity Register, with Earl Blackwell
  (Harper & Row, 1963)
Man Kind? Our Incredible War on Wildlife
  (Harper & Row 1974)
A Treasury of Great Recipes: Famous Specialties of the World's
  Foremost Restaurants Adapted for the American Kitchen
  Cleveland Amory, Vincent Price,
  Mary Price and Martha Amory, editors
  (Grosset & Dunlap, 1974)
Animail
  (E. P. Dutton & Co., 1976)
The Trouble with Nowadays: A Curmudgeon Strikes Back
  (Arbor House, 1979)
The Cat Who Came for Christmas
  (Little, Brown and Co., 1987)
The Cat and the Curmudgeon
  (Little, Brown and Co., 1990)
The Best Cat Ever
  (Little, Brown and Co., 1993)
Ranch of Dreams
  (Viking, 1997)

Burke, Coleman, 154
Burr, Raymond, 74
Burro rescue in Grand Canyon, 165–67,
    190, 193, 194, 206
Burrows, Abe, 104
Butcher, Fanny, 42
Byrne, Christopher, 159, 193, 205, 206

Cagney, James, 180
Capote, Truman, 62
Carlson, Carolyn, 198
Carroll, Diahann, 98
Cat and the Curmudgeon, The (Amory):
    on acting job in *Mr. North*, 196; on
    Anderson, 183–84; on book tour
    opportunities, 40; on financing
    Harvard education, 20; on Probst,
    176; writing and publication of,
    187–89
Cat book trilogy, 176, 185–90. *See also*
    individual books
Cats: Amory's fondness for, 143, 148,
    159–60, 185–86; Peg, 193–94; Polar
    Bear, 176, 185–90, 199; Polar Star, 201
Cat Who Came for Christmas, The
    (Amory): on Amory's brother, 19,
    174; audience response to, 189–90;
    movie idea for, 196; writing and
    publication of, 185–87, 188
Cavett, Dick, 145
CBS, 86, 133–35
CBS Morning News, 100
CBS Reports, 101
Celebrity and celebrities: Amory as
    commentator on, 55, 60–62, 157–58;
    Amory as member of the club, 43,
    44, 45, 46, 59; Amory's definition,
    61; and Amory's role as TV critic,
    92–93; Amory's writing and speaking

on, 52, 58, 59, 178–82; as animal rights
    supporters, 4, 63–64, 105–6, 121,
    145–46, 166, 178, 181; as anti-Vietnam
    War tool, 74–76; *Celebrity Register*,
    55, 60–62; evolution of concept, 58;
    hunting and gun advocates' criticism
    of, 136; network of friends among,
    107–8; as new high society, 55–59;
    Status Quotes column, 157, 158
Celebrity Register (Amory and Blackwell,
    eds.), 55, 60–62
Cerf, Bennett, 96
Charo, 158
Chess, Amory's love of, 16, 24
Chicago Sun-Times, 39
Chicago Tribune, 39, 42, 58, 87, 134
Chico and the Man, 95
Children, Amory on, 145–46, 176
Children's shows, 101
Christian Science Monitor, 58, 127, 131,
    146
Clem (timber wolf), 126
"Cleveland Amory and the Kingdom of
    the Kind" *(Field & Stream)*, 136–37
Cleveland Amory Black Beauty Ranch,
    195. *See also* Black Beauty Ranch
Cobb, Henry Ives (grandfather), 13
Cobb, Leonore (Mrs. R. Amory)
    (mother), 12, 13–14, 19, 20
Color television, 88
Commonweal, 37
Conga the elephant, 193
Conservation groups, political agendas
    of, 127, 166
Cooper, Wyatt, 75–76
Coronet, 34
Cousins, Ellen, 65
Cousins, Norman, 65–66, 69, 73, 139,
    148, 196

Huston, Danny, 196
Huston, John, 196

In Defense of Animals (Singer), 152
Internet, 201
Inverse snobbery, 15–16
Ironsides, 101
Irwin, Paul G., 154
Israel, Amory's support for, 77–78, 111–13
Ivan the Terrific (pet dog), 54
Ives, Burl, 103, 104

Jasper, James M., 63, 151
Jericho, 97
Jerry Lewis Show, The, 101
Jethro (timber wolf), 126
Journalistic writing: Amory's early
    interest in, 22–26; Animail column,
    124, 142–43; in Arizona, 32–34;
    as beneath upper-class Bostonian
    society, 17; drying up of outlets in
    1980s, 173; *Harvard Crimson*, 22–23,
    25–26; *Holiday* article on Texas
    oilmen, 78–80; *Nashua Telegraph*, 27;
    New York Herald Tribune, 64; *New
    York Times* book reviews, 57; *Parade*,
    2, 80–81, 177–84; Status Quotes
    column, 157, 158; Sun-Times/Daily
    News syndicate, 60; *Washington Post*,
    82. See also *Saturday Evening Post*;
    Saturday Review
Julia, 97–98
Juvenile crime story in Arizona, 33–34

Karras, Alex, 95
Keats, John, 204
Kennedy, Jacqueline, 11
Kennedy, John F., 11, 22, 168
Kennedy, Joseph, Jr., 22

Kennedy, Robert F., 76
Kennedy, Rose, 11, 179
Kilgallen, Dorothy, 96
Kirkus Reviews, 198
Knickerbocker, Cholly, 51
Koala protection project, 172
Kojak, 95
Kung Fu, 100

Laboratory animals: and Amory's
    debating skills, 128; legislative
    ineffectiveness in protecting, 127,
    146; medical experiments debate,
    63; Nim Chimpsky as, 195; radical
    activism against abuse of, 119; Singer
    on, 151–52; vivisection debate, 10,
    69–72
Ladies' Home Journal, 29
Language of upper-class Bostonians, 15
Last Resorts, The (Amory), 41–43, 46
Laurent, Lawrence, 87
Lectures and speeches: Amory on the
    circuit, 83; Amory's distaste for
    criticism during, 64; Amory's style,
    59, 147; and animal-rights crusade,
    72; audience response to, 59, 146–47;
    book tours, 40, 59, 61, 187; Hadassah
    banquet, 113; later in life, 157; lecture
    bureau conflicts, 111–12; radio
    commentary, 124, 148; *Today* show,
    6–10, 41–43, 60, 66, 67, 68, 72
Leghold traps, 131–32
Legislation for animal protection:
    Airborne Hunting Act, 125; Amory's
    tracking of for audience, 76–77;
    Animal Welfare Act, 72; ineffective-
    ness of, 127, 146; lobbying for, 69;
    Marine Mammal Protection Act,
    120, 126, 162; and politics of wildlife

Index ◁ ◁ ◁ 245

Morgan, Al, 68
Movie projects, 44, 196
Movin' On, 100
Moynihan, Daniel Patrick, 168
Mr. North, 196
Murchison, Clint, 79–80
Murchison, Texas, 80, 190–95
Murphy, Charles, 46, 50
Murray, Jim, 76
Murrow, Edward R., 16, 45–46, 52
Music Country USA, 98
Mustang rescue project, 170
My Man St. John, 103–5

Nahant, Massachusetts, 6, 12, 15
Nashua Telegraph, 27
Nation, 37–38
National Animal Interest Alliance, 208
National Catholic Society of Animal
    Welfare, 34
National Geographic Society, 127
National Park Service, 166
National Review, 131
National Rifle Association (NRA), 133,
    145–46
Nazi sympathizer, Duke of Windsor as,
    47, 51
NBC network. See *Today* show
Nelkin, Dorothy, 63, 151
News programs: Amory's reviews of,
    100–101; CBS, 86, 100, 101, 133–35;
    evolution of, 41, 86. See also *Today*
    show
Newsweek, 49
New York, residing in, 35, 38, 44, 45,
    150–51
New York Daily News, 49
New Yorker, 42
New York Herald Tribune, 39–40, 64

New York Herald Tribune Book Review,
    38, 42
New York Journal-American, 49, 51
New York magazine, 78, 157
New York Marathon party, 17
New York Review of Books, 151
New York Times: Amory's book criticism
    in, 57; on *The Cat Who Came for
    Christmas*, 187; *Celebrity Register*, 61;
    on *Cousins*, 65; Gould's television
    criticism, 87–88; on *Home Town*,
    39; on *The Last Resorts*, 42; on *Man
    Kind?*, 131–32; Maxwell's obituary
    in, 57–58; on *The Proper Bostonians*,
    37; on *Today* show debut, 41; on *The
    Trouble with Nowadays*, 150
New York Times Book Review, 189
New York Times Magazine, 82–83
Ney, Edward, 117, 155, 166, 167–68, 173
Ney, Judy, 122, 154, 173
Nichols, Mike, 182
Nielson ratings, 84, 85
Nim Chimpsky (chimpanzee), 193,
    194–95
Nixon, Richard, 61–62
Novel (*Home Town*), 38–41, 44
NRA (National Rifle Association), 133,
    145–46

Oakes, John, 132
O.K. Crackerby!, 102–5
Opre, Tom, 133
Outdoor writers, 125

Paar, Jack, 145
Pacelle, Wayne, 121, 207–8
Palm Beach Post, 59
Panitt, Merrill, 83, 85–86, 92, 110, 115,
    148–49